CONTROVERSIAL ISSUES

in Presidential Selection

SUNY Series on the Presidency:
Contemporary Issues
John Kenneth White, Editor

CONTROVERSIAL ISSUES

in Presidential Selection

Gary L. Rose, Editor

STATE UNIVERSITY OF NEW YORK PRESS

Published by State University of New York Press, Albany

Printed in the United States of America

For information, address State University of New York Press, State University Plaza, Albany, N.Y., 12246

Production by E. Moore
Marketing by Theresa A. Swierzowski

Library of Congress Cataloging-in-Publication Data

Controversial issues in presidential selection / Gary L. Rose, editor.
    p. cm.—(Suny series on the presidency)
    Includes bibliographical references and index.
    ISBN 0–7914–0747–0 (acid-free).—ISBN 0–7914–0748–9 (pbk. : acid
–free)
    1. Presidents—United States—Election. 2. Presidents—United
States—Nomination. I. Rose, Gary L., 1951– . II. Series: SUNY
series in the presidency.
JK528.C73 1991
324.5—dc20   90–46019
                                                                  CIP

10 9 8 7 6 5 4 3 2

I wish to dedicate this book to my wife Laurie, my son Garrison, and my daughter Meredith.

Contents

Preface / ix

Introduction
A Presidential Selection Process in Crisis / 1
Gary L. Rose

Chapter One
Is the Nominating Process Representative? / 23
Yes—John S. Jackson III / 25
No—Sarah McCally Morehouse / 40

Chapter Two
Should Convention Delegates be Formally Pledged? / 57
Yes—Robert T. Nakamura / 59
No—Elaine Ciulla Kamarck / 67

Chapter Three
Should Vice-Presidential Candidates be Selected from the
Also-Ran Category? / 79
Yes—John Kenneth White / 81
No—Landis Jones / 93

Chapter Four
Do the Media Inform? / 107
Yes—John Orman / 109
No—Kant Patel / 118

Chapter Five
Should Campaign Commercials be Regulated? / 131
Yes—Curtis B. Gans / 133
No—Marion R. Just / 143

Chapter Six
Is Public Financing a Desirable Policy? / 155
Yes—Herbert E. Alexander / 157
No—Mitch McConnell / 169

Chapter Seven
Should Presidential Debates be Required? / 181
Yes—William Carroll / 182
No—James I. Lengle and Dianne C. Lambert / 192

Chapter Eight
Should the Electoral College be Abolished? / 203
Yes—Lawrence D. Longley / 204
No—Denny Pilant / 216

Chapter Nine
Is On-Site Voter Registration Desirable? / 227
Yes—Peverill Squire / 229
No—David B. Hill / 237

Chapter Ten
Should Political Parties Govern the Presidential
Selection Process? / 249
Yes—W. Wayne Shannon / 251
No—Allan J. Cigler / 266

Conclusion / 281
Gary L. Rose

Notes / 291

Suggested Bibliography / 323

Contributors / 331

Index / 337

Preface

While teaching a course entitled "The Politics of Presidential Elections," I became inspired to organize a number of thought-provoking and highly debatable issues associated with the process of presidential selection. The various texts used in class, articles in professional journals, seminal works of political scientists, guest speakers (political and academic), the evening news, and the insightful questions and comments of my students served to crystalize what appear to be the most current and controversial issues associated with the selection of the American president. Although a wide variety of substantive and theoretical issues affect the process by which we choose the president, the major controversies of the selection process can be distilled into ten clear and debatable issues. Moreover, these ten major issues span the entire process of presidential selection: the nominating process, the national nominating convention, and the general election campaign; no part of the selection process is immune from controversy and debate.

The issues examined and debated in this book are associated with what political scientists refer to as the "modern" process of presidential selection. This process is marked by the decline of political parties as electoral institutions, candidate-centered campaigns, open and fluid nominating procedures, media-based campaign communication, presidential debates, and public funding of presidential campaigns. The modern process of presidential selection can be attributed to demands for egalitarianism and representation in presidential contests, the merger of politics with technology, and a fundamental change in attitudes among the American electorate toward the role of political parties within the context of American politics.

At the risk of oversimplification, but important for the purpose of establishing a baseline for analysis, it can be argued that the modern process of presidential selection spans approximately twenty years. The turning point appears to be the Democratic National Convention of 1968, a fractious and, according to some, illegitimate nominating convention. It ultimately led to broad reforms and changes in the process of presidential selection. Following those tumultuous summer evenings in Chicago over twenty years ago, the process of presidential selection underwent a series of dramatic changes. The modern process, or new system, of presidential selection that subsequently evolved has given rise to a myriad of debatable issues that impact directly on the quality of American democracy, presidential leadership, and good government.

The Introduction to this book argues that the modern process of presidential selection is a process that is failing. It is my position that the process has evolved to a point of crisis and that collapse appears imminent; a process in crisis is this work's central premise and empirical data have been incorporated to document such a condition. Following the Introduction, the controversial issues associated with presidential selection are then examined in a debate format through a series of ten chapters, each chapter centering on one controversial issue. While several issues examined in this text are relevant to all phases of the presidential selection process, I have attempted to organize and present the issues in a fashion that parallels the sequence of the selection process. Thus, as the process unfolds from the selection of convention delegates to the national nominating convention and through the fall campaign, there are a series of controversial issues that simultaneously unfold. The chapters are therefore organized in the following fashion: Chapter 1 debates the question "Is the Nominating Process Representative?" Chapter 2, "Should Convention Delegates be Formally Pledged?" Chapter 3, "Should Vice-Presidential Candidates be Selected from the Also-Ran Category?" Chapter 4, "Do the Media Inform?" Chapter 5, "Should Campaign Commercials be Regulated?" Chapter 6, "Is Public Financing a Desirable Policy?" Chapter 7, "Should Presidential Debates be Required?" Chapter 8, "Should the Electoral College be Abolished?" Chapter 9, "Is On-

Site Voter Registration Desirable?" And Chapter 10, "Should Political Parties Govern the Presidential Selection Process?" This last question debates in essence the entire character of the modern process of presidential selection. To avoid accusations of criticizing the selection process without suggesting plausible alternatives, I use the Conclusion to summarize what has thus far been examined, and to endorse a proposal that should serve as the first step toward improving a presidential selection process gone awry. Here I advocate the preprimary national convention followed by a national primary, a proposal, needless to say, which is also controversial and very debatable.

The issues under examination in this book will more than likely occupy the attention of political scientists, political strategists, political pundits, and national decision-makers during the decade of the 1990s. Indeed, the currency of the issues can be seen in the recent concern of the Democratic Party to improve the representativeness of the party's presidential nominating process. At the very time of this writing, the Democratic National Committee has approved of a proposal to move the California primary in June, traditionally the last primary of the nominating campaign, to the very beginning of the delegate selection process, perhaps immediately after the New Hampshire primary in February or March. This proposal is now before the California General Assembly. At the same time, the United States Congress is debating the National Voter Registration Act, also known as the "motor voter bill." Such a bill, if passed into law, will allow individuals to become registered as voters at the same time they acquire their drivers' licenses. There is also in Congress the controversial Hollings-Danforth bill, which, if passed, would place legal regulations on campaign commercials. The reader should therefore recognize that the issues addressed in this book are quite pressing and are currently the subject of extensive debate and review at the highest levels of American party organization and government.

While recruiting my team of essay contributors, one of the common questions that surfaced concerned the style of the individual article. Should an article be primarily a provocative, theoretical essay, or should it be buttressed with extensive data and substantial documentation? My response was normally flexible. What was important to me was that the author of an article produce a clear and cogent point of view in a style most comfortable to him or her. It was my view that rigid stylistic requirements could potentially impede effective argumentation. What was critical was that a persuasive affirmative or negative position be articulated. As such, the result is a text consisting of twenty interesting and original articles, some depending heavily on research and empirical data, some on broad theoretical premises, and some on personal feelings, observations, and experiences. The variation in style should demonstrate to the reader that positions on issues can in fact be developed through different approaches. While some prefer stylistic symmetry, I believe flexibility in style has contributed to a more diverse, original, and sincere set of arguments.

Another dimension of this book that lends itself to diversity and interest is the fact that the various contributors offer perspectives not only from the towers of academia, but also from the real political world. Contributors include a United States Senator, a former member of the Electoral College, a full-time and nationally recognized political consultant, a former special assistant to a vice-president, a former candidate for Congress, a Democratic Party strategist, as well as directors or members of research oriented foundations, institutes, and committees. Indeed, the credentials of numerous contributors often reveal an impressive record of scholarly achievement as well as a history of direct involvement in the political process. The result is a body of work that contains the perspectives of those who teach and write about presidential politics, those who actually practice the art, and those who do both.

I recommend to instructors who adopt this book for classroom use to employ the chapters in a fashion that encourages students to actually debate the controversial issues under survey. My own experience suggests that debates between small panels of students is the most effective; each panel should have the opportunity to investigate the issue well in advance and conduct additional research if necessary. Panel members, of course, should meet to select a team leader and to develop an organized and cogent argument. Following the point counterpoint debate, other members of the class should be allowed to offer additional insight into the issues by directing questions to panel participants, or by freely speaking on behalf of the affirmative or negative position. To raise the stakes, the class can be allowed to cast a vote for the panel that presents the most effective argument. As one who employs this format in several political science classes, and as the coach of an energetic debating team, I can state with great confidence that today's students genuinely enjoy opportunities to advocate, defend, and debate controversial political issues. More importantly, political argument conducted in an organized forum with proper moderation inevitably brings to life seemingly abstract issues, enhances learning, generates higher levels of interest in the subject matter, and increases the critical listening and verbal skills of the student. In short, there is much to gain by debating the controversial issues that face the presidential selection process.

A book of this nature could not have been completed without the advice and support of a number of very fine individuals. First and foremost, I wish to acknowledge the extraordinary support of John Kenneth White of the Catholic University of America. John is without a doubt one of the most helpful and insightful persons I have ever worked with. From the conceptual stage of this project through the final editing, he offered excellent guidance, constructive criticism, and superb professional advice. John is the editor of the SUNY Press presidency series, of which this text is a component, and it is with great pleasure that I include his insightful perspective concerning vice-presidential selection as well.

I am deeply indebted to the individual contributors to this book. It was truly a learning process for me to work with such a fine collection of professionals. I commend each of them for their attention to deadlines, detail, and expertise in the field of presiden tial selection. I also appreciate their confidence in me as editor and the project generally.

Many thanks go to my colleague in political science at Sacred Heart University, John F. Kikoski. Known affectionately as "Dr. K" among the student body, John has been very supportive throughout all stages of this particular project as well as other facets of my work at the university. In a program consisting of only two full-time political scientists, I am indeed fortunate to have my one and only colleague so genuinely helpful and supportive. I also would like to thank John for providing me with the wonderful opportunity to return to my home state of Connecticut; there is indeed something very special about teaching and residing in a state that is truly your "home."

I wish to acknowledge three administrators and colleagues at Sacred Heart University: the chairman of the Faculty of Financial Studies, Government, and Law, Thomas Corrigan; the acting academic vice-president and provost, Lucjan Orlowski; and the president of Sacred Heart, Anthony J. Cernera. Collectively, they have been extremely supportive of this project from start to finish. I am particularly grateful for their unanimous approval of my request for a reduced teaching load from twelve to nine credits in the spring of 1990. The three credit reduction was critical for meeting the contract deadline and I am indeed appreciative of this decision.

I would like to thank and acknowledge my former secretary, Julie Pavia. Julie's attention to the fine details, deadlines, and revisions was simply extraordinary. I was indeed fortunate to have such a conscientious and industrious individual work with me from the beginning to nearly the completion of the project. Valerie Canada has ably placed the finishing touches on the final draft, and I wish to acknowledge her very fine and competent efforts also.

My thanks extend to the anonymous reviewers of the final manuscript. I have no knowledge of their names or affiliations but I do know that their suggestions and criticisms contributed to a better product; their expertise was certainly impressive. At the same time, I wish to acknowledge those individuals at SUNY Press who were directly involved in this project. In particular, I would like to express gratitude to Ms. Peggy Gifford, the acquisitions editor, and her interim replacement, Ms. Dana Foote, for being so professional and helpful.

I also acknowledge those students at Sacred Heart University who took the time to read parts of the final manuscript for the purpose of evaluating readability, organization, and argumentation. I also express thanks to former and current members of the Sacred Heart University Debating Society who every Tuesday from 3:00 to 6:00 P.M. and on numerous weekends during the academic year stand toe to toe to debate the pressing issues of American democracy. The society's dedication and energy has served as a source of inspiration for this particular project.

Last, but certainly not least, I thank my entire family for their love and encouragement. It is difficult to imagine being professionally productive without a caring and supportive home environment; I am indeed grateful.

Introduction

A Presidential Selection Process in Crisis

Gary L. Rose

The presidential selection process in the United States is the foundation of American democracy. Without this pivotal and dynamic event, American democracy would lose much of its vitality and uniqueness—a uniqueness, it should be added, that contributes significantly to the image of the United States as the world's model democracy. Filled with controversy, emotion, scandal, and drama, the election of an American president is an event unlike any other on the entire planet.

Unfortunately, however, the presidential selection process, so often identified as the foundation of America's political system, is a foundation that is crumbling. Indeed, to describe the process by which American presidents are selected as a process "in crisis" may not at all be an exaggeration, for the term "crisis" can confidently be applied to a system characterized by frequent and repeated failure. Clearly, as we reflect upon the modern presidential selection process, which spans approximately the last two decades, we find a substantial amount of evidence strongly indicative of a process plagued by recurrent failure. First, the process is failing with regularity to effectively link the American people to the political system. Second, the process is often failing to yield presidential candidates capable of governing in the tradition of great American presidents. What is also distressing is that the presidential selection process remains in a crisis state despite repeated attempts by political reformers to democratize, refine, and improve the manner in which we choose our president.

A CRISIS IN LINKAGE

Theoretically, the presidential selection process should be the key event in American politics that stimulates political participation, facilitates an awareness of important policy issues, and generates positive feelings toward candidates who emerge as presidential nominees. The empirical evidence, however, strongly suggests serious failure in this respect. Voter turnout, for example, is unimpressive in presidential election years. Turnout in primary elections, a device unique to American politics, remains dismally low. In 1988 the evidence reveals that only 24 percent of the eligible electorate voted in primary election contests, a figure hardly indicative of an enthusiastic public.[1] Voter participation in precinct caucuses is substantially lower. One study conducted by Austin Ranney revealed a mean of 1.9 percent of the voting age population voting in the precinct caucuses of twenty-one caucus states.[2] During the general election, voter turnout further reveals an unenthusiastic and disinterested electorate. In 1988 voter turnout was recorded at 50.2 percent, the lowest recorded turnout in presidential elections since the election of 1924, an election year that recorded turnout at 43.8 percent.[3] The repeatedly low level of voter participation in primaries, precinct caucuses, and the general election should be viewed as a clear indication of a presidential selection process in crisis.

In addition to low voter turnout, we find an American electorate quite disenchanted with the presidential nominees of the two major parties. Like voter turnout, we see a fairly steady decline in the percentage of the electorate who give highly favorable ratings to presidential nominees. Consider the following findings from the Gallup Poll. In 1952, 84 percent of the voters surveyed rated the two presidential nominees as "highly favorable" candidates; in 1956, 92 percent of voters rated the party nominees as highly favorable; and in 1960, 82 percent of voters surveyed rated the two presidential nominees in such terms. Clearly, from 1952 to 1960 the American electorate was very much impressed with those candidates who emerged as the nominees of the two major parties. Following 1960, however, one notices a marked decline in the ratings of presidential candidates, with 65 percent of the voters in 1964, 63 percent in 1968, 62 percent in 1972, 69 percent in 1976, and 53 percent in 1980 rating the Republican and Democratic nominees as "highly favorable" presidential candidates. From 1952 to 1980 the empirical evidence reveals a 31 percent drop in the highly favorable rating, a disturbing development to say the least. Such evidence is hardly suggestive of a presidential nominating process that is functioning well, particularly from the perspective of representation. Analyzing the Gallup data, Anthony King, a renowned scholar of British politics, stated the following: "The bizarre outcome in 1980 was that the most open, most 'democratic' leadership selection system ever devised resulted in the nomination of the two least-respected and least admired presidential candidates in modern American history."[4]

Public attitudes toward presidential nominees in 1984 reveal a short-lived resurgence in positive perceptions among the electorate. Following the nominating process, a Gallup Poll discovered that 71 percent of the American electorate collectively rated the two nominees as "very favorable" candidates, the most favorable perceptions of candidates since the 1960 election. A word of caution should be noted, however. In 1984 President Reagan was an extraordinarily popular president. Indeed, the impressive percentage of voters rating the nominees as very favorable was essentially attributable to the president. The data, when analyzed by party, reveal President Reagan receiving very favorable ratings from 43 percent of the voters and Walter Mondale receiving very favorable rating from only 28 percent of persons polled.[5]

In 1988 the American electorate appeared once again unimpressed with the nominees of the two major parties. Among those persons polled, only 39 percent rated the nominees as "very favorable" candidates. When examined by party, the data reveal George Bush receiving very favorable ratings from only 23 percent of the respondents and Michael Dukakis very favorable ratings from a mere 16 percent of persons polled.[6] Such perceptions continue to indict the process by which presidential candidates are nominated.

To further demonstrate the current displeasure among the American electorate regarding the final products of the presidential nominating process, one should consider the results of yet another Gallup Poll. Rather than rate presidential nominees, the respondents in this particular poll were asked if the presidential primaries actually produced the "best" presidential candidates or if "better qualified" candidates should have been nominated. Sixty-six percent of the respondents believed that better qualified candidates should have been selected.[7] Needless to say, the results of scientific public opinion polls raise serious questions and doubts about the process devised by both political parties for nominating presidential candidates. Surely one would expect public perceptions of presidential nominees to be more positive within the world's model democracy.

Further evidence of a presidential selection process in crisis surfaces in the attitudes of the American electorate toward political parties and elections, institutions central to American democracy, and certainly central to the process of presidential selection. In 1964 survey data gathered by the Survey Research Center/Center for Political Studies discovered that 44 percent of the American electorate viewed political parties as effective political linkage institutions. In 1980, however, the percentage of the electorate who expressed such an orientation declined to an astonishing 18 percent. Positive perceptions of elections as linkage mechanisms also declined from 1964 to 1980, although not as precipitously. In 1964, 68 percent of the electorate viewed elections as institutions that effectively link the people to their government, while in 1980 this view was expressed by 52 percent of the electorate.[8] The results of the survey data lead to a logical conclusion: the American people are dissatisfied with political parties and elections due in large part to the presidential candidates and presidents such institutions have been routinely producing.

The decline in voter turnout, the decline in positive perceptions of presidential nominees, and the decline in support for political parties and elections firmly point to a presidential selection process in crisis. The behavior and attitudes of the American electorate are indicative of a process that is systematically failing to meet the expectations, ideals, and hopes of the American people. The symbiotic relationship between the system of presidential selection and the negative orientations that exist among the electorate is expressed in clear terms by Gerald Pomper:

> The capacity of voters, while considerable, is not unlimited or permanent. The electorate reacts to events in the political and social environment. It is not able to structure the choices presented, but must depend on parties and candidates to provide appropriate stimuli. The character of voting behavior therefore varies with the events and alternatives presented.[9]

Given the negative perceptions expressed by the voters toward presidential nominees and the concomitant low level of interest and participation during presidential election years, one must seriously question the "stimuli" that presidential candidates, parties, and elections are providing during the presidential selection process. There appears sufficient reason to question the "alternatives" that emerge from the selection process as well. The failure of both political parties to generate enthusiasm specifically is succinctly noted by Everett Carll Ladd, Jr.:

> Both of the major parties are now weak. . . . Neither can achieve sustained coherence in the development and implementation of governmental policy. Neither possess a public philosophy or programmatic approach that rallies the populace to its standard, as New Deal liberalism once brought a national majority to that of the Democrats. Thus partisan and electoral drift continues.[10]

A CRISIS IN GOVERNANCE

Indication of a presidential selection process in crisis also surfaces in the performance of recent American presidents. In this respect, it is the failure in governance that casts a dark shadow over the process by which American presidents are selected. Unlike the presidential selection process that existed prior to 1972, the "modern" presidential selection process, as it is often referred to, is a more open and democratic process, a clear reflection of the goals and objectives of the reform movement that prevailed following the tumultuous Democratic National Convention in 1968. Outcomes in primary elections and caucus contests now determine the nominees of both political parties, as opposed to independent and private decisions reached by party elites in national nominating conventions. Although both parties continue to conduct national conventions, they are hardly the forums for determining the party nominee. The "modern" process of presidential selection is also a very porous process in that persons with minimal experience in party politics, what some refer to as "political amateurs," can emerge as meaningful and key actors within the context of nomination contests. Party organization officials or "political professionals" have to a significant extent been sidelined as the principal actors. It is the openness of the process and the decline of political party influence that characterize the modern process by which presidents are selected.

What is ironic, however, is that it is precisely during such drastic reforms in the selection process that we notice serious problems developing with presidential leadership. Indeed, there now appears to be enough evidence to suggest an association between the reforms that have theoretically "democratized" the presidential selection process and the declining quality of presidential leadership. Public approval ratings of American presidents have declined over the course of the last two decades. Calculations from the Gallup Poll by Richard Rose reveals a 65 percent average public approval rating for Dwight D. Eisenhower, 71 percent for John F. Kennedy, 56 percent for Lyndon B. Johnson, 49 percent for Richard M. Nixon, 47 percent for Gerald R. Ford, 46 percent for Jimmy Carter, and 52 percent for Ronald Reagan. It is evident from Rose's calculations that the average public support scores for our recent American presidents have demonstrated a downward trend. The one exception was Ronald Reagan, although even his score does not approximate that calculated for Eisenhower or Kennedy.[11]

The ratings of American presidents by presidential scholars also suggest an association between the modern process of presidential selection and poor presidential performance. The Chicago Tribune Poll in 1982 discovered President Carter and President Nixon, two products of the modern selection process, rated among the ten worst presidents in American history—the only American presidents since World War II to be rated among the bottom ten presidents. Presidents Truman and Eisenhower, however, were rated among the ten best. The Murray Poll, also conducted in 1982, ranked presidents from one to thirty-six. From this poll we find President Nixon ranked thirty-fourth, President Carter twenty-fifth, and President Ford twenty-fourth—three presidents in a row ranked in the bottom third. President Kennedy is ranked thirteenth, President Eisenhower eleventh, President Lyndon Johnson tenth, and President Truman eighth.[12] The important point to be made from such data is that American presidents who have emerged through the "modern" presidential selection process, which is theoretically a more "democratic" and representative process, have not been rated very favorably by experts on the presidency. Quite to the contrary, our recent presidents have been rated very poorly and in some cases as the very worst in the history of the United States.

The relationship between ineffective presidential leadership and the process by which we currently select our presidents has not gone unnoticed by close observers of the American presidency. Robert Shogan, a well-respected Washington correspondent for the *Los Angeles Times*, describes the dynamics of the modern selection process as resulting in "instability in politics and government, exaggerated expectations and excessive responses from the presidency and a deepening cynicism among the voters."[13] Writing during the 1980 presidential contest, President Gerald Ford noted the negative consequences that have emerged from political party decline specifically: "The parties today are really more or less impotent . . . and if you do not have party responsibility, the system does not work."[14] Ted Sorensen, a former counsel to President Kennedy, also views the current dynamics of presidential selection as being very incompatible with the requirements of modern presidential leadership:

> The very process of campaigning for the Presidency under the present system weakens the winner's ability to govern effectively. The special talents demanded by a Presidential campaign are for the most part not the skills needed in the White House. . . . Once there was a closer relationship between running and ruling. Twenty-four and more years ago, the qualities required to win the Presidential nomination and reelection resembled many of those required to govern the nation effectively.[15]

In Sorensen's view, critical differences between the modern presidential selection system and the selection system in use several decades ago include an excessive concern with generating the support of voters in primary contests as opposed to cultivating the support of party and elected officials, a heavy reliance on pollsters, media consultants, and professional fund-raisers rather than policy advisors, simplification of complex policy issues for communicative purposes rather than thorough policy articulation, an overemphasis on image and personal appearance as opposed to intellect and experience, and the replacement of campaign volunteers with computerized mailing lists, automated phone banks, and other technological devices designed to mobilize voter support. Such developments, according to Sorensen, have done little to bring to the forefront talented presidential leadership.[16]

VOTING BEHAVIOR AND PERCEPTIONS IN 1988: FURTHER EVIDENCE OF CRISIS

As we examine data regarding voting behavior and perceptions of the characteristics of the two presidential nominees during the 1988 presidential election, we find additional evidence of a presidential selection process in grave crisis. In this respect, the high incidence of negative voting behavior is most disturbing. Among those voters who cast their vote for Michael Dukakis, the evidence shows that 49 percent voted for Dukakis due to their dislike of George Bush. At the same time, 45 percent of voters who voted for Bush did so because of their dislike for Dukakis.[17] Such a high incidence of negative voting behavior suggests considerable displeasure with those candidates who emerge as party nominees through the long, arduous, and fractious nominating contest. One would expect more genuine support for presidential nominees particularly since the nominating processes of the two major parties are theoretically constructed to ensure fairness and representative outcomes.

Additional empirical evidence that sheds doubt on the virtues of the modern presidential selection process concerns popular perceptions of the presidential nominees' "best" characteristics. Polling during the 1988 presidential contest discovered only 14 percent of those who voted for Bush perceived his best characteristic to be that of a strong leader, 11 percent believed his best characteristic was good judgment, 5 percent perceived Bush to be a man of vision, and only 1 percent cited his best characteristic as being able to get things done. Bush's experience in government was identified as his best characteristic by 47 percent of his voters. Among those who voted for Dukakis, we find that only 3 percent cited his experience as his best characteristic, 12 percent cited strong leadership, 14 percent good judgment, 14 percent vision, and 3 percent as being able to get things done. Twenty-eight percent of Dukakis voters believed his best characteristic was his ability to care for people.[18]

Generally speaking, the evidence is not at all impressive with respect to popular perceptions of the two presidential nominees. Strong leadership, judgment, vision, and getting things done are the characteristics one tends to associate with presidential greatness. Yet we find that voters in 1988 did not perceive such traits to be present in the candidates for whom they cast a ballot, compelling evidence of a presidential selection process that is failing to meet the expectations and ideals of the American people.

PRESIDENTIAL SELECTION IN 1824: A PARALLEL?

To proclaim that American history is in the process of repeating itself is perhaps on the bold side and even somewhat imaginative. However, a historical examination of the presidential selection process can discover a specific time period during which the process evolved to a point of extreme crisis, followed by a total collapse of the existing system. In this respect, it is the presidential selection process of 1824, recorded as the most discredited selection process in the history of the United States, that bears a disturbing resemblance to the modern presidential selection system.

The United States Congress from 1800 through 1824 had assumed the responsibility of nominating presidential candidates. The presidential nominating caucus within Congress was unaffectionately known as the "King Caucus." In 1824, following the two-term presidency of James Monroe, four distinct factions within the Democratic-Republican party, the only major party at the time, emerged to compete for the presidency. Factionalism was intense and the King Caucus became the center of deep controversy. Deemed by many to be an elitist and thoroughly illegitimate means of selecting presidential candidates, the caucus, when convened, was boycotted by close to three-fourths of Democratic-Republican congressmen. William Crawford was nominated by the poorly attended caucus, while Andrew Jackson, John Quincy Adams, and Henry Clay were nominated by state legislatures, such nominations reflecting strong regional biases.[19] With four regional candidates contesting the presidential election, no candidate was able to garner a majority of the electoral vote, thereby requiring the House of Representatives to select the president. Quite incredibly, Adams, who ran second to Jackson in the popular and electoral vote, emerged from the House as president due to a secret deal struck with Clay. Briefly, Clay negotiated the post of secretary of state in an Adams administration in return for mobilizing his own congressional support on Adams's behalf. The deal was struck and when Adams emerged as president the election result was perceived as grossly illegitimate, leading to sharp accusations of fraud, deals, and deceit. The King Caucus in particular became the focus of severe criticism as the nominating process was identified as the root cause of the illegitimate election result.

Following the election of 1824, an election deemed a complete failure in representative government, the presidential selection process underwent a radical revision regarding nominating procedures. For a short time, the nominating process became the responsibility of state conventions. State conventions, however, accomplished little in terms of party unity and before long the process gave way to the centralized national nominating convention, a nominating structure in use to this day. In short, as the result of a process that failed, a fundamentally new process was created and institutionalized.

When we examine the selection process in its current form, it is difficult not to see a parallel to the circumstances that existed in 1824. Certainly, the mechanics of the modern process are different from what existed in 1824, yet the process, as it is currently constituted, is yielding results that are in many ways perceived as illegitimate and unrepresentative. Indeed, it is uncanny how scholarly descriptions of the crisis in 1824 are more than appropriate to today's presidential selection process.

George Dangerfield described the 1824 election in these terms: "Then, too, the year 1824 was the great year of indecision, which found both candidates and voters struggling in the same cobweb."[20] In Dangerfield's words: "It was not an election that expressed the wishes of the electorate."[21] Robert V. Remini portrays the events of 1824 in this fashion: "By 1824 all semblance of unity, vigor and discipline within the party had vanished."[22] Reflecting on recent presidential elections, it is difficult to avoid the evidence suggestive of candidates and voters struggling in "cobwebs," nomination and even election outcomes that do not truly reflect the "wishes of the electorate," and internal party processes that reveal a breakdown in "unity, vigor, and discipline." In 1824 the presidential selection process collapsed.

As we approach the 1990s, the evidence continues to mount that once again our selection process is on the verge of disintegration. The crisis in linkage is real: participation in presidential primaries and precinct caucuses is extremely low, voter turnout in presidential elections is clearly on the wane, and American presidents are coming to power with mandates of less than one-third of the eligible electorate. In addition to such trends, we find an electorate increasingly dissatisfied with key linkage institutions, particularly political parties and elections, as well as presidential candidates who emerge as party nominees through the torturous nominating process. The crisis in governance is also a reality: presidential support scores, which are general indicators of presidential performance, have declined to disturbing levels. An alarming number of presidents since 1968 have been rated quite poorly by presidential scholars, and scientific polling data demonstrate that Americans do not perceive the qualities of presidential greatness to be present among the nominees of the two major parties.

The crisis in linkage and the crisis in governance, when taken together, point to but one direction: the presidential selection process is in a severe state of crisis and the process appears to be on the verge of collapse, a strikingly similar situation to what existed in 1824. It is absolutely imperative, therefore, to examine those rules, institutions, forces, and processes that condition and determine the outcome of the current presidential selection process. It also seems appropriate to examine proposals that should theoretically improve the quality of presidential selection. More specifically, as we enter the decade of the 1990s, it appears that ten pressing and controversial issues involving presidential selection warrant a thorough and scholarly review. Such issues clearly span the three phases of the American presidential selection process: the nomination process, the national nominating convention, and the general election campaign. The ten controversial issues in presidential selection are the following.

Is the Nominating Process Representative?

The representativeness of the presidential nominating process is perhaps the issue that has sparked most debate among political scientists and political practitioners.[23] The central issue here concerns the extent to which the modern nominating process yields Republican and Democratic nominees who are in fact representative of their political party's rank and file and who are capable of forging broad electoral coalitions conducive to effective presidential leadership.

Critics of the nominating process often point to the rules and regulations that govern the process by which delegates are chosen to represent presidential candidates at national nominating conventions, as well as the formal mechanisms adopted by the various states for delegate selection purposes. In the latter respect, primary elections and caucus contests have been the subject of considerable debate, with a number of scholars suggesting that such delegate selection mechanisms are simply not conducive to nominating presidential candidates who reflect the values of their party and the American people. Critics of the current nominating process often point to the openness and fluidity of the process that, it is argued, allows for "political amateurs" as opposed to "political professionals" to dictate the course of nominating events.[24]

The defeats of Democratic presidential nominees in 1972, 1980, 1984, and 1988—four of the last five presidential contests— are quite relevant to the issue of representation. Have recent Democratic nominees been truly representative of the Democratic rank and file? How representative was the Democratic nominating process in 1988, which catapulted Michael Dukakis, a relatively obscure governor from Massachusetts, to the forefront of Democratic presidential contenders? One should also not forget the Democratic nominating contest of 1976. Although the Democratic Party did in fact capture the presidency that year, the Democratic nominee was often referred to as "Jimmy Who?" The question of representation is particularly pressing not only because the values of recent Democratic nominees often appear incongruent with the values of the Democratic rank and file but also because Democratic defeats in presidential elections are normally recorded as major Republican landslides. Although the question of representation can also be raised in conjunction with Republican nominating procedures, the issue is particularly acute within the context of Democratic party politics.

Other issues that raise doubts about the current presidential nominating process include the incredibly low level of voter turnout in primary elections and caucus contests, as well as the demographic characteristics of those who do vote in primaries and caucuses.[25] At the same time, another controversial dimension of the nominating process involves the sequence of presidential primaries. Should New Hampshire, a New England state whose population is not at all a cross section of the nation, be allowed to create the tremendous momentum necessary for a presidential candidate to capture the presidential nomination?[26] It should be evident that the representativeness of the presidential nomination process contains a myriad of controversial issues worthy of debate and discussion.

Should Convention Delegates be Formally Pledged?

Another controversial issue that periodically surfaces during the presidential nominating process involves the issue of "pledged" as opposed to "unpledged" convention delegates. To what extent should convention delegates be bound to presidential candidates at the national nominating convention? Convention rules normally require convention delegates to remain pledged, either formally or morally, to their respective candidate for at least the first round of convention balloting. Such procedures have been the subject of much dispute and every so often we witness an attempt to modify the rule governing the status of delegates.

One of the more recent and notorious attempts to challenge the rule governing the status of delegates on the first round of balloting occurred during the 1980 Democratic National Convention. The struggle for convention delegates erupted between supporters of Senator Ted Kennedy and President Jimmy Carter. While the Carter forces prevailed and delegates were therefore required to remain pledged through the first round of balloting, thereby securing the renomination of Carter, a fundamental issue regarding the democratic spirit of national nominating conventions was raised. Should convention delegates who are chosen in primaries and caucuses be required to remain pledged to candidates from the time of their selection as a delegate all the way through the first round of balloting at a national nominating convention conducted in July or August? For some delegates, the length of time during which they must remain pledged to one candidate might be as long as five or even six months.

A convention delegate selected during the Iowa caucuses or the New Hampshire primary in February could conceivably arrive at the party's nominating convention during the summer with very different perceptions of candidates as compared to several months prior. It is possible that a delegate might come to appreciate the policies of another candidate, or it is possible that over the course of the lengthy primary and caucus season a character flaw might surface in the candidate to whom the delegate is pledged. Indeed the strenuous nominating contest can be quite revealing with respect to the ability of a presidential candidate to withstand physical and emotional stress, an important clue to future behavior in the Oval Office. The issue in this particular case involves not only discretion, choice, and judgment, but more fundamentally questions the proper role of convention delegates within the context of the presidential selection process.[27]

Should Vice-Presidential Candidates be Selected from the Also-Ran Category?

The issue of vice-presidential selection also merits considerable attention. Due to the recent "Quayle factor" the issue appears to be more pressing now than at any other time in recent American history. Should presidential nominees be pressed to choose a vice-presidential running mate from the "also-ran" category? After all, those candidates have already been subjected to intense media scrutiny and throughout the lengthy nominating season they have come into extensive contact with the American people. Although ultimately rejected by the voters in the various nominating contests, several candidates tend to establish a certain rapport with the American people and, in some instances, become household names; Senator Robert Dole and the Reverend Jesse Jackson are prime examples in this respect. Consider the 1988 Republican presidential and vice-presidential ticket of George Bush and Dan Quayle, or the 1984 Democratic ticket of Walter Mondale and Geraldine Ferraro. Neither Quayle nor Ferraro were familiar faces to the American people and their personal character and policy preferences were known only to their immediate constituents and congressional colleagues. They were, in other words, total strangers to the American people.

Given the distinct possibility of a vice-president becoming president,[28] is it not a wise and more democratic policy for the presidential nominee to select a familiar face as a running mate? Granted, the argument can also be made that those candidates who emerge from the nominating contest as the party's presidential candidate should be trusted to exercise independent judgment regarding the choice of a running mate, and if such judgment cannot be trusted then, what does this suggest about the presidential capacity of the individual? One can also point to the fact that those on the "also-ran" list have already been formally rejected by the voters in primaries and caucuses, and perhaps one of the most undemocratic decisions the party's presidential nominee can make is to include a presidential reject on the ticket. The issue of vice-presidential selection is obviously controversial, quite current, and requires a full examination.

Do the Media Inform?

The role of the mass media within the context of presidential selection currently stirs a great deal of debate. The fact that so many Americans are dependent upon the media, particularly television,[29] to help form political opinions and opinions about presidential candidates that it seems more than appropriate to examine the informational capacity of the media. Do the media serve to inform the American electorate during the course of the presidential selection process? Do the media truly contribute to rational and sophisticated voting behavior during presidential elections? Is American democracy, which is deeply tied to the presidential selection process, currently being served by the mass media?

Reflecting upon the 1988 presidential campaign, one cannot help but notice the unusual amount of attention focused on the private lives of presidential candidates. Was it truly the public's right to know what the private sex life of a presidential candidate involved? Was it truly in the best interest of leadership selection to know the fine details associated with a candidate's decision as a young man to enter a National Guard unit in Indiana? Was it really in the best interest of leadership selection for the public to be informed that a presidential candidate plagiarized a research paper while in law school?

In the 1988 presidential campaign, five Republican and seven Democratic candidates contested primary elections and caucus contests in an effort to secure their party's nomination. Following the nominating contest, the nation witnessed the Democratic and Republican national nominating conventions, which also offered the first real opportunity to review and evaluate the two vice-presidential running mates. From September to November, the American people watched the presidential candidates and their respective running mates campaign vigorously throughout the country. The selection process resulted in a victory for the Republican presidential ticket of George Bush and Dan Quayle. Without a doubt, the entire winnowing process, from the Iowa caucus and the New Hampshire primary to election day in November, was very much influenced by the reporting of the mass media. It seems fair, therefore, to ask if in fact the media, in coverage of the American presidential selection process, enhanced the ability of the average American voter to make educated and responsible choices regarding national leadership? Were the American people properly informed of the various candidates' positions on domestic and foreign policy issues? In this author's view it certainly seemed as if the American people knew far more about Gary Hart's encounter with model Donna Rice on the yacht Monkey Business than they knew about Hart's budgetary recommendations for resolving the massive deficit that currently haunts decision-makers; interestingly the former senator was the only candidate to offer a completed written recommendation for the budget crisis.

At the same time, Democratic Senator Joseph Biden, referred to by his Republican colleague on the Senate Judiciary Committee Strom Thurmond as the Democratic Party's most articulate spokesman, will long be remembered as the presidential candidate who plagiarized a paper in law school and who verbally plagiarized a speech delivered by a member of the British Parliament. Senator Biden was a member of the Senate Foreign Relations Committee and chaired the Senate Judiciary Committee, two committees deeply involved in national policy-making. Unfortunately, however, the American people remained uninformed with respect to Senator Biden's position on pressing and complex national issues. Like former Senator Hart, Senator Biden was forced to withdraw from the presidential nominating contest. To think of the possible precedents that have been established from the 1988 campaign, and the negative impact such scrutiny will have on the decisions of some of our most talented congressmen and governors to enter future presidential campaigns, is disturbing to say the least.

Should Campaign Commercials be Regulated?

Should legal regulations be placed on campaign commercials? This policy has been proposed not only by political scientists and close observers of the political scene but also by current members of the United States Congress. While campaign commercials contribute to the national visibility of presidential candidates, which is a positive aspect of such commercials, the disturbing dimension of campaign commercials concerns their substance and the forces responsible for their production. An examination of a typical campaign commercial in the presidential campaign will discover a commercial very short in length. The commercial will either promote the virtues of the presidential candidate, often with the skillful use of imagery, or depict the opposition candidate in an extremely negative light.

In 1988 the general perception of the American public was that presidential campaign commercials were very negative and did little to promote issue awareness. Indeed, the preponderance of negativism in campaign advertising is apparent not only in modern presidential campaigns but has surfaced in congressional and gubernatorial contests as well. Even the 1989 mayoral contests were tarnished by elements of negative campaign advertising, suggesting that such tactics are becoming an integral feature of national and subnational campaigns. What is also unsettling is the raw fact that modern presidential candidates expend over half of all campaign funds on campaign commercials,[30] such funds supplied by the American taxpayer. Campaign commercials are the clever products of paid media consultants, the "hired guns" of presidential campaigns who are employed by presidential candidates to strategically market their candidate.[31]

Caution needs to be exercised, however, with respect to the proposal to place legal regulations on campaign commercials, for such a measure comes into conflict with the freedoms of expression and press contained within the First Amendment of the United States Constitution. While the regulation of campaign commercials might be viewed as the proper approach to cleansing presidential campaign politics, one must necessarily be sensitive to the words contained within this cherished component of the Bill of Rights: "Congress shall make no law . . . abridging the freedom of speech, or of the press." As such, the issue of commercial regulation is constitutionally complex, very controversial, and worthy of serious debate.

Is Public Financing a Desirable Policy?

Another key and very debatable issue facing the American presidential selection process involves the policy of public funding for presidential candidates. Public funding, enacted under federal law in 1974 as a result of campaign finance reform efforts, has been utilized with regularity by presidential candidates in the nominating contest and the general election since 1976. Although not a legal requirement, all major presidential contenders, with the one exception of former Texas Governor John Connally in 1980, have chosen to use public campaign funds.

The goal of the public funding provision is to eliminate the influence of "fat cat" contributions and special interest money in presidential elections, thereby making the American president less beholden to wealthy forces behind the political scene. At the same time, presidential candidates should theoretically be tied to the will of the people who, through a federal income tax check off system, supply the public funds.[32] Four presidential elections have now occurred under the provisions of public funding, enough presidential contests to allow serious thought and reflection on the merits of this particular policy. Has the presidential selection process been improved as a result of this novel experiment? Have we witnessed the emergence of a more effective presidential selection system? The issue is controversial and debatable.

Should Presidential Debates be Required?

Are presidential debates a necessary forum for evaluating presidential leadership? In what way does a presidential debate assist the American voter in developing a more sophisticated opinion regarding the capabilities and leadership potential of presidential candidates? Since the 1976 presidential election, presidential debates have become an institutionalized component of the presidential selection process. Americans now witness debates between the Democratic and Republican nominees, debates between vice-presidential candidates, and a series of debates between candidates contesting the nomination.

There is reason, however, to question the true utility of presidential debates and the extent to which debates should be required. It is well understood that presidential candidates tend to exercise considerable control over the format of a debate and that a number of arguments and counterarguments have been rehearsed well in advance; there is little spontaneity according to critics of presidential debates. One also needs to ask whether performance in presidential debates is a good indicator of a candidate's ability to manage a crisis and, more generally, if presidential debates provide clues to leadership capabilities.[33] The fact that presidential debates have become practically a requirement during the presidential campaign, and the fact that serious questions pertaining to the quality and utility of debates currently exist, necessitates a full review of the arguments for and against the institutionalization of presidential debates.

Should the Electoral College be Abolished?

No review of controversial issues facing the American presidential selection process can possibly ignore the perennial question regarding the Electoral College. Should the Electoral College, an institution created by the framers of the United States Constitution for electing the American president, be retained or abolished? This issue surfaces during every presidential election year, receives extensive scholarly and journalistic attention, and then recedes until the next presidential election.

Those in favor of retaining the Electoral College generally focus on the stabilizing impact the institution has on the presidential selection process. Indeed, advocates of the Electoral College view it as one of the very critical pillars of American democracy. Conversely, those who believe the Electoral College should be abolished appear to be particularly concerned with the inherent flaws that lurk beneath the surface of this complex institution and, more importantly, how such flaws can potentially produce undemocratic results. Despite the familiarity of the Electoral College controversy, it would be remiss not to provide a full review of the arguments for and against this most controversial mechanism of presidential selection.[34]

Is On-Site Voter Registration Desirable?

One of the more recent controversial issues in presidential selection involves the proposal to allow on-site voter registration. Movement in favor of on-site registration reflects a growing concern among reformers of American politics with the declining trend in voter turnout. Indeed, it is universally recognized that declining voter turnout is one of the most discernible trends in American electoral behavior. As it was previously noted, among the eligible American electorate voter turnout in the 1988 presidential election was recorded at 50.2 percent. Proponents of on-site registration attribute the low rates of turnout to the current procedure of voter registration used in most states. Such procedures, which normally require a verification of residency, a personal visit to the town hall, and normally an oath, are deemed by reformers as too time-consuming and unnecessarily bureaucratic. Reformers argue that the procedure for voter registration should be as simplified and as expedient as possible. In the view of on-site proponents, many of whom are Democrats, voter turnout will increase substantially if a citizen is permitted to register as a voter at the polling booth on the day of the general election. It is apparent that advocates of this policy subscribe to the notion that mass political participation in American politics is a desirable goal.

With voter turnout in a state of decline, and with voter turnout in the United States recorded as among the lowest of all democracies on earth,[35] it is plausible that the issue of on-site voter registration will remain on the agenda of electoral reformers. It may possibly surface as the most controversial issue in presidential selection during the 1990s.

Should Political Parties Govern the Presidential Selection Process?

At one time, political parties, more specifically political party elites, governed the presidential selection process. Political party leaders, such as national, state, and county party chairmen, congressmen and senators, and state governors, were very significant actors in determining who would serve as the party's presidential nominee. It was the party leaders, often operating in "smoke-filled rooms," as lore would have it, who constructed the party's presidential and vice-presidential ticket. Party leaders not only controlled the outcome of the presidential nominating process, but presidential candidates normally waged their election under the supervision and guidance of party organization leadership. Clearly, until the 1960s and what some refer to as the age of "new politics," political parties essentially governed the presidential campaign from start to finish.

With the rise of television as a campaign mechanism, the appearance of media consultants, the proliferation of presidential preference primaries, public funding in presidential elections, and reforms in nominating rules and procedures, the role and influence of party leadership, particularly within the context of the presidential selection process, suffered a serious decline.[36] Campaign functions, once considered the principal responsibility of party organizations, were now assumed by the presidential candidate's own staff of campaign workers. Presidential campaigns became more independent of the political party, with media consultants in particular surfacing as key figures in the course of campaign decision-making. Rather than depend on the party organization to mobilize voter support, presidential candidates were now able to harness television to build a winning coalition. Television not only freed the presidential candidate from reliance on the party organization during the presidential election campaign, but also allowed presidential candidates to largely bypass the party organization during the course of the nominating process. One can point to the nominations of Senator George McGovern from South Dakota in 1972 and Governor Jimmy Carter from Georgia in 1976 as prime examples of presidential candidates who, due to significant changes in the nature of the presidential nomination process, were able to become Democratic presidential nominees without the full support of the Democratic Party.

The fundamental question that emerges from such recent developments is whether or not the role of political party leadership should be restored and strengthened within the context of the presidential selection process. Are we more likely to get meaningful choices, attractive presidential candidates, and leadership more representative of the parties and the American people if we strengthen the hand of the parties in the process by which we select our presidents? It seems only proper, therefore, to debate whether or not political parties should govern the presidential selection process.

The issues to be reviewed and debated in the following chapters should promote critical thinking on the part of students concerned with presidential selection. Although there are additional issues, it is my perspective that the ten issues under survey are perhaps the most current and pressing issues facing the modern system of presidential selection. It is important for the reader to grasp the significance of each issue and comprehend how each individual issue deeply affects the outcome of the presidential contest. Who emerges as the Democratic or Republican nominee and which political party occupies the American presidency is significantly determined by one or more of the issues and positions presented in this book; the reader should never lose sight of this important fact. How each individual issue is resolved in the years ahead and what positions ultimately prevail will have a very deep and long-lasting consequence for the process by which we select the American president. To go one step further, how we govern ourselves as a free people will also be determined by the issues examined in this book and the positions subscribed to. With such thoughts in mind, it is the controversial issues that currently face the American presidential selection process, a process deep in "crisis," to which I now turn.

CHAPTER ONE

Is the Nominating Process Representative?

Our examination of controversial issues in presidential selection begins with a debate regarding the representativeness of the presidential nominating process. Clearly, the presidential nominating process, characterized by primary elections, caucus contests, and elaborate rules and regulations, constitutes the dimension of the selection process that has received the most attention and alteration by reformers in the years following the 1968 presidential election. The representativeness of the nominating process in particular has been the principal concern of those who have spearheaded nominating reforms.

Ironically, despite the almost obsessive concern of reformers with improving the representative character of the presidential nominating process, extensive debate continues regarding the extent to which the process is in fact representative. John S. Jackson III defends the current process of nominating presidential candidates. In Jackson's view, the process by which the political parties currently nominate presidential candidates produces, for the most part, representative results. Jackson explores the multidimensional and complex nature of representation demonstrating that the concept of representation is by no means simplistic and requires evaluation from more than one perspective. Employing Hanna Pitkin's philosophy of representation, Jackson analyzes the representativeness of the process by focusing on the extent to which convention delegates "stand for" and "act for" their respective political party. While Jackson's analysis of convention dele-

23

gates reveals a mixed set of findings, the evidence does suggest a nominating process more representative than what critics would have us believe.

Sarah McCally Morehouse presents a number of arguments that cast doubt on the current process by which presidential candidates are nominated. According to Morehouse, recent political reforms involving nominating rules, the forces at work in nominating campaigns, and the mechanisms by which convention delegates are selected, have combined to create a nominating process incapable of producing presidential candidates representative of their political party. Morehouse focuses on the deleterious contributions of the post-1968 Democratic reform commissions, the negative consequences of media coverage during the nominating campaign, the inherent unfairness that results from frontloading primaries and caucuses, the unrepresentative character of primary elections, and the fact that convention delegates tend to be unrepresentative of the party rank and file. In Morehouse's view, the unrepresentative characteristic of the nominating process reflects the diminished role of political parties within the context of presidential selection.

Part 1

YES—
The Nominating Process is Representative

John S. Jackson III

The concept of representation is usually applied to legislative bodies in philosophical debates and empirical research. The idea that Congress or the state legislatures "represent" the American people is central to our form of representative democracy or the "republican" form of government. The concept has less often been applied to political parties; however, it is eminently applicable to political parties operating in a mass democracy as well. Most experts agree that political parties serve an important systemic function of "linking" the mass public to the decision-makers in the government. If the parties are to perform such a linkage function, there must be some sense in which the party elites are representative of the party identifiers, and of the public at large. This is particularly important with respect to the role of party elites within the context of the presidential nomination process. Party elites selected to attend national nominating conventions have been criticized in recent years for being "unrepresentative" of their respective party and the American people. Critics often point to the process in which party elites, or, more specifically, national convention delegates, are selected to attend national nominating conventions. The process, it is argued, produces convention delegates who are ideologically unrepresentative of their party's rank and file, and the nation.

While there is a substantial body of literature critical of the representative dimensions of the presidential nomination process, this article will argue that the presidential nominating process is in fact more representative than critics would have us believe. To substantiate the representativeness of the nominating process, I will focus on the degree to which national convention delegates are representative of those they are supposed to represent. Before proceeding to an analysis of national convention delegates, it is first important to address what is meant by the term "representation."

THE PHILOSOPHY OF REPRESENTATION

Hanna Pitkin, the foremost modern theorist of representation, differentiates between two components of the concept. One is the "standing for" component, by which she means that the representative mirrors in some respect the characteristics of the represented. This could be via the representation of demographic characteristics, as in race and sex, or it could be via faithful representation of the attitudes and values of those being represented. Pitkin further observes that the ability of the representative to "act for" the represented—that is, to act on behalf of the represented and as they would act if they were making the decision—is the more advanced form of representation. "Standing for" representation is relevant to "acting for" representation to the extent that personal characteristics or attitudes and values, on the one hand, influence behavior, on the other.[1]

How representative, at least in the "standing for" sense, are delegates to the Democratic and Republican national nominating conventions? In essence, this is a question about the extent to which the elites of the two parties reflect the demographic backgrounds and views of their mass memberships and of the public at large. An examination of the demographic characteristics, ideological values, and issue positions of convention delegates compared to members of their party and the general public will reveal mixed findings regarding representation.

Demographic Representation

The issue of the representative nature of national convention delegates has been important for both parties and unusually compelling for the Democrats over the past two or three decades. As early as Lyndon Johnson's national convention in 1964, the Democrats started trying to eliminate racial discrimination in the delegate selection process and outlawing the almost all-white delegations from the South. The unspoken premise behind the political debates was that substantively and symbolically it was important for the many black voters supporting the Democratic Party to have people of their own race gaining delegate seats and access to the process of selecting presidential nominees and writing party platforms. In short, black voters should be represented by at least some black delegates in the national conventions, or so went this line of argument. This is a place where remote philosophical debates combine quickly with very practical questions of power politics, and the debate continued in the Democratic Party.[2]

In the aftermath of the contentious 1968 Democratic National Convention in Chicago the Democrats appointed the McGovern-Fraser Commission to study and improve their delegate selection process. Among the many requirements for the 1972 convention produced by the McGovern-Fraser Commission was that minorities, women, and young people should be represented in the national convention delegations, "in reasonable relationship to their presence in the population of the state".[3] This is a simple extension of the earlier position regarding the removal of racial barriers to prospective convention delegates. At first, it resulted in de facto "quotas" for minorities, women, and young people for the 1972 convention. Later, through a combination of action taken by various subsequent party reform commissions and the Democratic National Committee, a quota of 50 percent was provided for women delegates in the Democratic national conventions (since 1980), while minorities were left to the vagaries of affirmative action and young people have largely fallen by the wayside. These battles over prescribed representation for various demographic groups have not been as important in the Republican Party; however, the Republicans have responded to some political pressure to provide increased representation for women, and to a lesser extent minorities, in their national conventions. Thus, the issue of demographic representation has been important for both parties, although so far it has been more decisive for the Democrats.

The conflict over demographic representation was long-standing. Analysts have tracked the data on this issue for a substantial period. Table 1 provides demographic data for the three most politically salient groups for the entire period of twenty years and six presidential elections between 1968 and 1988.

There are some very interesting trends evident in these data. First, it is quite evident that women in both parties have been the

TABLE 1

Women, Black, and Young Delegates to the Democratic and Republican National Conventions 1968–1988

	1968		1972		1976		1980		1984		1988	
	D	R	D	R	D	R	D	R	D	R	D	R
Women	13%	16%	40%	29%	33%	31%	49%	29%	49%	44%	48%	33%
Black	5	2	15	4	11	3	15	3	18	4	23	4
Under 30	3	4	22	8	15	7	11	5	8	4	4	3

Source: Martin, Plissner and Warren J. Mitofsky, "The Making of the Delegates, 1968–1988," *Public Opinion* (September/October 1988):47.

group whose status has changed the most over those twenty years. The year 1968 is ordinarily used as a baseline year, for it predated the most significant reform movement and the 1968 election is generally agreed to be the last presidential selection held under the old system. That year 13 percent of the Democratic delegates were women and 16 percent of the Republican delegates were women. This percentage increased dramatically for the Democrats (up to 40 percent) in 1972 under the influence of the McGovern-Fraser rules. Republican women also increased in 1972 (up to 29 percent), although the more informal pressure used by the Republicans to increase the number of women was not as effective as the Democratic requirements.

Obviously, the fortunes of women delegates have waxed and waned somewhat ever since. About one-third of the delegates to both conventions were women in 1976. Then in 1980 the Democrats mandated equal division and almost achieved it, while the Republican women declined a bit. In 1984 the GOP women reached their highest level, 44 percent, but their percentage declined again in 1988. The Democrats have never achieved exactly equal division, probably due to their provision of the automatic (or "superdelegate") status for party and public officials; however, they have come very close since 1980. Inasmuch as the census data indicate that 51 percent of the population is female, clearly the Democratic convention delegates are representative on this dimension and the Republicans are somewhat less so.[4]

The story on black delegates in these six conventions is somewhat more mixed. There is some political dispute over the proper yardstick to use to judge the representativeness of black delegates. The Census Bureau reports that the national population is 11.2 percent black.[5] In arguing for more delegates, black leaders often advocate use of the percentage of black voters in the party as an objective to be reached. This, of course, increases the Democratic target substantially. Either way it is evident from Table 1 that black delegates started at about the same low levels of representation in 1968, 5 percent for the Democrats and 2 percent for the Republicans. This percentage increased dramatically for the Democrats and changed very little for the Republicans over the ensuing twenty years. The conventions of 1984 at 18 percent and 1988 at 23 percent were the apex for black Democratic delegates, and their success was undoubtedly influenced partially by Jesse Jackson's success. The Republicans feel less political pressure on this matter, partially because they have far fewer black Republican party activists and supporters. Nevertheless, there are occasional calls within the Republican Party for a "broadening of the base" by being more inclusive of minorities. Both President Bush and Republican National Chairman Lee Atwater issued such calls after the 1988 election. If that objective were to be pursued, the Republicans would face some of the same internal pressures for minority representation that the Democrats have struggled with for years.

Finally, for Table 1 there is an interesting point to be made about demographic representation for young people. This was an important issue in both parties in the Vietnam War era. In 1972, 22 percent of the Democratic delegates were under thirty; in 1976, 15 percent were in this age group. Since then the percentage has declined back to 1968 levels. There was never substantial increase of young delegates among the GOP, although their ranks did double to 8 percent in 1972 and 7 percent in 1976.

Inasmuch as the Census Bureau indicates that 46 percent of the total population is under thirty, it is evident that party delegates are not representative on this dimension.[6] Young people are not a self-conscious group complete with group leaders in the same way as women and blacks are (at least at the activist level), so their lack of representation is explainable in political terms. Overall the trends among these three demographic groups are reasonably clear and are indicative of the larger political and social trends that have included these three groups during the 1968 to 1988 era.

Ideology of the Delegates and the Public

The first and in many ways the most basic values question is the degree of mass-elite congruence in political philosophy. Members of the party elites tend to be well educated, accustomed to dealing with the world in ideological terms, and able to assess their own positions on an ideological continuum. Earlier research demonstrated that such elites can place themselves and political candidates on the ideological spectrum and can make fairly fine distinctions between their own position and that of a given candidate.[7]

While most Americans may not be terribly sophisticated about matters of political philosophy, they do recognize and relate to the terms "liberal" and "conservative." In fact, there is considerable evidence that these concepts constitute a factor in the voters' electoral decision-making—a tendency the Bush campaign

TABLE 2
Philosophical Position of the 1988 Democratic Delegates vs.
the Mass Public

	1988 Democratic Delegates	Democratic Identifiers	American Public in 1988
Liberal	43%	26%	20%
Moderate	43	42	48
Conservative	5	28	32

Source: Assembled from: CBS News poll of national convention delegates. Plissner and Mitofsky, "The Making of the Delegates, 1968–88," p. 47. Also Andrew Rosenthal, "Poll Finds Atlanta Delegates More Liberal Than the Public," *New York Times* (July 17, 1988, pp. 1 and 17, the source of data on the mass public).

seized on when it effectively painted Dukakis into a corner by portraying him as a "liberal" (a term that now carries derogatory connotations for a large portion of the American public).

As is obvious from Table 2, more than twice as many Democratic delegates (43 percent) as members of the mass public (20 percent) called themselves liberal in 1988. Members of the public who identified with the Democratic Party fell in between, at 26 percent. The remainder of the Democratic delegates were almost exclusively "moderates" (43 percent), with only 5 percent calling themselves "conservatives." By contrast, 32 percent of the American public and 28 percent of Democratic identifiers considered themselves to be conservatives. Obviously, on this highly symbolic ideological dimension Democratic delegates were out of step with their party's mass membership and even more out of step with the public at large. The Democratic Party in 1988 was an ideologically diverse coalition with a substantial block of voters in each philosophical category. As we have seen, this is one of the Democrats' problems, especially since that diversity was not fully reflected in the philosophical leanings of the party's elite.

These findings are consistent with earlier reports that convention delegates tend to be predominately from the left of the ideological spectrum if they are Democrats and the right of the spectrum if they are Republican.[8] It would therefore come as no surprise to learn that in 1988 Republican convention delegates were as far out of step on the conservative end of the continuum as Democratic delegates were on the liberal end.

TABLE 3
Philosophical Position of the 1988 Republican Delegates vs.
the Mass Public

	1988 Republican Delegates	Republican Identifiers	American Public in 1988
Liberal	0%	11%	20%
Moderate	36	44	48
Conservative	59	40	32

Source: CBS News poll. See Plissner and Mitofsky, "The Making of the Delegates," p. 46, for data on the delegates and party identifiers. The *New York Times* survey was the source for the mass public. See the Rosenthal article cited in Table 2.

According to Table 3, the 1988 Republican delegates were hardly paragons of representativeness on the matter of their own political philosophy. Fifty-nine percent of Republican delegates, versus only 32 percent of the American public, considered themselves to be "conservatives." Less than one percent of the Republican delegates called themselves "liberal," as compared to 20 percent of the public. Thirty-six percent of the Republican delegates, but 48 percent of the mass public, considered themselves "moderates."

Based on these comparisons, it is obvious that neither party's convention represented a cross section of either the American public or, perhaps more problematically, of the party's mass membership, at least insofar as the liberal-conservative dimension is concerned.

Issue Positions

Beyond broad positions on the left-right continuum, there are important domestic and foreign policy issues that divide the American electorate. Some of the specific issues in American campaigns tend to divide the party elites much more sharply than they do the mass electorate.[9] In general, we expect Democratic elites to take issue positions to the left of their party's mass base, Republican elites to take positions to the right of the Republican mass base, and the total electorate to fall in the middle, between the two sets of elites and the two sets of partisans. However, the question then becomes what this pattern tells us about how gen-

TABLE 4

1988 Democratic and Republican Delegates' Views on Smaller Government Providing Fewer Services vs. Larger Government Providing More Services Compared to Party Identifiers and Mass Public

	Democrat Delegates	Democrat Identifiers	American Public	GOP Identifiers	GOP Delegates
Smaller Government	16%	33%	43%	59%	81%
Larger Government	58	56	44	30	4
"It Depends"	15	5	5	11	15

Source: Calculated from Plissner and Mitofsky, "The Making of the Delegates," p. 45, and from the results of their general survey provided by the CBS News poll.

eral election campaigns are run and how voters react to those campaigns.

The 1988 *New York Times* survey asked convention delegates and party identifiers whether they preferred bigger government providing more services or smaller government providing fewer services. One of the most interesting facets of the responses (see Table 4) is how evenly divided the public was on this question. In 1988, 43 percent of the mass public favored a smaller government performing fewer services, and 44 percent favored larger government. This divided result suggests that the "Reagan revolution" against government either never took hold in a large portion of the public or ran its course by 1988. Pressing national problems like drug abuse, homelessness, AIDS, environmental pollution, nuclear waste, and so on, were on the minds of many Americans, and the polls showed that the public supported some government action to deal with these problems.

There were marked differences between Republicans and Democrats in their preferences for more or fewer government programs. Some 59 percent of the Republican identifiers and 81 percent of the Republican convention delegates favored smaller government. On the Democratic side, 56 percent of the Democratic identifiers and 58 percent of the convention delegates favored bigger government providing more services. In this domain, then, the Democratic party elites mirrored their party's mass base fairly closely, and certainly more accurately than the Republican elites did theirs. The Democrats, elites and followers alike, were much closer to public opinion at large on this issue than the Republicans were; however, this was not an advantage the Democrats were able to exploit in the fall campaign.

If my analysis of the representativeness of the presidential nomination process were to end here, the reader would more than likely conclude that demographic representation is apparent in certain respects within the nominating process of both political parties. The clear exception of course is participation of persons under thirty. Here, there is little indication of representation. With regard to the ideological and issue aspect of representation, the empirical evidence is mixed and not terribly suggestive of a true representative process. Generally, national convention delegates are not mirror images of the party's rank and file, nor of the mass public, in terms of political values. However, to focus on only demographics and values is to restrict the analysis to the "standing for" component of representation. As it was noted, the "acting for" component of representation offers the more advanced analysis of representation and the more definite indication of whether or not national convention delegates are properly representing their party and the public. Behavior as opposed to characteristics offers the more complete picture of representation and necessitates an examination of strategic considerations at the nominating convention.

The Strategic Dilemma of the Delegates

The important strategic consideration is how members of the party elite ultimately behave at the convention. This is where the idea of "acting for" representation becomes relevant. American party elites have tended to represent the ideological wings rather than the center of the political spectrum. Somewhat anomalously, however, the classic presidential strategy is for the party to nominate a candidate who steers more toward the middle of the political road than do party activists. More than three decades ago, Anthony Downs (1957) and V. O. Key (1958) explained this behavior as a case of rational action resulting in the desired electoral payoffs, since the middle is where the most voters tend to be in American politics.[10]

Following this logic, the strategic drive toward the middle became the conventional wisdom among observers of American presidential politics. In fact, two apparent exceptions to this rule seemed to provide conclusively the wisdom of the norm. In 1964 the Republican Party seemed to be in jeopardy. In 1972 the Democrats nominated the liberal George McGovern, and again a defeat of landslide proportions followed.

Critics denounced the internal Democratic Party reforms of the McGovern era as opening up the party to a takeover by far left activists with little loyalty to the party.[11] Subsequent events and research, however, have shown the situation to be a good deal more mixed than that.[12]

In 1976 the Democrats nominated a virtual unknown, Jimmy Carter, who developed a considerably more moderate image than George McGovern. While Gerald Ford was also fairly moderate, he carried the baggage of the scandals of Watergate and his pardon of Nixon. Carter's victory, coming only four years after the McGovern debacle, seemed to provide further support for the thesis that the Democrats needed to nominate moderate candidates. In fact, Carter in 1976 and Johnson in 1964, both southerners who appealed to the middle of the political spectrum and both able to rally personal support in the black community, are the only Democrats who have won in the last seven presidential elections. Thus, a drive toward the middle without losing at least the black portion of the traditional base has been the essential ingredient of the Democrats only recent presidential victories.

The 1980 presidential election raised substantial doubts about the conventional wisdom for the Republicans. In 1980 the Republicans nominated Ronald Reagan, who was clearly the champion of the party's conservative wing. In Reagan's 1980 victory, the conservative activists who were first attracted to the Republican Party by Barry Goldwater in 1964 consolidated their takeover of the party organization.[13] Reagan went on to a landslide victory over Carter, who was wounded by the Iranian hostage crisis and by double-digit inflation and other economic woes.

In 1984 Reagan won another landslide, this time over Walter Mondale in an election that did little to enhance the Democratic Party's long-term presidential prospects. In both 1980 and 1984 the Republican delegates did what their own ideological positions rather than the Downsian imperative toward the middle would seem to dictate. The Republicans nominated one of the most conservative and ideological candidates of the twentieth century, yet they were rewarded with handsome electoral victories on other than ideological grounds.

Notwithstanding the Downsian imperative, there can be ample philosophical rationale for party activists to nominate a presidential candidate from the party's characteristic ideological wing. The "responsible parties" school of thought advocates that a party should stand for something meaningful in terms of basic philosophy and public policy.[14] In a fundamental sense, the Republicans in 1964, 1980, and 1984 were only engaged in the kind of strategic behavior demanded by the responsible party model by offering the public an ideological candidate. So the pull of these two competing electoral models—the idea that it is rational to select centrist candidates in a system where middle-of-the-road thinking predominates, and the notion that the parties should offer distinctive choices to the electorate and then try to govern according to an electoral "mandate"—continues to pose a dilemma for the party elites.

The 1988 experience suggests support for an elaboration on the conventional, centrist, or Downsian strategy. More specifically, the Bush campaign exemplifies a two-stage strategy: (1) win the support of the more ideological party regulars or elites before and during the primaries and national convention, but (2) leave room to move toward the middle in the general election campaign. Such movement must be done in such a way as to broaden the ticket's appeal without losing the support of party loyalists. In 1988 Bush accomplished this balancing act; Dukakis did not.

Certainly Bush's campaigners had no room to move to the right. If they wanted to pick up votes or to avoid alienating those to their left, the campaign had to position itself somewhat toward the middle on the question of the role of government. This is the conventional Downsian strategy. Undoubtedly poll results helped inform the Bush campaign, and they suggest why Bush seemed to favor some form of child care program, drug treatment and interdiction programs, continuation of cost-of-living adjustments for Social Security recipients, support for the homeless, and some form of environmental program. Bush also announced that he wanted to be known as "the education president," and confessed in his nomination acceptance speech that he "did not hate the government," which, he said, could be instrumental in achieving a "kinder, gentler America." In short, Bush's general election campaign dealt with the issue of the role of the government in a manner that more closely reflected the views of the mass public than did the views of the 1988 Republican delegates who nominated him. Moreover, the Republican elites gave Bush relatively wide latitude during the general election campaign, permitting the smaller of the two major parties to broaden its electoral coalition during the general election campaign.

While Bush is somewhat harder to classify ideologically than Reagan was, he spent eight years courting the conservative wing of the Republican Party. The "conservative" label that Bush applied to himself certainly did not hurt him in 1988, and it may have been crucial in his primary victories. On the other hand, Bush successfully labeled Dukakis a "card-carrying northeastern liberal," and this theme really came into prominence during the Republican National Convention. Being a liberal meant, as the Bush campaign told it, being soft on crime, in favor of prison furloughs for convicted first-degree murderers, weak on national defense, opposed to weapons systems, in favor of abortions, and opposed to "traditional values." In short, it meant being outside the American mainstream. To these charges the Dukakis campaign never mounted an effective response. Late in the campaign Dukakis agreed that he was indeed a liberal and tried to define in positive terms what that meant. But by then his response was too little, too late.

The strategic challenge for each party is to maintain its own traditional party base while appealing to the middle of the political spectrum, which is populated by members of the party, by potential crossovers from the other party, and by large numbers of the independents who can hold the balance of power in presidential elections. The data in Tables 2 and 3 indicate how difficult and delicate this balancing act can be. Data regarding demographic and ideological profiles of convention delegates simply do not answer the complex question of representation in the nomination process. It is the behavior of the convention delegates in conjunction with the Downsian model of rational behavior that is the more stringent measure of representation.

CONCLUSION

Clearly over the two decades between 1968 and 1988 the Democratic convention delegates became more representative of the national electorate on the matter of demographic representation. On the male vs. female and black vs. white dimensions of representation, the Democrats, through a combination of mandated quotas, affirmative action, and the political fallout from actions taken by various presidential candidates accomplished a relatively high degree of demographic representation. Democratic constituency groups feel that such representation is definitely important to them in symbolic terms and potentially important in attaining more faithful representation of those groups' policy preferences and values. The Republicans have moved somewhat in this direction on representation for women, although they backtracked somewhat in 1988. They have made virtually no change on the matter of black representation and apparently feel very little political pressure to do so.

The matter of the representation of values and public policy preferences is infinitely more complex than that of demographic representation. Consequently, as we have already seen, the picture on the representativeness of the party elites is a very mixed one. On some indicators the elites of both parties are fairly close to their mass base and to the public as a whole. On most indicators the party elites, in the form of the convention delegates, are much closer to the ends of the ideological continuum. The party leaders are more and more offering the voters "a choice, not an echo" to borrow from Barry Goldwater's phrase in terms of their own issue positions and ideology, and the party leadership is becoming more polarized. So the answer to whether the party elites are "representative" in a "standing for" sense varies depending on which question is asked.

Finally, the most important question revolves around the "acting for" dimension. What do the convention delegates do at the convention? Here the matter is more difficult to address. However, if the delegates follow a Downsian imperative and vote toward the middle in candidate support and platform adoption, the chances are that they are acting rather faithfully *for* the values of the greatest majority of their partisans and of the American electorate. To the extent that they do this, they and their candidates will probably enjoy greater long-term electoral success. If they fail too consistently to "act for" the interests of the voters at large, or at least are perceived to fail, the parties will lose presidential elections and access to the rewards of holding power. In that sense, then, the governed retain at least some check on the actions of the governed. When we explore the outcome of nominating contests over the past two decades, it becomes apparent that the Downsian mode of behavior with respect to candidate selection and platform construction has been apparent, although not always, in Democratic and Republican nominating conventions, certainly more so than critics of the process currently claim.

Part 2

NO—
The Nominating Process is Not Representative

Sarah McCally Morehouse

An astounding process recruits and nominates the president of the United States. In many other democracies an acknowledged leader stands ready to govern should that party win the election. In these countries each party already has a leader whether it be in the majority or the minority. In the United States, nobody knows who their national party leader is unless he or she is president. Hence, every four years each party searches for a leader with the hope that he or she will be elected to this highest office. In the last twenty years this search has been unstable and risky.

Can a constantly changing and unpredictable process be representative? The presidential nominating process cannot guarantee that candidates representative of their party's identifiers and voters will be selected. Hence the people of the United States are at risk every four years when a nominating process, which has not operated by the same set of rules since 1968, produces a Republican and Democratic nominee. Citizens have the right to have confidence in the institution that gives them candidates for president. Turnout for presidential primaries is about 27 percent of the eligible voters, which at best indicates a lack of interest in the process and at worst means that nominations are made by an unrepresentative minority of the American people.

This grave picture is not without hope, however. Political parties are largely reactive organizations. They are in the business of winning votes from an electorate that is more educated and informed than ever before. They must adjust their operations to the needs and demands of this electorate. While there were many reasons for the succession of reforms that engulfed the nominating process in the last twenty years, the parties have begun to make incremental changes calculated to restore representation and predictability. The Democrats have instituted a system of ex officio delegates—those who make up 15 percent of their convention and who are officeholders and party officials. Both parties have tried to give more control over the nominating process to the party organizations and leadership.

In this paper I will discuss the post-1968 changes that have made the presidential selection process different from before and the impact of these changes. I will analyze the implications for the political parties as they attempt to represent the American people in candidate selection and governing. The issue of representation is fundamental. Representation is institutionalized in our system of competing party organizations. The vast increase in the number of primaries by which we nominate the president tends to undermine such representation, making the nominee responsive to a small segment of the electorate that has no responsibility for governing. A primary electorate cannot be held accountable; a party organization can.

CHANGING THE RULES CHANGES THE GAME

The time-honored delegate selection process began in the precincts as meetings of local party officers who elected representatives to the next level in the hierarchy of conventions that eventually chose national delegates. This "caucus-convention" system gave party leaders influence or control over the delegate selection process and hence over nominees. Before 1968, sixteen or seventeen primaries for each party were used by an occasional candidate as an appeal to party leaders. Very few delegates were selected in these primaries. But in 1988 there were Republican primaries in thirty-three states and Democratic primaries in thirty-two, all producing committed delegates.

There is no doubt that the change in the rules by which we nominate a president has changed the presidential selection game. These rules came about as a result of a much longer process of party decline, according to Howard Reiter.[1] Indeed it is hard to imagine how a healthy party could have submitted to the reforms put forward by the Democratic Party's Commission on Party Structure and Delegate Selection, commonly known as the McGovern-Fraser Commission, which was mandated by the Democratic National Convention in 1968. Observers had noted the impact of a combination of public opinion polls, primaries, and media on the nominating process. Rather than indulge in a more gradual change, which would have responded to the polls, the media, and public participation without massive institutional dislocation, the Democratic Party set itself on a course of reform for the next twenty years.

The year 1968 had brought forth a series of profound shocks to the American political system, which fueled the demand for change. The war raged in South Vietnam, President Johnson said he would not run for reelection, and Vice-President Hubert Humphrey declared his own candidacy. Martin Luther King, Jr., was assassinated and on the last day of the primary season Robert Kennedy, a major contender for the nomination, was shot and killed. Hubert Humphrey, the choice of the party leaders throughout the nominating process, was nominated at the Democratic convention in Chicago. But the party was seriously divided and the American viewing public saw Mayor Daley's Chicago police clubbing young anti-Humphrey demonstrators in the streets outside the convention hall. Humphrey had been nominated without contesting one primary and hence he appeared unrepresentative of the party. In this environment it is not surprising that the party leaders could not control the extent of the reforms.

The McGovern-Fraser Commission and subsequent commissions, which have followed each Democratic convention, attempted to make the nominating process more representative of the wishes of those who identify with and support the Democratic Party. This was to be accomplished in the following ways: (1) prohibit the common practice of providing delegate positions automatically to certain party or public officials; (2) guarantee by affirmative steps opportunities for participation by certain minorities (blacks, women, and young people) in reasonable relationship to their presence in the population; (3) prohibit the use of the unit rule, which allocated all of a state's delegates to the candidate receiving a plurality of votes in the state. The commission encouraged the adoption of proportional representation systems in which any candidate receiving at least 15 percent of the primary vote in a state would get some delegates. The "loophole" system in which the unit rule is applied at the congressional district level is still allowed if delegates are elected directly.

What of the Republicans? They were more willing to remain "unreformed." They have no enforceable demographic quotas or affirmative action standards. But many of the reforms of the Democratic Party had to be accomplished by changes in state election laws. Where state laws were changed, Republican practices had to be changed as well.

Both parties have had to accommodate to the Federal Election Campaign Act Amendments of 1974, which created a federal subsidy for candidates in primary elections. In order to qualify for the subsidy, candidates have to raise $5,000 or more in small amounts in twenty different states—hardly a difficult task. Although the actual payments do not occur until the election year begins, candidates begin early to acquire the money in as many states as possible to gain favorable news coverage. In addition, candidates need to start early because heavy financial backing by a small circle of friends was also forbidden by the 1974 law. Hence candidates need to raise money in small approved amounts (up to $5,000) through direct-mail advertising, fund-raisers, and dinners.

The Democratic Party reforms as well as the Federal Election Campaign Act of 1974 have brought about the following results, which have had a major impact on the representativeness of the nominating process:

1. Consistent instability.
2. Rapid growth in the number of presidential primaries, first among Democrats but subsequently among Republicans as well. (Note that the Republicans had one more state primary than the Democrats in 1988.)
3. Increase in the number of delegates selected in primaries from 40 percent in 1968 to 66.6 percent for the Democrats and 76.9 percent for the Republicans in 1988.[2]
4. Earlier starting campaigns due to the need to raise money and gain publicity.
5. "Frontloading"—the practice of a growing number of states to move primaries and caucuses to the beginning of the nominating process.

The remainder of this paper will discuss the implication of these results singly or in combination for the representativeness of the nominating process. The impact of the news media on the nominative system has major implications as well.

The Mass Media: Do they Represent or Control?

Advanced technology, not reform, gives us a further element of the contemporary nominating process—the central importance of television. It impacts on all facets of the presidential selection process. Two-thirds of Americans claim that television is their most important source of campaign information, about one-fourth cite newspapers, and the rest are divided between magazines and newspapers. Television is the most trusted and clearest source.[3] Now that over two-thirds of all delegates to the national nominating conventions are chosen by presidential primaries, candidates must rely upon the media, especially television, to inform the voters. Television has taken the place of the political party in presenting the candidates for nomination to the party's most important race. Television informs the electorate; the electorate chooses the nominee. The media are asked to organize public choice, a task for which they were not designed. Walter Lippmann, Journalist, said that public opinions must be organized *for* the press, not *by* the press.[4] How can we be sure that the election opinion presented by the media is representative of the desires of the party's voters?

The presidential nominating races attract large numbers of contenders, except when an incumbent is seeking reelection. Most candidates are not nationally known in advance of the race. In the first few primaries, voters are asked to choose quickly on the basis of what they have learned through the media. According to Thomas Patterson, the media leave voters inadequately informed for two reasons.[5] First, election news concentrates on the "horse race" aspect of the campaign and not about policies and leadership. This is particularly likely to occur in the early stages of the campaign when the voters have their greatest need for information about the candidates' political positions. Second, the election news does not provide the candidates with equal exposure. In 1988 five Republican candidates sought to inform the voters through the media, but received vastly different coverage. The amount of attention each candidate received until the primary season began was in proportion to their standing in the national polls. Thus previous popularity determined coverage until the day of the first event in the nominating season. It would not be surprising if the candidates selected in the first contests closely reflected this coverage.

Another limitation on the ability of the media to cover all self-declared candidates is their supply of people, space, and time. These were severely strained for the Super Tuesday round of primaries, which occurred on March 8, 1988, and involved twenty states for the Democrats and seventeen for the Republicans. David Broder, dean of national political reporters, admitted that the above limitations would prevent coverage of more than two or three candidates in each party. He said that the press would have to reduce the number of candidates treated as serious contenders. Those who finished first or second in Iowa or New Hampshire would be eligible for the next round, with the possible exception made for Jesse Jackson and Pat Robertson, who had their own church-based communications networks.[6] Are the results of the early caucuses and primaries satisfactory winnowing devices for the nominating races?

Iowa and New Hampshire now compete for preeminence as the first two confrontations between candidates. In 1980 Robinson and Sheehan found that Iowa and New Hampshire together accounted for 28 percent of all primary coverage by television and newspapers.[7] Larry Bartels reports that about 30 percent of the total newspaper coverage in 1984 came in the first eight weeks of the campaign, a period ending one week after Hart's New Hampshire upset. During the same period less than 1 percent of the season's primary votes were cast. The 4 million votes cast on June 5, the last big day of the primary season, generated about half as much coverage as had the 100,000 votes cast in New Hampshire more than three months earlier.[8]

The attention the news media give to these two states, coupled with their tendency to emphasize winning, ensures that winners in these two contests have the momentum to carry them fast forward into the race. In addition to covering primary winners, the media tend to give attention to some candidates who do "better than expected." Coverage was lavished on Gary Hart in Iowa in 1984. Although Walter Mondale beat him three-to-one, Hart got more coverage than Mondale in the subsequent week, and was launched on his campaign. Two days after his New Hampshire victory, criticisms of him began to appear, which slowed his progress. The greatest danger of the existing nominating process, depending as it does on the media, is that an unknown candidate like Gary Hart may emerge in the early stages when substantive political information is in short supply and horse race reporting plays a crucial role in shaping choices. In 1984 reconsideration of Hart came in time for Mondale to survive and eventually win the nomination, but the Democratic Party was perilously close to losing its tested candidate to one who would have proved to be dangerous.

Frontloading: Iowa and New Hampshire

Recognizing the influence that states with early primaries have over the presidential selection process, more states have moved to place their candidate selection events near the beginning of the season. In 1968 only New Hampshire held its primary before the middle of March; in 1988 twenty states did so. In addition, eleven states had caucuses before that date.[9]

This means that candidates must start early to raise money and secure publicity so essential for the nomination. Now there is no other choice. A candidate who decides not to enter the first two races in Iowa and New Hampshire is crippled from the start. It was not like this before 1972 when candidates could use various strategies, which included some primaries and caucuses but not others. Influencing party leaders does not matter any more. Influencing voters in two states, Iowa and New Hampshire, has become the key to the nomination because of the momentum they give the candidate. George McGovern in 1972 and Jimmy Carter in 1976 proved that strategic early wins were essential to the nomination. Both ran well in Iowa and New Hampshire, gaining the media attention, financial contributions, and organizational volunteers that carried them to further victories and hence to the nomination. In 1988 momentum gained in Iowa and New Hampshire was predicted to carry the candidate into Super Tuesday, a day on which there were primaries in sixteen states and caucuses in four. The primaries were held in almost every Southern state and were planned to "frontload" the nominating schedule to give the South an advantage at an early stage. Vice-President Bush's momentum did carry him through Super Tuesday and he essentially secured the nomination. Dukakis's momentum from the New Hampshire primary undoubtedly helped him win two populous states, Florida and Texas.

Losers in New Hampshire are crippled because they receive negative publicity, money begins to dry up, and volunteers look elsewhere. Therefore it is important to take a look at the two states that launch presidential candidates. Are partisans there representative of their party's rank and file? Can a candidate who wins in New Hampshire appeal to the identifiers and voters of his or her party in the general election?

In Iowa and New Hampshire, small numbers of voters have a disproportionate effect on the nominating process. In Iowa roughly 235,000 voters turned out for the Democratic and Republican caucuses in 1988, and about 280,000 voters went to the polls in the Democratic and Republican primaries in New Hampshire. Compare that with the 5 million voters who participated in the California primary on June 7 who had no effect on the results, because Dukakis and Bush already had their nominations sewed up.[10]

Some political scientists believe these two states offer the possibility for dark horse candidates to prove themselves in the small-market environment in which personal campaigning counts. Then with the publicity that accompanies a win or a place, they can count on money and momentum. In 1972 McGovern was publicized as the "winner" (he did better than expected) in both states although he lost both to Senator Edmund S. Muskie, the front-runner. It is my belief that the presidential nominating contest is not the place for dark horse candidates to emerge. They should prove themselves as capable and electable leaders before the presidential selection process begins.

Democratic Iowa and New Hampshire partisans are not representative of their party's identifiers. Republican voters are reasonably representative. Mayer has compared the registered voters in New Hampshire and nationally for each party. For the Republicans, the registered voters are white, middle-class, Protestant, and suburban, both in New Hampshire and in the country as a whole. For the Democrats, there are important differences between the New Hampshire primary voters and the national party. Nationally, 19 percent of all voters who think of themselves as Democrats are black but in New Hampshire only 2 percent of Democratic voters are black. The New Hampshire Democrats are better educated, wealthier, more Catholic, and less urban than the national Democrats.[11] This means that "middle-of-the road" Democrats—those who vote for the party most faithfully—are not accurately represented in New Hampshire. In the past twenty years, those who won or placed well in the state—McCarthy in 1968, McGovern in 1972, Carter in 1976, and Hart in 1984—have all been dark horses and aligned with a nonregular faction of the party. In 1988 Dukakis, governor of the neighboring state of Massachusetts, won the primary with 35.8 percent of the vote. His campaign managers had counted on name recognition, due to neighborliness, as his major asset, not that he was from the middle-of-the road faction. In this case, the Democrats were able to produce momentum for the candidate who was most representative of their party primarily because of geography.

Perhaps if Walter Mondale had been fortunate enough to come from Massachusetts, he might have won the New Hampshire primary four years earlier. It was his misfortune to have to campaign first in his two worst states (those in which his underlying support was lowest).[12] New Hampshire and Vermont provided optimal conditions for Hart momentum. To conclude, it is an ironic twist of fate that a party that committed itself to twenty years of reforms to make itself more representative should be at the mercy of the nominating contests in two of its most unrepresentative states.

CAN PRIMARY VOTERS BE REPRESENTATIVE?

There is a difference of opinion about whether primary voters, who make up 20 percent of the voting age population, are representative of their fellow partisans. Since they select between two-thirds (Democratic) to three-fourths (Republican) of all delegates to the national convention, it is important to know whether they can be representative of their party. V. O. Key's study of state-level politics concluded that primary voters were unrepresentative of their respective parties and these differences could be based on geography, ideology, occupation—almost any possible source of division that would bring out the fervent few to nominate in their image.[13] Ranney found that presidential primary voters were better educated, wealthier, and with stronger partisan ties.[14] Lengle concluded that Democratic primary voters were ideologically more liberal than the party's constituency.[15]

On the other hand, two recent studies indicate that the voters in presidential primaries have not been unrepresentative of their parties. Geer used results from exit polls to define party following instead of the more traditional survey of self-identified partisans, a data source that could account for the difference from earlier results.[16] Bartels discovered that each party's primary voters were not noticeably different from party identifiers on domestic as well as foreign policy.[17] He did find that primary voters scored higher on "social stability" indicators insofar as they were older, more established in their communities, more likely to own their homes, and more frequent church-goers. Additionally, they were more interested in politics, more informed, and more frequent users of the media.

This suggests that primary voters could represent their respective party electorates well. However, the question remains: Can primary voters be expected to gain enough information about the candidates to make an informed choice? Bartels suggests that the momentum generated in the early races matters much more in some contests than others. It is, after all, the job of the primary voters to select a candidate who will be intelligent as well as popular, virtuous as well as presentable, and upright as well as inspiring. If Iowa and New Hampshire generate momentum, primary voters in the remaining races must evaluate substance over dynamics. It is in contests where none of the candidates are well known that momentum can be most compelling. In contests where there is one major candidate, momentum can also matter if a dark horse comes from behind and tries to stop the front-runner. It is only in races where there are two major candidates that momentum does not play a major role.[18]

In 1976 Jimmy Carter won the nomination on the first ballot in the Democratic convention. He was not popular with the party leaders—county chairpersons, national and state committee members, and other party notables. His pollster Patrick Caddell said: "My position is, unless we can put together a first-ballot victory or damn close to it, this party will deny us the nomination. Popular with the elites, we are not."[19]

Bartels's analysis suggests that without momentum Jimmy Carter would not have won Wisconsin, Pennsylvania, Indiana, Florida, Illinois, or North Carolina, and would not have put together a first-ballot victory. In this case, it was dynamics rather than substance that mattered. Over half of Carter's support in primaries came from his early successes. The conclusion of this is that primary voters may not be able to size up a candidate before it is too late to stop him. I believe that Jimmy Carter did not have the experience to govern, as his administration proved.

The second case where momentum matters is when a well-known candidate is challenged by a relatively unknown candidate who emerges in Iowa or New Hampshire. This was the case in the

Mondale-Hart contest in 1984. Hart was lucky in having early primary contests in congenial states. He was able to capitalize on his early successes in later primaries. Substantive political information was slow in catching up with the Hart momentum. Perceptions about the horse race dominated the choice at first. This is where an irrevocable mistake could be made. It is clear that the sequence of primaries does not allow for informed decision-making. Primaries come at a speed too rapid for substantive information to inform primary voters. They need time to evaluate the dark horse as a political leader, not a charismatic. In 1984 reconsideration of Hart did come in time for Mondale to survive, but his fate hung in the balance for several weeks. Voters in primaries may be reasonably representative of the party's rank and file, but the choices that they are asked to make by the structure of the nominating process may prevent selection of representative candidates.

ARE CONVENTION DELEGATES REPRESENTATIVE?

Over the last twenty years the Democrats have experimented with various ways to make their nominating process more representative. I have discussed the impact of these reforms on the Democratic Party as well as the Republican since many of the changes were enacted into state law, and even if they were not, the GOP felt the pressure to follow suit. The purpose of the McGovern-Fraser Commission was to take control of the presidential nomination away from party leaders gathered in the convention and give it to party activists attached to candidates who would be selected in primaries or caucuses open to all party members.

In addition, the commission assured representation of groups previously slighted: women, youth, and minorities. Women and blacks have fared rather well: among convention delegates they represent 75 to 85 percent of their strength in their respective parties.[20] Youth (ages 18–29) are seriously underrepresented in their respective conventions, although there was a surge in the three conventions following the reforms. However, disparities between income and education levels of delegates and of rank and file voters have remained largely unchanged during the era of reform. While the percentages of teachers and union members reached an all-time high at the Democratic convention of 1980, blue-collar workers and farmers to whom the Democrats wished to appeal could each claim less than 4 percent of the convention seats.[21] Since delegates are bound to their respective candidates, demographic representation does not matter a great deal. It may send a message to television viewers that the delegates are properly representative of minorities, but certainly more prosperous than the mainstream.

What matters more than demographic representation of the rank and file is the ideological representation. Here the national conventions are not representative of party identifiers. While ordinary voters of both parties tend to be centrist, Republican delegates are generally conservative and Democratic delegates are normally more liberal. Hence we discover a substantial gap between convention delegates and a party's rank and file. According to Miller and Jennings, the 1980 delegates supporting Senator Edward Kennedy were furthest from the party's identifiers, but not nearly so far as the Reaganites were from rank and file Republicans.[22] Polsby and Wildavsky believe that there may be some relationship between the reforms and the ideological elite-follower gap, for the Democrats at least. In 1972, the first year of the reform effects, McGovern delegates deviated significantly from Democratic followers. After that, the more moderate delegates dropped out of the process and those who returned became more ideologically committed. Apparently the same process occurred in the Republican Party, although it was not brought about originally by delegate selection rules.[23]

I believe that it does matter if convention delegates are ideologically unrepresentative of the party's followers. In the first place, a brokered convention, one in which no candidate arrives with a sufficient number of delegates to be nominated, is certainly a possibility, given the mandate for proportional representation within the Democratic Party and its emulation by Republicans. In 1976 that possibility existed if Jimmy Carter had not achieved the momentum that brought him a majority of the primary vote. The convention delegates would have had a choice between Carter, Wallace, Udall, Brown, and Jackson. If the Democratic delegates are considerably more liberal than their followers, an unrepresentative nominee is likely. A second way in which the difference between delegates and followers matters is that in the attempt to persuade delegates to support the party ticket in the fall, nominees must prove their ideological credentials. Dukakis was a moderate, but he had to appease the liberal activists in the party and this was not his best approach to the millions of uncommitted voters throughout the nation. At the Republican convention, Bush stressed conciliation with the right wing of his party rather than a broader appeal.[24]

In another way the delegates of both conventions have been unrepresentative. After 1968 the proportions of elected officeholders dropped drastically. In 1968, 92 percent of Democratic governors, 67 percent of the senators, and 36 percent of the congressmen attended the party convention. In 1972 these percentages had dropped to 67 percent, 35 percent, and 15 percent, respectively. And they dropped even further for the convention of 1976. The Republicans also experienced a drop, but not as severe.[25] It matters whether the delegates to the national nominating conventions are representative of the officeholders in their respective parties. Officials have been successful in their election attempts. They are better able to judge the electability of potential candidates. No doubt their proportions went down because they were required by the reformed process to compete for delegate seats like everybody else. This means competing among each other as well as declaring early for a candidate, both requirements distasteful or inappropriate to a top officeholder. Thus for two or three conventions, top officeholders in each party were denied the right to attend the convention and provide a moderating influence.

Fortunately, both parties have reacted to this loss by encouraging their top party people to return, with noticeable success. Republican governors and representatives are increasing in attendance. Beginning in 1984, the Democratic Party created several hundred "superdelegate" slots for Democratic members of Congress and state party leaders. These delegates do not have to run in their state's primary or caucus and can vote for any candidate they wish. While these superdelegates occupied 15 percent of the seats at the 1984 and 1988 Democratic conventions, they loyally supported the front-runner in the primaries: Mondale in 1984 and Dukakis in 1988. However, this first step to bring back peer review into the nominating process signals a reaction of the party to its weakened condition and an attempt to alter the trend. This sends signals to elected officials throughout the party as well as to potential nominees. They need to build alliances and coalitions among these officials in order to receive support in the election as well as in the governing process.

ARE NOMINEES REPRESENTATIVE?

In 1988 the nominating process produced candidates who were moderates, thus representing the centrist positions of their respective parties' flock. Bush and Dukakis were experienced politicians with many years of public service. Both strove for unity among all party factions. Was this a result of the increased effort on the part of the political parties to reenter the nominating process? While the increase in party leaders as convention delegates may have played a minor part, it could hardly be responsible for the fact that both parties chose "textbook" nominees: those who could build a coalition in the electoral process that would carry over into the governing process. I conclude that there is no guarantee that the nominating process will produce representative candidates as it did in 1988. We are at risk that a future presidential election year will again give us ideological extremists or insurgents.

Any discussion of the characteristics of nominees must begin with those who choose not to run because of the rigors of the preprimary period. Fund-raising and campaigning in Iowa and New Hampshire must start so early that it is impossible to hold a responsible job and run for nomination. New Jersey Senator Bill Bradley gave that as his reason for not running. Governor Cuomo withdrew his name from the race claiming that he did not wish to subject his family to the intense personal scrutiny necessary to campaign in a succession of primary elections. Hence two qualified Democrats chose not to enter the race because they did not want to build their own candidate organizations, raise their own funds, and otherwise engage in the highly personalized effort required of contemporary candidates for nomination.

Does the nominating process give us candidates who are electable? Certainly not. George McGovern, an outsider who was not favored by party leaders, proved that he could capture the nomination without their support. He had his base in the insurgent anti-Vietnam war wing of the party. The electorate feared his extremism and he received a bare 38 percent of the popular vote.

Even acknowledged vote-getters such as incumbent presidents are having a harder time being renominated. Since 1972 there has been an increase in the anti-incumbent vote at the conventions, as Howard Reiter has demonstrated.[26] Ford and Carter were able to overcome Reagan and Kennedy's preprimary leads in the polls, but the fact that incumbent presidents are seriously challenged indicates again the decline of party support for acknowledged vote-getters. President Reagan spent significant amounts of time at party-building, which may explain his overwhelming renomination in 1984. Reiter also indicates that the present nominating process does not encourage coalition-building for the election. He shows an increase in the extent to which those partisans supporting candidates who lost the nomination were likelier to defect in November than those who supported the winner.[27] This is true for both parties since 1972. The evidence indicates that it becomes harder to elect a presidential nominee, especially one who is an ideologue and unrepresentative of the party's rank and file.

Can nominees selected by the nominating process represent the needs and demands of the voters once they are in office? Lester Seligman claims that a president's influence depends upon his electoral coalition. The groups that played an important part in the nomination stage usually play an important role in presidential policy-making and administration. The president chooses principal members of the White House staff and other key officials based on their participation in the campaign.[28] In this regard, Jimmy Carter exemplified lack of coalition-building for nomination and election, and hence lack of ability to govern once elected. What it takes to achieve the nomination differs sharply from what it takes to govern. Carter did not believe in the reality of the interest group composition of the Democratic Party. As Nelson Polsby points out, the litany of presidential mistakes toward Congress was nearly endless.[29]

He had a reluctance to bring Congress into the process of bill-formulation before it reconvened on Capitol Hill. He appealed to the people over the heads of congressmen who had run well ahead of him in their home districts. Hence the presidential nominating process does not ensure that candidates who can build coalitions to represent the needs and desires of the people will be elected. In fact the process discourages this effort, for when Walter Mondale attempted to a build a coalition of labor, teachers, and other groups within the Democratic Party, he was criticized for being a "captive" to special interests.

CONCLUSIONS

In this paper I have stated that I do not believe the presidential nominating process gives us candidates representative of their party's rank and file. It is a process totally dependent upon the media for information. The party as an organization gives the voters no cues as to its preference, nor can it, because an overwhelming percentage of the delegates are selected in primaries the parties cannot control. The first primaries, held in small states, can give a potential candidate the momentum he or she needs to be the front-runner. The voters in the following sequence of primaries are not given enough information to make the vital choices they must make to nominate a representative candidate. In the convention itself, delegates are not representative of the party's rank and file but are ideologically far away. This could mean that a brokered convention could not fulfill its role of agreeing on a candidate who would represent the voters, or indeed agree on a candidate at all. The unrepresentative character of convention delegates also means that those who did not support the winner may "sit on their hands" in the forthcoming election. While it is riskier to state that nominees are not representative of the mainstream party identifiers, we have the example of Jimmy Carter who did not believe in coalition-building and hence could not govern. He lost the following election, the first time that an incumbent had been defeated since 1932 (I do not count Ford). Both parties have had a hard time recently in renominating incumbents, presumably those who are acknowledged vote-getters.

No set of rules is foolproof. General rules operate within a set of constraints: issues, party loyalties and images, the press, the record of the administration, public opinion. But it is possible to increase, however marginally, the odds of a favorable outcome, one that will guarantee candidates who are mindful of and appeal to the rank and file voter. The Democratic Party will need to make more changes to bring about a central role for public officials. Both parties must work toward coalition-building in order to give the people a nominee who can be elected and govern in their interests.

CHAPTER TWO

Should Convention
Delegates be Formally Pledged?

The issue of pledged convention delegates brings us deep into the heart of one of the most current controversies facing national nominating conventions. Should convention delegates who arrive at a national nominating convention pledged to a specific candidate be allowed the opportunity to break their pledge and exercise independent judgment in the choice of a presidential nominee? Robert T. Nakamura argues that a convention delegate should remain pledged to a candidate for at least the first round of convention balloting, a position that endorses the current rules of both political parties. In Nakamura's view, nominating conventions in which convention delegates are independent decision-makers are not a practical consideration in the modern age of party politics as party elites are fragmented and there is an absence of true power brokers. Conventions, therefore, are not the best forums for developing a consensus on who will be the presidential nominee. Nakamura also argues that the current policy of pledged delegates is consistent with the principle of popular consent, maintains the important distinction of a "front-runner," contributes to party unity during the presidential campaign, promotes stability, and enhances democratic legitimacy in the nominating process.

Elaine Ciulla Kamarck believes that convention delegates should have independent discretion on the floor of the convention regardless of previous commitments in primaries or caucuses. Of interest is that Kamarck in 1980 argued in favor of pledged dele-

gates to ensure the nomination of President Carter. Following a detailed examination of the history and politics associated with the Democratic nominating convention in 1980, when the pledged delegates rule was at the center of controversy, Kamarck proceeds to articulate her position. One of Kamarck's chief concerns is that nominating conventions, by upholding the policy of pledged delegates, are slowly but surely evolving toward the status of the Electoral College, an institution predictable in behavior and not worthy of news coverage. Kamarck views this development as having unfortunate consequences for political parties as electoral institutions. She also argues that perceptions of candidates can change over a five- or six-month period and that discretion is an effective check against candidates who eventually surface as incompetent or even extremist. Kamarck believes that the Democratic rule of proportional representation can potentially deadlock conventions, which, she argues, necessitates free will and independent judgment. Kamarck expresses optimism over the relatively new rule of the Democratic Party, which ensures some influence for unpledged party regulars, known as "superdelegates."

Part 1

YES—
Convention Delegates Should be Formally Pledged

Robert T. Nakamura

Yes, convention delegates should run as pledged to a candidate and they should be bound to vote for him or her at least for the first ballot. In practice this is the current situation for most delegates, the largest exception being the superdelegates who comprise about 15 percent of the Democratic convention. Presently, the degree to which delegates at either convention are bound depends on a complex combination of state laws, party rules, and the personal commitments of the delegates themselves. While the Democrats have relaxed the party rule binding delegates, the candidate commitments of the delegates themselves—reinforced in many instances by state laws and expectations of those who participated in delegate selection—have kept them faithful.

This brief essay will deal with the desirability in principle of binding delegates rather than the mechanisms for accomplishing it. And, on a more general note, the essay argues for retaining a more participatory nominating system over one that is more controlled by party and elected officials or other elites.

Ultimately, preferences about the degree of discretion that delegates should have turns on broader conceptions about where conventions fit into the larger nominating process. All other things being equal, conventions with larger numbers of delegates free to change their votes are more likely to be decision-making bodies than those in which delegates are more constrained. Those who want a larger role for party elites in the nominating process favor a model of the nomination convention in which it functions as a decision-making body choosing the nominee. The other view, which holds that the convention is the last step in a more participatory process, sees it more along the lines of an electoral college registering preferences determined elsewhere.

As a practical matter, however, the world also constrains the degree to which a favored nominating system can be achieved. An elite-centered process—in which party and elected officials have a larger say—assumes a more coherent and integrated elite environment than currently exists. Traditional state party organizations continue to wane, legislative parties are fragmented by concerns about the interests of individual constituencies, and the notion of national party power-brokers seems more a product of press attention than an occupant of command positions.

A more participatory vision of the nominating process also suffers from weakness in real world referents: voters, particularly in early primaries, operate on the basis of low information and they react to short-term events. This may produce popular preferences that are often unstable to the point of volatility. That, of course, leaves open the question of who and what is being represented at the convention.

Why, then, prefer a system in which delegates are pledged and bound over one that leaves larger numbers free to decide? This position rests on both normative and practical considerations.

FIVE ARGUMENTS

First, voters should have the choice to send pledged delegates. Giving voters and other participants the choice between delegates pledged to candidates provides them with a means for registering their presidential preferences directly and in a form that all can understand. Presently, popular participation in primaries and caucuses produces—with some distortion due to cutoff points for awarding delegates—the rough distribution of candidate strength at the nominating convention. Candidate success depends on how much support one can muster in primaries or caucuses. Presently, the way to win the nomination has been to win the largest share of pledged or committed delegates in events where the public can participate.

There is some practical evidence that voters want their votes to go for candidates with a chance, and they choose not to support those who want to use their votes to empower them to make choices for them. The voters have overwhelmingly chosen to support real candidates over those running as "favorite sons," regional candidates, single-issue candidates, and other strategems for accumulating delegates who are uncommitted to the major contenders for the purposes of bargaining. And voter events intended purely to ascertain preferences—"beauty contests" and other nonbinding primaries—have usually yielded lowest participation rates. In short, voters—by their decision to participate and by voting for those whom they perceive to have a chance—have expressed their preference for participating directly in the process and their preferred means has been voting for pledged delegates.

Second, the strongest claim that convention delegates have to exercise power is that they represent voter preferences about candidates. Pledged delegates should be bound to support their candidate at least for the first ballot. Delegates should be committed to reflecting the preferences of those who sent them to the convention in the first place. Delegates—according to convention research—are rarely demographically or attitudinally representative and few would claim to have been selected for their qualities of deliberation. People get to be delegates because they support candidates whom voters or other participants want, or because they occupy formal positions. In short, most delegates have few strong claims to serve as individual deliberators, while the ones who sent them do have a strong claim on delegates to vote as instructed.

Furthermore, delegates should be bound by popular preferences because those preferences constitute about as informed a choice as the electorate is capable of making. Whatever the participatory shortcomings of the delegate selection system—low participation in caucuses and low turnout in primaries—the selection process is the most participatory aspect of the nominating system. Indeed, according to the conventional recommendations for gaining popular consent, the delegate selection process has most of the elements thought to produce informed choice: highly visible and well-organized competition among campaigns with strong incentives to inform voters about alternatives and consequences. On the other hand, the claim of delegates to speak for themselves and to exercise their own judgments has almost no foundation in popular consent.

Third, the system of pledging delegates to candidates should be retained because it has made the front-runner's status clear and it helps to make candidate organizations the central actors at the nomination convention. Both of these factors contribute to the achievement of party unity.

This is a practical preference based on the place of the nominating convention in contemporary politics. Most people agree that nominating conventions—in addition to serving to represent the party or voters—should perform two main functions: selecting nominees with a chance to win and uniting the party behind the candidate. As a practical matter, in both the prereform and postreform eras, the candidate leading just before the convention has nearly always been the nominee. In the prereform period candidates led by their capacity to gain support of party leaders and in the postreform period they have led by beating their opponents in popular contests for delegates. In the most recent Democratic conventions, superdelegates—uncommitteds who have gained seats on the basis of their status—have reflected the cleavage of committed delegates in casting most of their votes for the leading candidate. Thus the real work of most modern nominating conventions has been to build support for nominees who have all but won prior to the convention.

The leading candidate's status derives from having more pledged delegates than any competitor, delegate votes unlikely to be lost and whose possession usually puts the leader close to or over the plurality required. Everybody knows who the front-runner is and that he or she can count on the loyal support of delegates. The system has worked—in both parties—to make the leading candidate's organization the central actor in organizing the convention. And the leading candidate organization has had strong incentives to unite the party and to incorporate losing candidates and their supporters into its fold. And the organizations of losing candidates have played a role in helping the party to achieve a degree of unity for the general election.

Advocates of a more elite bargaining process want the convention to be a real decision-making body and gain room for greater discretion by reducing the number of people committed to cast their ballots according to the dictates of a previously determined allocation. They reason that such a body, led by the natural leaders of the party, would be more likely to engage in peer review and to consider last-minute developments damaging to the front-runner in making their final choice. Such a convention is unlikely to occur, depending as it does on the existence of a body of natural leaders, motivated by long-term concerns, capable of commanding the loyalties of delegates selected by various candidate organizations, and facing a situation in which the nomination is in doubt. None of the required antecedent conditions have existed in the recent past and it is unlikely that freeing delegates from their commitments would establish them in the future. And moving in the direction of such conventions, releasing delegates from pledges would do little to increase deliberation but would diminish the prospects for party unity.

The degree of conflict at the convention clearly affects the amount of legitimation the nominee can hope for. Insofar as unbinding delegates creates uncertainty about the outcome of the nomination, that uncertainty will fuel conflict at the convention. While it may not alter the outcome, the opportunities for protracted conflict would increase. Indeed, in the Democratic and Republican Parties, many recent demands for freeing committed delegates have been made by losing candidates shortly before the convention as a means of forestalling the front-runner's nomination. A convention in which the nominee seems already determined is one in which the business of reconciling losers can begin earlier.

The units that must be reconciled to the nominee for legitimation to occur are the supporters of the losing candidates. Here again pledging delegates to candidates may have some advantages. Convention research shows that the units that organize the bulk of delegate activity at the conventions are the candidate organizations. They bargain over platform items, mobilize delegates for floor votes, and speak for the interests represented at conventions. The formal binding of delegates, augmenting the already strong personal ties that delegates feel for their candidates, helps to make candidate organizations the effective units for convention dealings. When legitimation has occurred—when losing delegates have rallied to the nominee—it has been led by candidate organizations accepting the victory of the nominee after extracting concessions symbolic and otherwise. Insofar as unbinding delegates is successful in turning individuals into decision-makers in their own right, the task of legitimation is likely to grow both more complex and difficult.

Fourth, insofar as delegates are freed to follow their own preferences, and the convention outcome becomes correspondingly more uncertain, the results are not likely to be good ones from the standpoint of legitimation or party health. The favored scenario of those who favor more flexible delegates has the following elements: a front-runner emerges out of the primaries, that person develops a number of weaknesses that were not visible earlier, the convention—with sizable numbers of delegates capable of changing their votes—deliberates and produces a more acceptable nominee. The losing sides opposing Ford in 1976, Carter in 1980, Mondale in 1984, and Dukakis in 1988 all made this argument. While each did lose the general election, they did beat their opponents for the nomination and by that measure they were the strongest candidates of their party.

More to the point, however, is an examination of what would have happened in the unlikely event that the leading candidate had been denied the nomination by the convention. The first, and most obvious, point is that the problem of legitimation would have been much bigger: the losing side would be the one with the largest block of voters supporting it, and the largest block of delegates would be disappointed with the result. Insofar as perceptions of the fairness of the process fuel legitimation—the acceptance of the nominee by the losers—accepting the verdict of voters and other mass participants is easier to swallow than accepting the results of a convention majority representing only itself.

Next, what units would organize the decision-making convention? Conventions are transient, temporary, and unstable bodies at the delegate level. Delegates have to be organized into larger groups, and the groups able to command delegate loyalties would be the units that control a decision-making convention. There are several problems here. The most likely contenders would be the party's leaders and elected officials, but there is little evidence that they can act in a unified fashion or that they command enough delegate loyalties to bargain effectively among themselves. Indeed, judging from how they have behaved at past conventions, these leaders reflect rather than cause cleavages in their own parties. Another set of groups that have tried—labor in the Democratic Party and women's groups and ethnic caucuses in both parties—to shape delegate behavior, on issues of interest to them, have not been notably successful in determining platform and other outcomes over the opposition of the dominant candidate organization. Arguably, their role in controlling delegates on nominations would be even smaller. In short, the strong possibility exists that a convention with the discretion to decide the nominee may face considerable difficulties organizing itself to use that power in ways that advance the party.

Fifth, the present system, based on pledged delegates, does contain elements of flexibility. After the McGovern nomination in 1972, and Carter's in 1976, a number of people expressed the fear that the system was one in which early momentum—and the accumulation of pledged delegates—would propel candidates to the nomination. Early front-runners—usually the most preferred candidates of party regulars—who lost a few initial contests might be doomed in this view. Of course, Reagan in 1980 and Mondale in 1984 both recovered after some initial reverses and went on to the nomination.

The system has elements of both stability and flexibility. Pledging delegates contributes to stability, candidates can accumulate dependable delegate votes over the course of the primaries and state conventions. At the same time, the very representativeness of the system produces elements that can put the outcome of the nomination into doubt. In the Democratic Party, for example, the principle of proportional representation—and prohibitions on winner-take-all systems—make it harder for leading candidates to deliver the "knockout" punches that guarantee them the nomination much before the end of the primary season. And while the Republicans permit winner-take-all primaries, Republican candidates have more primaries to run in making it harder for candidates to win everywhere at the same time. In both parties, the large numbers of primaries, and the differential regional and section appeal of candidates, also complicate the task of front-runners to win everything while advantaging those who follow a more limited strategy.

In short, there are plenty of opportunities for a party electorate, or for party activists, or for party and elected officials, who are profoundly divided over the choice of nominee, to assert their differences through the pledged delegate system. The inability of losing candidates to block the nomination of a leader before the convention is not a product of the system of rules leading to pledged delegates. Rather it is a sign of the capacity of the eventual nominees to overcome a system with considerable numbers of pitfalls to early victory.

CONCLUSION

Pledging convention delegates to vote for a candidate is an important element of a participatory nominating system. Voters do have candidate preferences and they rely on delegates to convey these to the convention. While not perfectly informed choices, these voter preferences are gained in highly competitive events conducted in an information-rich environment. And delegates, for their part, have a stronger mandate to reflect those participant preferences than they do to serve as individual deliberators on their own.

While a more democratic system is a normative preference, there is also a practical side to it. This system, I have argued, is one in keeping with the present state of the party system and electorate. Voters are not particularly loyal to the parties, but they do develop candidate preferences. Furthermore, the system in which candidate organizations build loyal corps of delegates—by achieving electoral success in the primaries and mobilizing activist support in convention states—encourages participation and reduces information costs for voters. By making participation easier and more consequential, the system produces a more informed electorate and one whose preferences ought to be taken seriously.

The system of pledged delegates also helps to make front-runner status clearer by convention time—reducing uncertainty about the outcome and diminishing prospects for further conflict—and at the same time shapes a convention organized by candidate organizations. These factors, in turn, help the convention to perform its important function of unifying the party. The resulting convention system, while far from perfect, is one that has produced about as high a level of legitimation—given the numerous opportunities for fragmentation—as can be expected, and it has produced nominees who have been tested against most of their plausible rivals.

The alternative system, in which delegates are free to make their choices at the convention, offers more limited prospects for legitimation. And the prospect that such a decision-making convention would produce a stronger candidate rests on rather unpromising premises about the capacity of party leaders to lead and of uncommitted delegates to follow.

Part 2

NO—
Convention Delegates Should Not be Formally Pledged

Elaine Ciulla Kamarck

Should convention delegates be formally pledged? No or at least not all of them.

But before I explain why, I feel it is only fair to warn the reader that during the summer of 1980 I devoted week after week of 16-hour days to arguing exactly the opposite position.

I would like to say that my change in position stems from having grown older and wiser. But in fact that is not the case. I have always believed that the postreform nominating system, which makes voters in caucuses and primaries more important than party officials, including delegates at conventions, needs modification. But in the summer of 1980 I was an official at the Democratic National Committee and (as with most officials of a political party that has an incumbent in the White House) a fierce partisan of President Jimmy Carter.

Thus when a version of the question—should convention delegates be formally pledged—became the focal point of Senator Ted Kennedy's last-ditch challenge to President Carter, I sided yes—with my candidate.

The question before us is best understood in the context of a discussion about modern nominating conventions. Thus is it worth taking a minute to review the events of the 1980 convention, because the resolution of the dispute between Carter and Kennedy says a great deal about the role of modern conventions in the presidential selection process.

RULE 11H

The most important vote at the 1980 convention was a vote over the following rule, Rule 11H in the Delegate Selection Rules for 1980. The rule read:

> All delegates to the National Convention shall be bound to vote for the presidential candidate whom they were elected to support for at least the first convention ballot, unless released in writing by the presidential candidate. Delegates who seek to violate this rule may be replaced with an alternate of the same presidential preference by the presidential candidate or that candidate's authorized representative(s) at any time up to and including the presidential balloting at the National Convention.[1]

The rule was adopted and passed by the Democratic National Committee as part of the delegate selection rules that governed the 1980 primary season. At the time it was not controversial, in spite of the rather unusual provision that allowed a presidential candidate or presidential representative to replace an unfaithful delegate.

The lack of initial controversy was an indication of the fact that the nomination system of the Democratic Party (and to a lesser extent the Republican Party) had become, in the years since the 1972 McGovern-Fraser reforms, a system totally dominated by presidential candidates. On the Democratic side, presidential candidates were allowed to give prior approval to anyone who wished to run as a delegate pledged to them, and in most states Democrats and Republicans awarded delegates to presidential candidates on the basis of how many votes the *presidential* candidate won, not how many votes the *delegate* candidate won.

With Rule 11H, the party had articulated what had become political reality for postreform conventions. The delegate was purely and simply a representative of the primary voters—he or she could exercise their own independent judgment on questions of party rules and the party platform, but in the era of presidential primaries delegates were not expected to exercise their own judgment when it came to the vote for a Democratic nominee.

Politics, however, has a way of disrupting consensus. As the spring of 1980 wore on, the primary battles between President

Carter and Senator Kennedy became more and more bitter. Carter developed a commanding lead in the number of delegates pledged to vote for him at the upcoming convention but, as was the case with Carter's entire presidency, his good fortune did not last very long. Starting with the New York primary, Kennedy began winning primaries and although he did not win by big enough margins to cut into Carter's delegate lead, the Kennedy wins in big states like New York and California gave him momentum going into the convention.

When the last primary was over, Carter hoped that Kennedy would concede that he had been beaten and throw his support to Carter in preparation for the race against the Republicans. But this was not to be. The Kennedy campaign decided to pursue the race for the nomination all the way to the convention. Because of this decision, the heretofore uncontroversial Rule 11H emerged as the test vote for the 1980 convention.[2]

Since Carter had more delegates at the convention, the Kennedy forces had to convince several hundred Carter delegates to switch their support to Kennedy in order to have even a chance of winning the nomination. But before Carter delegates could switch to Kennedy they had to revoke Rule 11H or risk being yanked off the convention floor and replaced by someone loyal to Carter. If the Kennedy campaign could convince enough Carter delegates to vote for a minority report, revoking Rule 11H it would be a serious blow to Carter and these same people might then switch and vote for Kennedy (or someone other than Carter) when the vote for the nomination came.

During the summer of 1980 the Carter and Kennedy campaigns organized massive campaigns around whether or not delegates to conventions should be bound. Delegates were phoned repeatedly to see where they stood on the issue. When they were not being phoned, they were receiving mail; when they were not receiving mail, they were reading about the controversy in a vast array of columns and editorials in newspapers around the country. As the preconvention campaign mounted in intensity, Kennedy forces dubbed 11H "the robot rule." Posters and buttons appeared with a picture of a robot in a red circle with a red slash across it. Other posters and buttons read "free the delegates."

The robot was a particularly appropriate symbol of what had happened to the role of delegates in a nomination process dominated by primaries and presidential candidates. Delegates to con-

ventions used to be important state and local politicians, elected
to attend the convention and settle on a nominee. Presidential primaries were few and far between, and when they were held they
tended to be "beauty contests," or elections that did not bind state
delegates to a particular presidential candidate.[3]

All that changed with the increase in binding presidential
primaries—primaries where delegates were awarded to a presidential candidate on the basis of how many votes the presidential
candidate won in the primary. Delegates were no longer expected
to exercise their own judgment; they were expected to go to the
convention and record the preferences expressed by the voters
at home.

As the debate over Rule 11H raged on, Carter ran into more
bad luck. In mid-July, the *Washington Post* reported that Carter's
beer-drinking brother Billy had been a lobbyist for the terrorist
government of Libya. "Billygate," as the scandal became known,
became one more embarrassment in a presidency for which embarrassment had become an almost constant companion. Rampant
inflation, high interest rates, the ongoing Iranian hostage crisis,
the bungled UN vote on Israel, the ongoing investigation of the
White House chief of staff for cocaine use—and now "Billygate"—
served to convince many Democrats that Carter at the head of the
ticket would be a disaster for other Democratic candidates in the
fall of 1980.

In July, Carter's approval rating hit a new low of 21%, the
lowest rating since 1938 when Gallup had started measuring presidential popularity.[4] In match up after match up with the Republican candidate Reagan, Carter lost by large margins. But
Kennedy, too liberal and personally flawed by the famous accident
at Chappaquidick and other personal problems, did no better
against Reagan.[5] Elected officials, especially junior members of
Congress, began to fear the impact on their own elections of *either*
candidate at the head of the ticket. If ever a party needed to free
itself of the options served up during the primaries, it was the
Democrats in 1980.

The Open Convention Movement

In late July, a group of forty House members, mostly young,
many from the independent-minded class of 1974, organized an
Open Convention Committee whose purpose was to try to draft a

candidate for president other than Carter or Kennedy. With a budget of $200,000, they opened offices, held press conferences, and recruited elected officials to try to convince delegates to abandon Carter and Kennedy, and draft someone else. Alternative names were floated, among them Vice-President Mondale, who quickly denied any interest in being nominated in place of Carter, and Secretary of State Ed Muskie, whose denial was somewhat less than Shermanesque.

It was the classic convention draft situation but for one problem: there were almost no delegates available to be drafted. By the end of June 1980, when most states had completed their delegate selection process, there were a total of 114 uncommitted and "other" delegates out of a convention of 3,331—hardly enough to begin a bandwagon for Muskie or anyone else.

Without a bloc of unaffiliated delegates to lobby, the open convention advocates were forced to start lobbying Carter and Kennedy delegates, a much more difficult task. Table 5 lists the twenty eight most active and prominent members of the open convention movement by state. If we assume that the influence of an elected official will be greatest on delegates from his or her own state, we can assess the efforts of the open convention advocates by looking at the vote in favor of opening up the convention and comparing it to the number of Kennedy delegates in that delegation (since almost all Kennedy delegates were in favor of opening up the convention).

In state after state the effect was minimal or nonexistent: in New York the governor, the United States senator, and three members of Congress made no impact on the open convention vote, and in fact one Kennedy delegate defected to the Carter position. In California five members of Congress could change only four votes in favor of opening up the convention.[6] The total net impact of the open convention movement was minimal, about 1 percent of the entire convention.

Thus in spite of all the efforts of the open convention advocates and the Kennedy campaign, in spite of all the signs pointing to electoral disaster for either of the two leading candidates for the Democratic nomination, the vote to open up the convention picked up only thirty five votes between the end of the primaries and the August convention.

Delegates to the 1980 convention were so thoroughly pledged to their presidential candidates—legally and psychologically—that

TABLE 5
Leaders of the Open Convention Committee—
Their Impact on the Vote by State

State Leaders	Net Impact
California; Reps. Dellums, Edwards, Lloyd, Stark, Waxman	+4
Colorado; Gov. Lamm, Reps. Schroeder, Wirth	+11
Connecticut; Rep. Moffett	−1
Illinois; Rep. Simon	+10
Maryland; Reps. Barnes, Mikulski	+1
Massachusetts; Rep. Markey	+4
Michigan; Reps. Carr, Conyers	0
Minnesota; Rep. Nolan	+30 or −7 (see text)
New York; Gov. Carey, Sen. Moynihan, Reps. Ambrose, Chisholm, Downey	−1
Oregon; Rep. Weaver	+1
Washington; Senator Jackson, Reps. Dicks, Swift	+3
West Virginia; Senator Byrd	+3
Wisconsin; Senator Nelson, Rep. Oberstar	0

Sources: Vote total for the open convention vote can be found on pp. 204–13, *1980 The Official Report of the Proceedings of the Democratic National Convention*, August 11–14, 1980 (Washington, D.C.: Democratic National Committee). Kennedy delegate count can be found in *Congressional Quarterly Weekly Report*, June 28, 1980 (Washington, D.C.: *Congressional Quarterly*).

Note: Net impact is calculated by comparing the "yes" vote on Minority Report #5 at the 1980 Democratic convention with the Kennedy delegate count as reported in *Congressional Quarterly*, June 28, 1980.

the party was unable to save itself from the defeat that followed in November. Of course, it is quite probable that the party would have been unable to save itself no matter what it did; incumbent presidents have never been easy to beat under any circumstances. But the point is that in 1980 it was futile to even try.

The Modern Nominating Convention:
New Role for an Old Institution

The 1980 Democratic convention is a good example of the fact that conventions are, by and large, no longer the place where presidential candidates are nominated.[7] They are nominated in primaries and caucuses that stretch out over a six-month period of time. More than any single party rule or state law on how delegates are to be bound, the existence of presidential primaries means that delegates to conventions are, for all practical purposes, limited in their choice of a nominee to someone who has at least contested and probably won the primaries. The days when presidential candidates (Adlai Stevenson in 1952 and Hubert Humphrey in 1968) could skip the primaries and still be nominated at the convention are long gone.

As the nomination itself moved from the convention into the primaries, the convention picked up another function. In the prereform era the convention was the place where the nominating majority was constructed and the nomination concluded. In the postreform era the convention became the place to begin the general election campaign. According to Byron Shafer, whose book *Bifurcated Politics: Evolution and Reform in the National Party Convention* is an excellent treatment of the postreform convention:

> The role of the convention in inaugurating the general election campaign grew enormously as the nomination receded. ... National news media, especially as embodied in full and national television coverage, became the means by which public presentations at the convention ... could be turned explicitly to the task of advertising the candidate, his party, and their program.[8]

Formally pledged delegates (the result of binding primaries) are at the heart of this transformation in the role of the modern convention. For the most part, a journalist can sit down at the end of the California primary (traditionally the last primary) and figure out, with a high degree of accuracy, who will be nominated without having to actually go to the convention, just as, on election night, he or she can add up the electoral votes won by each presidential candidate and figure out who the new president will be.[9]

The Electoral College still meets; real people, chosen to be presidential electors, travel to their state capitals to cast ballots for the president, but the fact that the outcome of the election is not in doubt means that media coverage is minimal. Tom Brokaw and Peter Jennings do not come on television, block out regular programing, and give us up-to-the-minute accounts of the progress of the Electoral College. If the actual meeting of the Electoral College is covered at all, it is to comment on the fact that it is an anachronism and to query whether or not it should be abolished.

And herein lies the paradox of the modern convention. Television coverage of conventions costs networks a great deal of money. Not only are the costs of coverage high but networks lose viewers (and advertising revenue) during those hours when the convention is being broadcast. Networks used to cover conventions "gavel to gavel," from the time they opened to the time they closed. But in recent years, with the outcome of the convention a foregone conclusion, networks have cut back on the amount of television coverage. In the 1950s and 60s television coverage had actually exceeded the amount of time that the convention was in session. Beginning in 1980, however, there have been dramatic drops in coverage by all three networks.[10]

In addition, network news executives are increasingly resistant to going along with the parties' desire to use the convention as a four-day advertisement for themselves and their nominees. In 1988 NBC developed a plan called the "convention without walls." As a means of bypassing the scripted and, in their terms, nonnewsworthy portion of the convention that was being served up by the Democratic Party, NBC arranged for a series of interviews with voters across the country—interviews that had little if anything to do with the convention. In the outcry that followed, Joe Angotti, executive producer of NBC News said "Our first and primary responsibility is to cover the news. I'd like nothing better than to throw all this out and cover a real breaking story."[11]

The convention without walls was pretty much a bust and the Democrats, thanks to Jesse Jackson, provided enough "hard news" to keep the networks tuned in. Similarly the Republican convention flap over the nomination of Senator Dan Quayle as the vice-presidential nominee ended up making the Republican convention newsworthy. Nevertheless when the conventions were over, ABC News President Roone Arledge opened up the question all over again by speculating that in the future networks would stop covering the conventions live.

Thus if political parties want to continue being able to use their conventions to advertise their candidate and party in preparation for the general election, they cannot take all "hard news" out of the convention and replace it with pure political advertising. This boils down to the fact that if they expect coverage, they cannot cede completely the power to nominate. If the translation from primary result to delegate vote is completely automatic, the news media will devote whatever air time they give to convention coverage to speculation on whether the nominating convention has become, like the Electoral College, a quaint vestige of the body politic.

Retaining the Power to Nominate

Keeping the power to nominate in the convention will guarantee continued news coverage, but it is also in the best interests of both political parties, which may find that, from time to time, they want to exercise the option of nominating someone other than the winner of the primaries.

The fortunes of a presidential candidate can change in many unpredictable ways over the six-month period of the primaries and caucuses. A candidate who looks fresh and exciting in New Hampshire in March may look too liberal, too conservative, dishonest, or just plain dumb come the Pennsylvania primary in April and a downright disaster come the convention in July or August. Yet if the awareness that he or she is an electoral disaster comes too late in the process and all the delegates are already chosen and pledged, party leaders really have no other option than to try and make the best out of a bad situation.

The second reason to preserve flexibility is the possibility that no one presidential candidate will come into the convention able to put together a delegate majority. This has not happened in recent times but the widespread use of proportional representation to award delegates to presidential candidates (in the Democratic Party especially) means that this is always a possibility.

Finally, because turnout in presidential primaries is, like turnout in primaries for other offices, very small, extremist factions can take over a primary by surprise and end up electing delegates pledged to a candidate who is clearly and obviously unacceptable. It has happened with some regularity in state and local primaries in recent years and could happen in presidential primaries under the right circumstances.[12]

In order to cope with all sorts of eventualities, the convention should retain the ability to nominate someone who may not have been the winner of the primaries or who may not have been in the primaries at all. Flexibility is enhanced by allowing a substantial portion of delegates to attend the convention without having to be formally pledged to a presidential candidate. If the unpledged delegates are high-level party and elected officials—as is the case currently—then so much the better.

In the years following the 1980 convention, the Democrats changed their rules in two important ways. The infamous Rule 11H was altered to read:

> Delegates elected to the national convention pledged to a presidential candidate shall *in all good conscience* reflect the sentiments of those who elected them.[13]

The presumption in the new rule reflects the reality of the current nomination system: as long as it was dominated by primaries and public caucuses, most delegates would enter the convention formally pledged to a presidential candidate. Barring anything unforeseen, delegates were expected to vote for the presidential candidate they had supported in the primary—but the current rule leaves open the possibility that delegates can change their minds at the convention.

More important than the new Rule 11H, however, was the inclusion at the 1984 and 1988 conventions of a bloc of delegates dubbed the "superdelegates." These delegates were drawn from the ranks of party and elected officials and were formally unpledged; they got a vote at the convention by virtue of their office, not by having chosen a presidential candidate who won the primary in their state. In both years the "superdelegates" constituted slightly less than 15 percent of the total convention delegates.

No one ever really expected that the superdelegates would overturn the results of the primaries and caucuses, especially under normal circumstances; rather their inclusion was sought to give the convention "ballast"—in other words, to make sure that the platform and other convention actions did not stray so far away from the political center that it would hurt the party's candidates in the general election.

But after the debacle of 1980, members of Congress were determined to write themselves back into the nomination process of the party. Since their fates were at least perceived to be closely connected to the fate of the presidential candidate at the top of the ticket, members of Congress lobbied for and got a bloc of seats at the Democratic convention.

In 1984 and 1988 preferences of the members of Congress followed the results of the primaries; most of the superdelegates in 1984 were for Mondale and most of the superdelegates in 1988 were for Dukakis. As long as the system is dominated by pledged delegates elected in presidential primaries and as long as the winner of the primaries is respectable, unpledged elected officials are not likely to lead the party toward a defeat. In order for that to happen, their numbers as a proportion of the total convention would have to increase dramatically—thus changing the common understanding that the nomination is won, not in the convention but in the primaries. Nevertheless, bringing the official party back into the nomination process is a step in the right direction.

CONCLUSION

As long as there are binding presidential primaries, there will be formally pledged convention delegates. But the inclusion at the convention of large numbers of formally unpledged delegates, especially if those delegates are drawn from the ranks of party and elected officials, is a safeguard against any number of predictable and nonpredictable disasters, as well as a means of ensuring a continued high level of media coverage. If party leaders and elected officials constituted an even greater proportion of both conventions than they do now, say between 25 and 50 percent, conventions would be amalgams of both the new and the old style of nominating presidential candidates. Presidential candidates would have to run in a primary and win formally pledged delegates in order to demonstrate vote-getting ability and popular appeal, but they would also have to meet the respect and support of their peers among the leadership of their party. Some mixture of the new and the old is probably the best and most prudent method of reforming the nominating process.

CHAPTER THREE

Should Vice-Presidential Candidates be Selected from the Also-Ran Category?

At no other time in the history of American politics has the process of choosing a vice-president been the focus of so much scholarly debate. Indeed, due to the events associated with George Bush's selection of Dan Quayle as a vice-presidential running mate, the procedure for vice-presidential selection has emerged as perhaps the most controversial issue facing the entire process of presidential selection. John Kenneth White argues in favor of selecting vice-presidential candidates from the list of viable presidential candidates, or what is commonly referred to as the "also-ran" category. In White's view, it is essential to have individuals of stature and competence occupy the vice-presidency, particularly in light of the potential for vice-presidents to become president and due to the important functions assumed by recent vice-presidents. In White's view, the tradition of allowing presidential nominees to exercise unilateral control over the choice of a running mate has not proved successful. White examines recent polling data concerning the "Quayle factor" to document a flawed vice-presidential selection process. White argues that selecting vice-presidents from the list of the also-ran would at once ensure executive competence and restore legitimacy to the process of selecting vice-presidential candidates.

Landis Jones believes that vice-presidential selection should be the exclusive choice of the presidential nominee. In Jones's view, the proposal to restrict a presidential nominee's choice to the list of the also-ran could have negative consequences for effec-

tive national leadership. Jones stresses the need for personal and ideological compatibility between presidents and vice-presidents in the modern age of governing. Such compatibility, according to Jones, can be guaranteed only by allowing the presidential nominee exclusive control over the choice of a running mate. Jones provides a full treatment of the development of the modern vice-presidency beginning with Henry Wallace in 1940 and extending to the present. Jones points to the constant growth of executive responsibilities in the vice-presidential office, which, he believes, necessitates cohesion, not diversity, between the president and vice-president. Executive cohesion and compatibility are desirable goals according to Jones and are most likely achieved by maintaining the current tradition of vice-presidential selection.

Part 1

YES—
Vice-President Candidates Should be Selected from the Also-Ran Category

John Kenneth White

Everyone in the nation's capital has a story about Dan Quayle. Mine goes something like this. At a 1988 gathering of political consultants, two spoke of an incident at the Republican National Convention. The night after George Bush announced his surprising choice of Quayle, these two GOP strategists made eye contact on the convention floor while each was fielding questions from inquisitive reporters about Bush's announcement. Although too far apart to speak, words were unnecessary. As one recalled, "Our eyes rolled back into our heads as if to say, 'How will we manage to extricate ourselves from this mess?' "[1]

The Quayle-bashing did not stop after the election. Joseph Canzeri, a Republican operative whose job it was to "handle" Quayle during the campaign, said of his charge: "He was like a kid. Ask him to turn off a light, and by the time he gets to the switch, he's forgotten what he went for."[2] Canzeri told reporters Jack Germond and Jules Witcover that Quayle was "immature," an adjective that by itself was a strong indictment of the forty-fourth vice-president's fitness to serve.[3]

Large numbers of Americans share Canzeri's doubts. According to a March 1990 Gallup Poll, 54 percent believe Quayle is *not* qualified to succeed Bush. Only 31 percent thought him fit to be a potential president—down ten points from August 1988.[4] When asked during the campaign what criteria he would use in selecting a vice-president, Bush responded, "I'd have to go with the generic: Who [would be] best to take over in case of something happening to the president?"[5] Using Bush's own yardstick, most Americans believe Quayle does not measure up.

As if to underscore the point, the same Gallup Poll contained more bad news for Quayle. Forty-nine percent, a plurality, thought Bush should change vice-presidents should he seek another term in 1992. Moreover, only 46 percent approved of the way Quayle was handling his job; 27 percent disapproved.[6] In a 1989 television interview, Quayle suggested public acceptance would grow over time.[7] But Quayle's approval ratings are among the lowest ever recorded. Contrast Quayle's numbers with his predecessor. In May 1981, 51 percent had a favorable impression of Bush. Even Spiro Agnew during the first year of his ignominious vice-presidency registered a 74 percent approval score.[8] Agnew later resigned his office pleading no contest to charges of income tax evasion. (Agnew never reported as income the bribes he received while he served as Maryland governor and U.S. vice-president.)

Once again, the vice-presidency is entangled in a crisis of confidence. Quayle jokes are bonanza items for late-night comedians. As Quayle himself says, "This Administration is in the job-creation business. And you have to say that this vice president has created jobs for comedians and writers [for] comedians."[9] But making fun of vice-presidents is nothing new. Thomas Marshall, vice-president under Woodrow Wilson, told what has become the most often-repeated vice-presidential joke: "Once there were two brothers. One ran away to sea; the other was elected vice president. And nothing was ever heard of either of them again."[10] In the 1930s play "Of Thee I Sing," the vice-presidential character was named Alexander Throttlebottom. Such depictions are reminiscent of Hubert Humphrey's 1968 television commercials castigating Nixon's choice of Agnew: "This would be funny. If it weren't so serious."

Such put-downs derive from the anomalous nature of the office. Political scientist Thomas E. Cronin writes: "Five hundred and thirty-seven elected officials are sent to Washington by American voters. Five hundred and thirty-six have a reasonably clear idea of their role and functions."[11] As Cronin indicates, only the vice-president is left to wonder what is expected. The framers of the U.S. Constitution created the office as an afterthought—not to ensure presidential succession, as is commonly believed, but to ensure a national president. By having two persons to vote for, the framers believed that voters would choose a local candidate first, and a person of national stature second.[12] Such carelessness led to difficulties from the outset. John Adams, the first to have the job, declared, "My country in its wisdom contrived for me the most insignificant office that the invention of man contrived or his imagination conceived."[13]

The vice-president's insignificance comes from an insufficient constitutional grounding. The first mention of the office is in Article One, that portion of the document dealing with *Congress*. Only two duties were given the vice-president: presiding over the U.S. Senate and casting a vote in the event of a tie. When some of the framers raised objections about even these meager responsibilities, delegate Roger Sherman responded that without them the vice-president would be "without employment."[14]

At first, vice-presidents took their constitutional duties seriously. Given the relative smallness of the Senate in its early days (26 members), tie votes were common. John Adams cast twenty-nine; John C. Calhoun, twenty-eight.[15] By contrast, Lyndon Johnson cast no tie-breaking votes during his tenure; Walter Mondale just one; and George Bush, seven.[16] Dan Quayle acknowledges the diminished importance of his constitutional obligations: "I do not spend very much time presiding in the Senate. I've been there for a few votes. The only important thing of presiding would be on a tie vote, or if you get into a problem with recognition [of a senator]."[17]

Article Two of the Constitution, that part describing the *president*, mentions the vice-president in connection with the Electoral College and the circumstances under which the vice-president can become president. By placing the office in both Articles One and Two, the founding fathers straddled the vice-presidency between Congress and the executive branch, resulting in a kind of political homelessness. Pious presidents excluded their vice-presidents from cabinet meetings, noting that the Constitution placed the vice-president in legislature; they sanctimoniously held that the "separation of powers" clause must be preserved. Harry Truman, for example, wrote in 1955 that the vice-president "is not an officer of the executive branch."[18] Truman's view is instructive since as vice-president he was uninformed about the development of the atom bomb, a weapon he would use against the Japanese four months after becoming president.

Some believe there was another reason for the presidential indifference: a vice-president is a constant reminder of a president's mortality. Thomas Marshall declared, "The only business of the vice president is to ring the White House bell every morning and ask what is the state of health of the president."[19] As Marshall suggests, innocuous questions like "How 'ya feeling?" take on a more ominous tone when asked by a vice-president of a president.

Legislators also shunned the office. Senators accepted its constitutional duties reluctantly, refusing to allow them to be transformed into enlarged sources of power. Any vice-president who attempted to use the Senate as a power base was promptly rebuffed. In 1961 Lyndon Johnson hoped that his Democratic colleagues would retain him as majority leader while he served as vice-president. Prior to his election in 1960, Johnson was the most powerful majority leader in history. But Senate Democrats would have no part of Johnson's scheme. They not-so-politely requested LBJ to get lost. Johnson did so, never to return.

The office humbled once proud men. John Adams wrote his wife: "I am vice president. In this I am nothing, but I may be everything."[20] Those men who, in Adams's phrase, "became everything" bitterly recalled their once lowly status. Harry Truman pronounced the position about as useful as a cow's fifth teat. Vice-presidents who, unlike Truman, never became president became embittered old men. The most famous was John Nance Garner, Franklin Roosevelt's first vice-president. He pronounced the office not worthy of a "pitcher of warm spit." Actually, Garner said something stronger than "spit," but historians prefer to quote a sanitized version.[21]

This lack of institutional grounding resulted in considerable tinkering with the Constitution itself. Since 1789 only twenty-six amendments have been added. Two involve the vice-president. The Twelfth Amendment, ratified in 1804, paired the president and vice-president in the Electoral College balloting.[22] The Twenty-Fifth Amendment was approved in 1967 after John F. Kennedy's murder. It provides for presidential appointment of a vice-president "upon confirmation by a majority vote of both houses of Congress" should the office be vacant.[23] It also outlines the circumstances under which the vice-president may become "acting president" should there be a serious presidential disability.[24] These two amendments are indications that the vice-presidency has never worked properly.

THE RESTORED VICE-PRESIDENCY

After two hundred years of neglect, presidents have finally taken vice-presidents into their bosoms. Franklin Roosevelt was the first. During World War II he made Vice-President Henry Wallace chairman of several boards, including the Economics Defense Board, the Supply Priorities and Allocations Board, the War Productions Board, and the Board of Economic Warfare.[25] Roosevelt also used Wallace as an overseas emissary, traveling to Latin America, China, and even Siberia, carrying important messages. Subsequent vice-presidents have acted as the president's eyes and ears in meetings with world leaders. Richard Nixon, for example, visited fifty-four countries during his eight years as vice-president.

Congress got into the act, codifying into law the vice-president's place in the executive branch. A 1949 amendment to the National Security Act placed the vice-president on the National Security Council. Another statute made the vice-president a member of the Smithsonian Board of Regents.

But congressional action was not enough to remake the office. Ultimately, the vice-president's position depends on the president. And recent presidents have been more forthcoming. President Eisenhower decided to give Vice-President Nixon several chores, telling him: "Dick, I don't want a vice president who will be a figurehead. I want a man who will be a member of the team. And I want him to be able to step into the presidency smoothly in case anything happens to me."[26] Eisenhower requested Nixon act as chairman of the National Security Council in his absence. He also asked that Nixon take to the hustings for Republican congressional candidates. President Kennedy put Vice-President Johnson in charge of the man-in-space program. After that, it was customary for a president to give his number-two a specific assignment. There matters rested until the Carter-Mondale administration.

Jimmy Carter and Walter Mondale reversed nearly two hundred years of presidential–vice-presidential bickering. Four days after his inauguration Carter confided in his diary, "I would like to delegate much more authority as President than I ever tried to do as governor."[27] Carter did not always live up to this wish. Speechwriter James Fallows mentions that Carter would personally approve each request to use the White House tennis courts.[28] But when it came to his vice-president, Carter made Mondale a true second-in-command. Carter noted that he was "astounded" to learn that previous vice-presidents had never been drilled on the procedures used in case of a nuclear attack.[29] Carter had Mondale promptly informed of what must be done in such an eventuality. Moreover, Carter insisted that every presidential document be shown to Mondale. Carter also allocated time to his vice-president, instituting a one-on-one Thursday lunch, and otherwise allowing Mondale unlimited access to the Oval Office. Finally, in an unprecedented move, Carter provided Mondale an office in the coveted West Wing of the White House. Proximity is power, and Carter's placement of Mondale in the suite once occupied by Nixon Chief of Staff H. R. Haldeman sent a powerful message to the power-brokers in the nation's capital.[30]

When Ronald Reagan and George Bush came to power in 1981, Bush hoped that Reagan would do for him what Carter had done for Mondale. Reagan, in fact, kept the Carter changes in place, thus lending greater institutional support to them. Reagan and Bush met weekly, Bush got his White House office, and he accepted a few specific assignments from Reagan.

But it was the Twenty-Second Amendment that, arguably, altered the vice-presidency forever. Approved in 1951, it limits a president to two terms. Since its passage nearly every incumbent vice-president has won his party's presidential nomination. Richard Nixon was the first, defeating New York governor Nelson Rockefeller in 1960. Hubert Humphrey won the Democratic nomination in 1968; Walter Mondale did so in 1984; and George Bush easily captured the GOP nod in 1988. Of the eight presidential elections held since 1960, only the 1980 contest did not have an incumbent or former vice-president heading the party ticket.[31]

This is in sharp contrast to the political dead end the vice-presidency represented in the late nineteen century. Its occupants were nondescripts whose names do not come easily to the tongue: Schuyler Colfax, Henry Wilson, William Wheeler, Levi P. Morton, Thomas Hendricks, and Garret A. Hobart.[32] None had a chance of becoming president unless their boss died or resigned. In fact, three of these men died in office. The resurrected vice-presidency prompted one Reagan aide to remark: "Twenty years ago, I wouldn't have advised my worst enemy to take the Vice-Presidency. It was God's way of punishing bad campaigners, a sort of political purgatory for the also-rans. Now, you'd be crazy not to take the job."[33]

Subsequent events have validated the observation. The selection of George Bush as president in 1988 marked the first time since 1836 that an incumbent vice-president was elected president. Bush's win increased the number of presidents who previously were vice-president to fifteen, more than one-third of the total.

THE PERILS OF VICE-PRESIDENTIAL SELECTION

Political scientist Barbara Hinckley writes, "It is commonly held at convention time that the presidential candidate always selects the vice presidential candidate."[34] Hinckley calls this a "myth," noting that presidents have rarely exercised an autocratic power in making the choice.

An earlier study by Paul T. David confirms the point. David studied the four party conventions held from 1896 to 1948 in which an incumbent president sought renomination at a time when the vice-presidency was vacant—due to the death of either the vice-president or the previous president.[35] In each case, David wrote that "the President was able to exercise only limited influence on the situation. . . . Seemingly, the choice tended to be made by the convention, with other leaders exercising as much influence as the President."[36]

Several Franklin Roosevelt biographies tell how the big-city Democratic bosses wanted Henry Wallace removed from the 1944 ticket and replaced by Missouri Senator Harry Truman or Supreme Court Justice William O. Douglas. Roosevelt acceded to their wishes—a historic decision, for he was to die within a year.[37]

Dwight Eisenhower revealed in his memoirs that he never handpicked Nixon as his vice-president. Instead, he carried a scrap of paper in his wallet containing the names of five men, including Nixon's, that were acceptable to him.[38] Ike shared the list with Republican party leaders, including New York Governor Thomas E. Dewey who vigorously argued Nixon's case.

In 1966 Gerald Pomper repeated Paul David's examination of vice-presidential nominations, using Lyndon Johnson's 1964 selection of Hubert Humphrey as his case study. Like David's previous work, Pomper studied the means by which an incumbent president filled a vacancy in the vice-presidential slot. He concluded that Johnson's recommendation of Humphrey to the Democratic convention was neither hasty nor arbitrary. Humphrey had gathered an impressive collection of endorsements, including a unanimous vote from the executive council of the AFL-CIO, the nation's largest labor union. Humphrey also won backing from the United Auto Workers Union, farm workers, and several Democratic state and local party chairs. Humphrey's staff neatly framed the criteria for his selection, saying Johnson was obligated, especially in the wake of Kennedy's assassination, to name "the next best man":

The sudden death of President Kennedy, the subsequent succession of President Johnson, the present vacancy in the office of the Vice-Presidency, have all underlined the necessity of the Vice-President to be the man next-best qualified for the Presidency itself. . . . [Other] factors—in the nuclear age—are overshadowed by the necessity of guaranteeing that should tragedy befall the President, the nation would be under the most experienced and capable leadership available.[39]

In naming Humphrey, Johnson maintained that he had chosen "the best man for the job."[40] Pomper concluded: "The nomination of Senator Humphrey points the way to the future of the Vice-Presidency."[41]

Pomper's forecast proved off the mark. In fact, Hinckley's "myth" was fast becoming a reality. In 1968 a new vice-president was chosen in an arbitrary fashion. Richard Nixon writes in his memoirs that in the several weeks prior to the Republican convention he and Campaign Manager John N. Mitchell secretly settled on Spiro T. Agnew. No list of potential vice-presidents was given to Republican leaders. Moreover, no pretense was made that their input was welcome. Nixon thought Agnew's incompetence an asset. Former staff member John Ehrlichman recalls that Nixon often referred to Agnew as his "insurance policy," saying: "No assassin in his right mind would kill me. They know that if they did they would end up with Agnew."[42]

The 1972 reforms in the presidential nominating process instituted by the McGovern-Fraser Commission removed Democratic party leaders from their once prominent role in writing their ticket. Several attempts have been made to restore their former luster, most notably those of the Hunt Commission.[43] But none were enough to restore the status quo ante. The result was to narrow the vice-presidential jury to a single person: the presidential nominee. This also holds true for Republicans, who have been reluctant accomplices to party reform. Sometimes the presidential nominee will consult others, but these are usually close friends and associates rather than experienced party professionals. Michael Dukakis, for instance, relied on childhood friend Paul Brountas to be, in Dukakis's words, "a committee of one" in selecting Lloyd Bentsen.[44] George Bush entrusted his vice-presidential canvassing to Robert Kimmitt, an attorney with limited experience in GOP affairs. Bush never sought the advice of

Republican professionals. If he had done so, the reaction might have given him pause. Veteran GOP operative Ed Rollins told Germond and Witcover:

> If any group of political reporters or other politicos had been asked [by Bush], "Hey, what do you think of Dan Quayle? I'm really serious about putting him on the ticket." In thirty-five seconds you'd have it all out there. There wouldn't have been a person in the room stand up [for his selection].[45]

It is easy to argue that Dukakis made a wise choice in Bentsen, and Bush the wrong one in Quayle. But such characterizations are too simplistic. If Bush had chosen any number of other Republicans, including Robert Dole and Jack Kemp, he might have received accolades for his selection. But Bush was under no compulsion to select his former rivals. His decision, like Dukakis's, was arbitrary. Moreover, the criteria used did not include "the next best man" thesis. Instead, Quayle's primary qualifications were his youth, loyalty, and subservience. The latter two qualities are ones Americans find tolerable in a vice-president, but not in a president. Bush himself once said that he would follow Reagan "blindly."[46] Bush expects no less from Quayle.

Convention delegates could change this. After all, they make the final selection of the vice-president. But their loyalties are often skewed, flowing first to the presidential candidate then to the party. Their predilection to accede to the wishes of the presidential nominee has led to the rubber-stamping of vice-presidential candidates heretofore unknown. A favorite question during the 1968 campaign was "Spiro who?" But the same query could have been directed at Edmund Muskie, Geraldine Ferraro, Thomas Eagleton, and Quayle.[47] Many Republican delegates and certainly the voters were unfamiliar with Quayle. He had never been a prominent senator, yet the GOP delegates approved his selection without a dissenting voice.

A MODEST REFORM

Arbitrary selection of the vice-president has contributed to the present crisis of confidence in the office. This loss of faith comes at a time when the vice-president has become a permanent member of the executive branch. Arguments are made that changing the selection procedures are untimely, given the job's new-found responsibilities. Advocates of the status quo contend that the president must have a "free hand" in designating his running mate. However, it is worth remembering that the Constitution does not give the chief executive much of a "free hand" in anything. Cabinet members, for example, must obtain Senate confirmation before assuming office. The Senate rejection of John Tower as Secretary of Defense in 1989 prompted President Bush to exercise greater care in designating his department heads. He did so, choosing a consensus candidate in Richard Cheney, who won easy Senate approval.

But no such check and balance applies to naming a vice-president. In fact, the American predilection for checks and balances is strangely absent as far as the nation's second highest office is concerned. This is most unfortunate. Presidents should have some limits placed on their vice-presidential choices, just as constraints are placed on nearly every other appointment. Party delegates are not predisposed to exercise their right of refusal when asked to ratify their nominee's choice of a vice-president, fearing that doing so would doom the ticket to defeat. Thus, placing some modest legal constraints on naming the vice-president seems warranted.[48]

In recent years, several proposals to enhance the legitimacy of choosing a vice-president have been advanced. In 1973 the Democrats created a Commission on Vice-Presidential Selection chaired by former vice-president Hubert Humphrey. It suggested extending the convention by one day to allow the presidential nominee more time to deliberate about the vice-presidential nominee. If that was not acceptable, the commission advocated delaying the selection of the vice-presidential candidate by three weeks or more after the convention adjourned. The eventual nominee would be presented to the Democratic National Committee for final approval.[49]

Other overhauls for choosing a vice-president have been advanced, including:

> Choosing the vice-presidential candidate sixty days before the national convention. The two would run as a "team" and delegates would cast a simultaneous vote for president and vice-president.[50]

Making the runner-up in the presidential contest the party's automatic vice-presidential candidate.[51]

Allowing the president-elect to name a vice-president after the election. The choice would be subject to the advice and consent of the U.S. Senate.

Abolishing the vice-presidency.[52]

These are drastic overhauls. Two would require amending the Constitution (here we go again!): one allowing a postelection vice-presidential choice, the other abolishing the office. All involve significant changes in custom. The chance of adopting any of these proposals is remote.

Change is required, but like many of the institutional alterations agreed to during the two hundred years of the republic's existence, modifying the selection of a vice-president should be done prudently. One modest proposal that does this is requiring the presidential nominee to choose from his party's also-rans for the presidential nomination. The nominee is under no obligation to select the first runner-up; indeed, someone else could be chosen. If this requirement existed in 1988, Bush would have named Robert Dole, Jack Kemp, Alexander Haig, Pat Robertson, or Pierre DuPont to the Republican ticket. Excluding Robertson and DuPont, each of these men would have had significant intraparty support. Dukakis would have chosen from Albert Gore, Jesse Jackson, Richard Gephardt, Bruce Babbitt, Paul Simon, and Gary Hart. With the exceptions of Hart and Jackson, each of these prospective Democratic vice-presidents would have won wide-spread acceptance from his party, the public, and the media.

The advantages of this idea are many. First, it requires a presidential candidate to select from a group of persons each of whom has achieved a threshold of political acceptance. By naming someone who has previously run for president, quiescent vice presidents will be replaced with forthright ones. Mondale and Bush are examples of the latter. Although Mondale did not run in the 1976 presidential primaries, he briefly entered the race. Moreover, over his long career Mondale had acquired a reputation as a New Deal Democrat. Bush held several high-level jobs prior to his selection by Reagan, including Chairman of the Republican National Committee. The relatively high standing of both men allowed each to bend his president's ear. And Carter and Reagan listened, for their vice-president represented an important political constituency.

Moreover, confining the presidential nominee to the also-rans guarantees that the vice-president will not have to play the "getting to know you" game that so many other presidents and vice-presidents have done. As a candidate, the presidential nominee learns the positions taken by rivals—agreeing with them sometimes, and challenging them on other occasions. During such jousts, the nominee gauges his competitors' respective strengths and weaknesses. Jimmy Carter wrote that if he had had to select from among his opponents in 1976, either Idaho Senator Frank Church or Washington Senator Henry Jackson would have been named:

> Since both had been opponents of mine in the primaries, I was familiar with their general political philosophy, their stand on particular issues, and their campaign strengths and weaknesses. I also knew them to be ambitious and willing to face a difficult political contest.[53]

In the end, Carter chose Mondale. But a Church or Jackson vice-presidency would not have prevented Carter from making the institutional changes in the office realized during Mondale's tenure.

SUMMARY

For two hundred years, the vice-presidency has been an anomaly in the American polity. During the past decade the position has been strengthened institutionally, making the vice-president an invaluable member of the executive branch. But these improvements have been undermined by questions raised about the method of vice-presidential selection. These doubts intensified in 1988, with Bush's surprise choice of Quayle. So profound were they that the newfound sense of vice-presidential institutional self-worth was put in jeopardy. A public crisis of confidence has arisen, not just in Quayle but in the office itself. By requiring the president to choose among defeated rivals, the enhancement of the vice-presidency begun by Jimmy Carter and continued by Ronald Reagan will be complemented by an enhanced public acceptance of the choice.

Part 2

NO—
Vice-Presidential Candidates Should Not be Selected from the Also-Ran Category

Landis Jones

During the past six decades the American presidency has assumed a unique importance. In the United States the office combines being head of state and head of government. Fast executive action or reaction is necessary, and compliance with our separation and sharing of powers becomes difficult. Primarily, this growth of the presidency stems from national security concerns, but the general executive responsibility has grown as well. Transition between administrations becomes more important, and transition from a disabled or dead president becomes very important.

The most important role of the vice-president is to prepare himself or herself to become president without need for much additional training or addition of information. The best way for a vice-president to prepare is to be active in the administration, to fill in the knowledge gaps and lacunae of experience. The only way that a vice-president can do this is to be allowed or encouraged to be active and to be given some important roles by the president. The only way that this will happen, short of its being mandated by Congress or constitutional amendment, is to have the president and vice-president compatible and not rivals. The best way to ensure this compatibility is to continue the practice of having a presidential candidate select a running mate.

The current practice—having a presidential candidate select a running mate—is fairly recent and is not a result of law or the Constitution. George Bush was free to select Senator Dan Quayle to run with him with no prior clearance from anyone. Bush had won the sufficient number of delegates to the Republican National Convention to assure his own nomination. The Republican convention, dominated by Bush delegates, was not likely to reject his choice of a running mate, whoever he or she might be. Although issues at the nominating convention might from time to time require an element of bargaining on the part of presidential nominees—platform planks, for instance—increasingly the question of a running mate is the presidential nominee's to answer.

As late as 1952, Dwight D. Eisenhower, a newcomer to politics but certainly not to government, was surprised to learn that he had a virtually free choice to name his running mate. From a list of names suggested to him, he fatefully chose someone he did not know well, Richard M. Nixon, a first-term senator from California. Nixon balanced the ticket: he was much younger, from the West not the East, and was championed by the stridently anticommunist and more conservative Republicans, many of whom had supported Robert Taft over Eisenhower for the nomination. Since 1952 television coverage of the conventions and the "democratization" of the presidential nomination process through primaries and caucuses have changed the national party conventions from decision-makers to ratifiers unsuited to independent decision-making, including a capacity to select a running mate for their newly named candidate. As the political function of national nominating conventions changed, presidential nominees essentially captured the nearly absolute right to select whom they wish.

Should the convention, rather than the party's presidential candidate, select the vice-presidential running mate? The argument of this author is that the convention or some surrogate such as the national committee should *not* select the vice-presidential candidate. This decision must be left to the presidential nominee whose first test should be to select a competent and compatible running mate. Based on past failures, such as President Nixon's choice of Spiro Agnew, who was forced to resign as vice-president, or George McGovern's choice of Thomas Eagleton, who was dumped from the ticket after previously undisclosed treatments for mental illness were revealed, we can say that improvement in the nominee's process of selection should be sought, but restricting the candidate's choice of persons from whom a running mate can be selected would be most unfortunate.[1] Getting more advice from larger numbers of consultants and requiring some pause after one's own nomination are procedures that have been raised and are worthy of consideration. However, the basic need for the presidential candidate to make the choice still remains. This argument rests on changes in the function and structure of the office of the modern vice-presidency, developments demanding that presidential nominees have freedom to select their own running mate.

DEVELOPMENT OF THE MODERN VICE-PRESIDENCY

Vice-presidents used to be considered relatively minor, if not laughable, choices for the electorate. Given any luck, a vice-president would be voted in and then not heard from. The vice-president would break a tie in the Senate on occasion and could preside over the Senate (both constitutional prerogatives), but had no role in the executive branch—unless the president died. Then, with little or no preparation, the vice-president would be transformed into the president. A vice-president was nothing or everything, as John Adams described it. Vice-presidents were legislative figures, if not by prior experience then by their virtual isolation to Capitol Hill, where they had their small staff and offices.[2] The running mates for presidential nominees were chosen by conventions that had one aim—to gain a majority in the Electoral College. Compatibility with the presidential candidate was not essential. Balancing the ticket for electoral effect might in fact ensure the incompatibility of the two candidates on the ticket.

In the premodern vice-presidency, even the eventual capacity to govern was not essential. The American presidency was not that crucial, just as the central government itself was not that active. Many of the important domestic functions of American government were the responsibilities of state governments, not the national government. A part-time Congress and a president with a very small staff and small number of cabinet officers could handle almost everything in a country whose domestic issues far outweighed any interest in international relations. A vice-president who had to succeed had plenty of time to learn the issues.

This antiquated form of the vice-presidency, caricatured in the bumbling personage of Vice-President Throttlebottom in "Of Thee I Sing," a Broadway musical, ended soon after the development of the modern presidency during the administration of Franklin Delano Roosevelt. In 1932 the Democrats had balanced their ticket traditionally with a former New York governor and a Texas congressman, John Nance "Cactus Jack" Garner. The Democratic team members were not chosen for compatibility, and as Roosevelt pushed through expansionist government programs as part of the New Deal and decided to run for a third term, the two split seriously. Their split did not affect Roosevelt's success significantly, but it symbolized the differences between a New Deal New Yorker and an unreconstructed Southern conservative. If Garner had succeeded Roosevelt, would the New Deal have continued under congressional insistence? It is possible, but unlikely. For his unprecedented race for a third term, Roosevelt pressured the convention into selecting a new vice-presidential candidate, Henry A. Wallace.

Wallace's election as vice-president, and President Roosevelt's use of him in the executive branch, described below, initiated the precedents for the "modern" vice-presidency, matching the vastly more active and important presidency also created by Roosevelt.[3] As we observe the growth of the vice-presidency, we observe that the growth is largely a creation of the presidents themselves and their willingness to give important or at least extensive executive roles to their vice-presidents.

The role of the vice-president has changed so significantly that the "modern" vice-presidency, since 1940, has become an integral part of the executive branch. Constitutionally, the vice-president is expected to have only minor legislative roles, presiding and breaking ties in the Senate, and only a potential role in the executive branch. The extraconstitutional executivization of the vice-presidency has both strengthened and weakened the office. The office has come to be recognized as more important by the public, and it receives more attention, but it has become very dependent on the will of the incumbent president for any prerogatives in the executive branch beyond the few provided for by law. Therefore, the vice-presidential selection process has changed from being one of the convention itself to that of the presidential nominee, who will set the parameters for the vice-president's executive roles. The nominee's degree of choice is essential in filling such a dependent office. Placing restrictions on the nominee's choice, such as requiring the vice-presidential nominee to come from the ranks of the runners-up for the nomination, would not necessarily increase the quality of vice-presidents or improve their training to become president.

The modern vice-presidency began with Roosevelt's selection of Henry A. Wallace. Wallace was F. D. R.'s personal choice, not that of the congressional party or the convention and its professional politicians. Wallace had been a cabinet member and was an executive type, not a congressional alumnus. During the war, Roosevelt put him in charge of coordinating part of the war effort and the vice-president got into serious conflict with fellow cabinet members. He traveled abroad on behalf of the president and reported back to the president.[4] He differed strikingly from his predecessor in the first two Roosevelt terms. He was compatible with Roosevelt and the New Deal. He was far more active in the executive realm than in the legislative. Pushed into replacing Wallace in 1944, Roosevelt agreed to select Harry Truman, who came from the Senate but had been a county executive. The Truman vice-presidency was too short-lived to characterize except for the abysmal ignorance in which the vice-president was kept, particularly about postwar planning and new weapons, such as the atomic bomb.

Truman came to the White House as the war was drawing to a close, but with prophetic decisions to be made about the future of the postwar world. He is now accorded high marks by many observers, but he regretted how ignorant he was and how much in the dark he had been kept. For almost four years he was a president without a vice-president. He got to select a running mate in 1948. Harry Truman's choice was Alben Barkley, an epitome of the old legislative type, a premodern, but even Barkley, who might have reverted voluntarily to the earlier Throttlebottom stereotype, could not. He traveled to Europe on behalf of the president.[5] He was made by law a member of the new National Security Council. He was not allowed to remain as ignorant of the progress of national security affairs as Roosevelt had allowed Truman to be. Perhaps, the neglect of Truman was as much a result of F. D. R.'s ill health and preoccupation as his not personally preferring Truman, but Harry Truman's own vice-presidency was to be the last neglected vice-presidency.

Vice-President Richard Nixon and all his successors in the office have been executive types even if they came with no past executive experience. Partly because of Dwight Eisenhower's lack of political experience and partly because of his own style, Ike gave lots of executive tasks to Vice-President Nixon. Nixon traveled abroad widely and received lots of publicity from narrow escapes in Latin America and debates in Moscow with Premier Kruschev. He chaired presidential commissions. He was perceived as doing the president's "dirty" work, the partisan attacks that left Eisenhower appearing above the fray. With several major illnesses of the president, Nixon became even more the executive oriented vice-president. He chaired substantial percentages of cabinet meetings and National Security Council meetings.[6] A fully modern and executive-dependent vice-presidency had been developed, and the office was never to be the same. A new expectation of utility and preparation of vice-presidents was created.

John Kennedy's vice-president, Lyndon B. Johnson, assumed a great many executive tasks and was present if not vocal in many of the critical decision-making sessions of the major foreign policy crises. Johnson chaired a number of presidential commissions: the President's Committee on Equal Employment Opportunity, the National Aeronautics and Space Council, and the Peace Corps Advisory Council. In his role in equal employment, he developed a reputation quite different from any he had had as a senator from Texas, basically a Southern state, and different too from his majority leader role in which he had tried to stake a somewhat more national role as he had run for the Democratic nomination in 1960. He got lots of hate mail as vice-president, telling him that he was a traitor to his region.[7] He was rebuffed in his efforts to chair the Democratic caucus in the Senate or otherwise retain a leadership role in the Senate (a not unreasonable expectation), so his recourse was to become an executive branch participant as Nixon had become. He was given a set of offices in the Old Executive Office Building next to the White House and a part of the White House—a first. Ensconced there, even this strongly legislative type of personality found it desirable to have a more extensive executive role.

Johnson's own vice-president, Hubert Humphrey, caught the full impact of the executivization of the vice-presidency. At the convention in 1964 where Johnson was nominated, the president toyed with Humphrey over his selection and made the senator from Minnesota wait until the last minute to know if he was the choice or not. Johnson continued to dominate Humphrey as his vice-president and once completely shut Humphrey out of the foreign policy decision-making for over a year, including de facto meetings of the National Security Council, when the vice-president seemed to disagree openly in meetings at the White House on Vietnam policy.

Humphrey was both refused access and humiliated. He was able to keep his Executive Office Buiding suite, but he was not part of the inner workings during his "banishment." Those who were his aides at the time say that this was an extremely distressing period personally for Humphrey.[8] He had been a serious contender with Kennedy for the presidency, as had been Johnson in 1960. He had been a majority whip when Johnson was majority leader of the Senate, but in the vice-presidency he had to toe the president's line or suffer his wrath. Obviously, to have access, to have a meaningful role, to avoid demeaning comments by the president, Vice-President Humphrey had to subordinate his own views to be in public agreement with the president. To retain his chairmanships of commissions, which proliferated in his term (President's council on Youth Opportunity, National Council on Indian Opportunity, and others) or to be involved in such a vital information flow as the National Security Council, Humphrey had to conform to an exceptionally strong and domineering president. An obvious price of meaningful executive involvement is compliance with the president's views.

Spiro T. Agnew had no independent standing in the Republican Party or the country when he was selected by Richard Nixon to be the vice-presidential nominee in 1968. Even more than Humphrey, who had been a leading contender for the Democratic nomination even before becoming vice-president, Agnew was dependent upon his president for a meaningful role. Vice-Presidents Humphrey and Johnson had retained many friendships on Capital Hill even if they were excluded from leadership there as vice-presidents. Former Governor Agnew soon learned that a vice-president, particularly a stranger to that body, was to be seen and not heard. His lobbying efforts were denounced, and he was embarrassed.[9]

Having been governor of Maryland for only two years before his election, the new vice-president did not have experience or perpectives on many national issues. He needed to work hard on a steep learning curve. He was briefed by Richard Allen and Henry Kissinger, and received daily national security briefings. He picked up the chairmanships of most of the councils that Humphrey had been given to chair. In addition, he was placed in charge of intergovernmental relations. Under Nixon's New Federalism, intergovernmental relations and cities were an important topic (as a number had suffered damaging race riots and extensive burning and looting in 1968). The vice-president was therefore placed in charge of the Office of Intergovernmental Relations and developed significant networks with mayors, county executives, and governors. The president made Agnew a participant and sometimes chair of the Urban Affairs Council and its eventual successor, the Domestic Affairs Council. When it became apparent that Agnew was developing his own support in the right wing of the Republican Party and with hard hats in the Democratic ranks, he was eventually, at the start of the second Nixon administration, cut out of these leadership roles. He was actively engaged in speech-giving for the administration and an obscure man became a "household" word. He became "Nixon's Nixon" (a hatchet man as Nixon had been for Eisenhower).

With the Twenty-Fifth Amendment in effect, President Nixon was obliged to fill the vice-presidency, which had always gone un-filled in the past when it became vacant by death or illness or the incumbent's becoming president. Gerald Ford was a well-respected minority leader of the House of Representatives. Both houses of Congress were quick to praise the president's choice and to vote to make Ford the vice-president. Ford picked up on all of Agnew's re-maining functions but spent much of his short vice-presidency traveling and speaking. He was in the awkward position of defend-ing his mentor but keeping his distance from Watergate issues as much as possible, for it was evident that he might well become president if Nixon was impeached.[10] He had to keep a low profile and not subvert a wounded president, but at the same time remain aloof and prepare to take over the reins of government. He became president in August 1974, when President Nixon resigned his office in disgrace and to avoid all but certain impeachment by the House and conviction by the Senate.

Ford in turn, when he did become president, had to select a vice-president, and his choice was a popular former Republican governor, Nelson Rockefeller. The long-term governor of New York was from the liberal wing and was a flashier person than Ford. He tried to play a low profile that would not overpower or hurt Presi-dent Ford's chances to get the 1976 Republican nomination, which was tightly contested by Ronald Reagan. Thus, he was a surpris-ingly inactive vice-president, living in his own Washington home rather than inaugurate the newly provided vice-presidential mansion at the Naval Observatory.[11] Rockefeller spent a lot of time in travel away from Washington and was something of a prisoner of the office. Ford dropped Rockefeller in favor of more conservative Senator Bob Dole of Kansas during Ford's own attempt at being elected to the Oval Office in 1976. Thus, a politically incompatible vice-president turned out to be a liability who could not be retained. Walter Mondale's tenure as Jimmy Carter's vice-president marks the beginning of a new pattern with even more dependency on the part of the vice-president. Walter Mondale came from the more liberal segment of the Democratic Party, but even though Jimmy Carter was viewed in 1976 as a relative conservative and was supported by the conservative wings of the party, there were not major substantive differences in Carter's and Mondale's views. Vice-President Mondale was fully trusted as a reliable aide in the innermost circles of the White House. His Senate experience and knowledge of Washington's mores were respected by the president. The vice-president did not take on any long-range assignments but was an active participant in day-to-day activities and planning. He was the most integrated of all vice-presidents to that day.[12]

Carter and Mondale set up a merged staff arrangement alleviating some of the staff-bred tension between the president and the vice-president. The vice-president was in the White House and a part of the staff. The vice-presidential staff was pared and merged with the President's White House staff. In the West Wing, the vice-president had fewer staff close to him, and a national security aide and others involved in military and national security are not likely to veer far from the official line developed in the National Security Council on which the vice-president serves. In the domestic area as well as on the National Security Council staff, Mondale appointees were placed to work right along with Carter's. They became indistinguishable, whether they were Carter campaign appointees or former Mondale Senate or campaign aides. This eliminated much potential strife. The president and vice-president met regularly, and there was not the sense of competition that appeared in earlier patterns of organization of the modern or executive vice-presidency.

President Ronald Reagan and his vice-president, George Bush, worked out a fairly similar arrangement. In spite of the surprising arrangement, in which a Bush aide, Jim Baker, became the very influential Reagan Chief of Staff, there was more expectation of differences of views between Bush and Reagan. Bush was from a more moderate wing or was thought to be more centrist than Reagan. They had been opponents for the nomination. However, differences were minimalized until Bush began to campaign for himself at the end of the second term. Even then, great care was taken to not have Bush get too far off the Reagan reservation, and Bush held to the policies of the administration very carefully. Early in the administration, Bush and his staff members were thought to be having some success in modifying the "evil empire" views and policies held by President Reagan about the Soviet Union.[13] If it were the case, it did not get much external note. Lots of speculation about the distrust of Bush by far-right Republicans and the role of moderation by Jim Baker arose, but on no major issues until the 1988 campaign were there open, publicized breaks between vice-president and president, and then fairly subtle.

The current model of full, integrated participation by the vice-president has been carried over into the Bush presidency. The president and his vice-president are perceived to be potentially of differing perspectives on some issues, Dan Quayle being more ideologically to the right than his pragmatic president. He had had no executive experience when he became vice-president. Quayle was not a front-bencher in the House or Senate. The few apparent instances of differences between the vice-president and his chief may be the result of early administration lack of coordination. The proclaimed model of Quayle's involvement is that of the Carter and Reagan models, but it is too early to judge the reality or success of that claim.

As we examine the development of the modern vice-presidency, it is hard to imagine severely competitive primary contestants being able to function together within the context of executive decision-making, particularly when close subordination and compatibility are required. A Bob Dole or a Ted Kennedy or a Jack Kemp or George McGovern could not have been expected to play the docile cooperative roles played by Mondale or Bush or a relative unknown like Dan Quayle. In most presidential campaigns, where there is a real contention for the nomination, it could not be expected that one of the major opponents of the successful candidate could be a successfully submissive vice-president.

The almost fanciful, television-inspired, possibility of a Reagan-Ford ticket in 1980 is an example of the ridiculous thought that a former (albeit unelected) president could be persuaded to be a vice-president.[14] Middle-of-the-road Jerry Ford could not have been expected to play a second to a far-right president, as the image of Reagan was at that point. Such a peculiar ticket might have made political sense, making Reagan more palatable, but it turned out to be as unnecessary an arrangement as it would have been unwise if there were hope of creating a productive vice-presidency.

The current vice-presidency is one of almost complete subordination to the president. Not much variance is allowed. One can ask whether this is a "good" or healthy situation, whether strong persons with real credentials for the presidency can play such a neutered role until their time comes to assume the presidency at death or disability of their president or to run for it in their own right. Early speculation about the Bush presidential campaign and subsequent administration raised this question. Does the current model of selection and utilization of the vice-president fulfill or support the main function of a vice-presidency—to prepare to take over in the event of death or disability?

THE WAY TO SELECT A VICE-PRESIDENT

The current system has many attributes. It cannot make a silk purse from a pig's ear, but as well as any other role, it can train for the presidency. A secretary of state or other inner cabinet officers are usually involved so deeply in their own major programs that they do not have the breadth of exposure that a vice-president acquires in domestic or political questions. Congressional leaders acquire their positions largely or solely (in the case of the president pro tempore) from seniority. They are not likely to have made foreign policy their main committee emphasis. An experienced vice-president is by far the most logical successor in case of incapacity or death. To succeed in normal fashion through election would appear productive as well, even though only one premodern and one modern vice-president has succeeded in doing that.

Vice-presidents must be chosen by the parties' presidential nominees because of the need for personal and political compatibility. There is always an underlying psychological phenomenon between an incumbent and a designated heir, even in monarchical succession. To add an artificial barrier that one must prepare a place for one's leading primary opponent is too much to require.

The relationship with and the training of a vice-president are difficult enough without adding more potential competition and continuing primary animosities of staff and principles. Would one be guaranteed a better quality vice-president who could do a better job in case of succession? This is not likely.

Even if one assumes that two years' or more of Holiday Inn residency and exposure to Iowa and New Hampshire are essential preparation for the presidency, it hardly follows that only the handful of final survivors has proven themselves for the vice-presidency. If one believes as this author that many excellent potential presidential candidates are loath to undergo our current initiation rights, one might presume that other demanding tests of legislative or executive leadership might be as good or better preparation for the vice-presidency or the presidency. It is a valid question: whether the current requirement for subordination leads to the best vice-presidents. If one is looking only for compatibility and submission, a new presidential nominee is not likely to place proper emphasis on the qualities necessary to be a good president, slippery as those might be.

The Mondale-Bush model for the vice-presidency is completely dependent upon presidential–vice-presidential agreement. It rests on custom and usage, not upon law and by no means the constitution. The formal constitutional position of the vice-president has changed very little, except for the Twenty-Fifth Amendment. This amendment infers a need for the vice-president to be informed. It does not mandate that and it certainly does not guarantee significant involvement by the vice-president prior to a disability or death. Such involvement, a need to look and feel useful and a need to be visibly close to the president, make most vice-presidents vulnerable. Only Alben Barkley and Nelson Rockefeller among modern vice-presidents seem to have been immune from this need. Once a precedent for intensive involvement was set, as with Eisenhower and Nixon, the expectation by the public and by the officeholder was escalated. This makes the vice-president increasingly vulnerable and necessitates the naming of someone who is compatible personally and ideologically. The usual list of presidential contestants is too short to ensure that a candidate for vice-president can be found there, particularly in the case of a semi-incumbent, such as the prior vice-president, who might run for the nomination.

The selection of a running mate should not be left to the convention, and if recent primary-dominated selections are indicative of the future, presidential candidates should have time to ponder and make an intelligent decision. Few people seem able to turn down the offer, even when they know as clearly as Agnew that they have reason not to run. Eagleton's failure to disclose his earlier mental treatment or merely its revelation got him bumped from the ticket. There are serious concerns about the way in which we select our presidents, but until we improve the quality of the final party nominees, we should not force selection of a vice-president from among those who have been competitors for the office of president. We have had a few avowed candidates for the vice-presidency itself, including Endicott Peabody, but attracting a larger crowd of contestants by the hope that they might be anointed with the vice-presidency and would be excluded if they do not compete will not improve the contest pool. Some of our best prospects for the presidency may not be willing to undergo the peculiarities of our current primary system and do not run. Should they be excluded from the vice-presidential pool? The relationship between a president and a vice-president is peculiar psychologically. Conflict between the principal and the heir-apparent would only be exacerbated by insisting that the heir had been a former competitor for the position. There must be a bond of trust and a willingness to sublimate one's will to another person's. That would be difficult to expect of most stiff-willed candidates. The presidential candidate of each party must have the final word, and this decision will be one factor for the electorate to observe and include in their decision to vote for or against a candidate for president and vice-president.

CHAPTER FOUR

Do the Media Inform?

An examination of the informational capacity of the mass media is relevant, given the increasing reliance of the American electorate on media throughout the course of the presidential selection process. In essence, the ability of the media to serve as a useful political linkage mechanism is under investigation in this chapter. John Orman argues that the media do inform the American electorate throughout the various phases of the presidential selection process. The media in Orman's view provide rich information regarding the viability of candidates, afford the electorate a look at the personal lives of candidates, establish the agenda with respect to campaign issues, add drama to the campaign, and offer analyses of the candidates' personalities. Orman recognizes that television could do more in the way of concentrating on substantive issues but contends that the American people are receiving the type of information which they demand. The media, according to Orman, are largely responding to the expectations of the viewers.

Kant Patel argues that the media have failed in their responsibility to inform the electorate. Patel draws heavily from empirically based studies to demonstrate that the media, particularly television, do not adequately inform the voters. Patel demonstrates the primary concerns of the media during presidential campaigns: the "horse race," the excessive importance placed on early primaries, overabsorption in character issues, and obsession with poll results. Patel believes that the commercial demands of the major networks tend to condition media coverage in campaigns and, as a result, the American electorate remains largely uninformed during the process of presidential selection.

Part 1

YES—
The Media Do Inform

John Orman

The mass media in the U.S. presidential selection process certainly have many problems, but one thing you *cannot* say about mass media is that they are "uninformative." Mass media, according to Holli Semetko, mean the "totality of mass mediated messages about the election, [including] national and local print and broadcast news coverage, candidate advertising, televised debates, and interview programs."[1] These forms of mediated messages may be biased, they may be sensationalized, they may be silly, or they may usurp the power of political parties in the election process, but they certainly are not "uninformative." Mass media in this country inform various targets in numerous ways at different times during the long drawn out process that we call the presidential selection process.

THE PREPRIMARY PHASE

During the preprimary phase of the election, which lasts about three years, the mass media can act to narrow the number of presidential candidates or can suggest the race would be better if other candidates entered the race. Although most citizens are not focused on the media events and commentary of the preprimary season, the key players in presidential politics are attuned to the media scorekeeping. The mass media inform candidates, political action committees, presidential watchers, other members of the media, pollsters, opinion leaders, and others how selected candidates are doing, judged by arbitrary mass media yardsticks.

In 1967, for example, Republican Governor George Romney of Michigan lost a promising presidential candidacy when the pack turned on the candidate for claiming he had been "brainwashed" by the Pentagon about how the war in Vietnam was progressing. In retrospect his comments were perfectly accurate, but no matter, the major media concluded that Romney was no longer presidential timber. During the preprimary period before the 1972 election, Senator Edward Kennedy was roundly criticized from 1969 to 1971 about Chappaquidick so as to make his candidacy in 1972 unthinkable. Finally, in 1987, Senator Gary Hart, front-runner for the Democratic nomination, was totally destroyed politically because the *Miami Herald* decided to stake out Hart to investigate whether he was having extramarital affairs. This was the first time in the history of the presidential selection process that a candidate had been staked out by the media in an investigative report into his private life. The media wasted no time in informing the public of the results of their investigative search into Hart's bedroom.

During the preprimary season, the media supply trial heats, give odds, discuss campaign fund-raising, and give some issue stands of various candidates. It is this kind of early "horse race" journalism that can have some influence on the chances of underdogs.[2] If you are not mentioned by the key presidential watchers as having a chance for the nomination, then in self-fulfilling prophecies your money fails to materialize, your support drops, your news coverage drops our of sight, and for all practical purposes you become a presidential campaign nobody. The problem, however, is not that the major media are uninformative. The problem is that they may be too informative about unimportant items.

PRIMARIES AND CAUCUSES

In the primary season, which also includes caucuses, the major media take on the role of "sports reporters." Americans watch politics much like they watch professional sports in this country. They rarely participate, and the media give them the score and massive commentary and criticism directed at each of the designated "major" candidates. It is during this critical period from the

Iowa caucus in January through the New Hampshire primary in February of presidential election years that the mass media may have their greatest impact in selecting nominees for the political parties. Many have argued that political parties no longer select the presidential nominees for their parties, but that the role has been taken over by the establishment media. I think that argument goes way too far and does not give credit to the power of the primary and caucus voters of each state. It is clear that massive doses of negative press over weeks or accumulation hurt the perceptions and expectations about a candidate; likewise, it is also clear that large doses of positive press over weeks of accumulation cannot hurt a candidate. Yet, in the end, as it should be, the voters, not the pack consensus of the media, decide the race for delegates.

Political reporters are important during the primary season in helping to set the campaign agenda.[3] The agenda setting function of the media has long been recognized. It is clear that the media inform citizens about which issues are worthy of discussion.[4] The media bring to task special skills in determining what is "news."[5] The broadcast media have a special set of requirements when compared to print journalism, and this means that citizens learn different things from television political news as compared to print reporting of the campaign.

Television news during the presidential selection process is guided by values of show business and entertainment.[6] However, this does not mean that citizens are not informed about policy differences between the candidates. What it does mean is that television just does not do as well as print media in covering issues. Television is constrained by time allowances, moving picture requirements, and sound-bite needs. The print media are constrained only by space requirements.

During the primary season both the television and print media spend much time in trying to weed out certain candidates and to establish the front-runner. Once front-runners are established the media attempt to make the contest as dramatic as possible by suggesting that the front-runner does not have the nomination locked up. It is in the interest of the media to make the story dramatic and sensational. Competition or projected competition allows the media to try to manufacture interest in the selection process. In order to manufacture competition, the media inform the passive audience that the front-runner has serious political "negatives" and that, on further inspection, the closest competitors have valuable "positives" that might outweigh the serious "negatives" exposed earlier by the careful analysis of the pack reporters.

The process is so drawn out and informative that some have argued that the regular citizen is bombarded with sensory overload. But the primary process only attracts presidential watchers, activists, political "junkies," and the citizens who have time for spring politics. Most Americans prefer to watch the long presidential selection show with attention spans that last two or three days at best.

Media consultants, public relations experts, and technological advisors try to come up with brilliant and creative ways to project presidential images to those few citizens who are still watching. Image specialists and their candidates try to portray issues like competency, honesty, credibility, composure, warmth, toughness, compassion, and other qualities. Media events and pseudo events help project these elusive qualities.[7] Yet images have to be filtered through the mass media presentation. Candidates do not control their own images.

In the 1988 primary season, citizens were informed by the media about a whole host of issues relating to the wide open field that sought nomination from both parties. Citizens learned about Gary Hart's womanizing and about Joe Biden's exaggerating and plagiarizing problems. They learned that Mike Dukakis was a short, competent, liberal governor who might be another Jimmy Carter. Citizens were informed about Paul Simon's bow tie and that he was a senator from Illinois, not Paul Simon the rock star. Citizens learned about Al Gore's "Southern strategy" for Super Tuesday, and they learned about Dick Gephardt's trade positions. Citizens learned that Pat Schroeder cried when she took herself out of the race. Most importantly for Jesse Jackson, citizens were informed that Jackson was running again, he was still black, he did not like Jews, and he was doing better than expected with his position on issues of education, drugs, jobs, peace, equality, environment, and tolerance.

With respect to Republican candidates, citizens were informed about Pat Robertson's religious views and Al Haig's egomaniacal personality. They learned that "Pete" DuPont was a rich preppie, and they were informed about Jack Kemp's football and economic past. Citizens were informed about Washington's best "power couple," Bob and Elizabeth Dole, and that Dole still had his "mean streak." Finally in dealing with the Republican candidates, citizens were informed that George Bush had the longest vita in the Western world and that he was a preppie wimp. Citizens were informed in detail of Bush's connection to the Iran-Contra scandal and his connection to the resupply network of Ollie North and Bill Casey. None of these candidates, the media pointed out, were Ronald Reagan.

The 1988 primary campaign provided a new wrinkle for media watchers in that Super Tuesday extended the media's influence from the Iowa-New Hampshire period for another month to reporting about the regional primary in the South. Instead of pronouncing winners after New Hampshire, the media informed citizens of the importance of Super Tuesday. Bush was declared the winner of the Republican nomination after Super Tuesday, but the pack still reported that the Democratic race was between Dukakis and the surprising "*black* Jesse Jackson, the *black* minister, who wants to represent more than *black* America." The media told the story of Jackson's incredible victory in Michigan and Dukakis's clinching victory in the brutal New York primary.

The media then turned to the question of who would get the vice-presidential nominations for both parties. We learned about Lloyd Bentson and more than we could possibly ever want to know about what Jesse Jackson wanted or did not want. Finally the media went into an absolute "feeding frenzy" over Dan Quayle's nomination for vice-president. The pack turned on Quayle in an effort to find out about his service record during the Vietnam war. Then his alleged extramarital story was resurfaced and stories about his college record came to the forefront. There was no lack of information about Dan Quayle.

THE NOMINATING CONVENTION

In the convention stage the mass media are very informative. Both political parties and their candidates receive an extraordinary amount of political coverage, which amounts almost to four days of free political advertising. In terms of viewership, however, the numbers of citizens who tune into the party conventions have been on the decline. So the more the media try to inform viewers of candidates and their position, the fewer the citizens who avail themselves of the opportunity to be informed.

THE GENERAL ELECTION

Finally in the general election phase, the mass media become the arena in which the entire campaign contest is played out. Everything that anyone knows about the candidates was culled from some mass media presentation somewhere. Mass media dominate the process and act as the national unifying agent for presidential election campaigns.

Exactly who does the media influence in their informative efforts? Certainly the phenomena of selective retention and selective perception act to limit the media's influence. But the media still play an important role of providing information to partisans to back up their previously held predispositions about the candidates. It is for the undecided, the independent, and the unaffiliated voter that the process of informing by the media takes on a special role.

There is evidence that suggests candidate preference-switching after the convention is minimal.[8] Contradictions in the voting literature are found when researchers try to sort the relative importance of long-term political predispositions and short-run, campaign-specific stimuli like candidate image, campaign events, and campaign issues.[9] The few citizens who do switch preferences, do so on the basis of new information. The goal of each major campaign is to create media events that are transmitted to voters as straight political information or "news."[10] Doris Graber described the phenomenon:

> At times, public meetings are arranged or conducted primarily for their propaganda value in swaying external audiences. As in public pageants, speakers unfold carefully planned scenarios before audiences who presumable are dazzled by the status of the actors or the solemnity of the setting.[11]

For the candidates the *coverage* of the happening, rather than the event itself, is of the greatest importance.

The impact of televised communications on political behavior and attitudes is a controversial discussion in communication research. Writers disagree as to the *degree* that media communications affect behavior.[12] The heart of this debate is whether the effects take a realigning or crystalizing effect on previous political views.[13]

The reinforcing view is supported by research done in selective exposure and selective perception.[14] The central position is that citizens seek out information that conforms to their own predisposition. When information opposes their positions, they will ignore this data. Maxwell McCombs observed:

> Implicit in these concepts of selective exposure and perception is the idea of motivation, that voters are actively motivated to attend to supportive messages. Conversely, this view suggests that voters are also motivated to avoid contradictory, non-supportive political messages.[15]

Although studies have indicated problems with this theoretical position, the majority of research on effects of the classic 1960 presidential debates concluded that voters judged each candidate's "performance" as an extension of predebate attitudes toward both parties and candidates.[16]

Citizens process news in different ways.[17] As Patterson and McClure have observed, the effect of political communication is not as "subconsciously subversive" as many writers would have us believe.[18] Yet some citizens do change their candidate preference when confronted with new information. These people have been a source of interest to scholars since the early voting studies.[19] "Changers" tended to have few contacts in the community and they were not linked to any political or social groups. Voters who are most likely to change preferences in light of new media information can be termed "rootless voters." Murray Edelman maintained:

> One of the most confident conclusions we can reach from the communication experiments and electoral studies is that people without enduring commitments are the most susceptible to persuasion, both by means of mass communications and by personal influence.[20]

The information that might change preferences in rootless voters more likely comes from print media. Television is more adept at communicating information that relates to personal characteristics rather than hard, issue-oriented data. Even though the election of 1984 was conducted by Reagan media advisor Roger Ailes in terms of generic patriotic television commercials and beautiful campaign backdrops, citizens were still informed by the print and broadcast media about Reagan's issue stands. Most polls showed that the electorate disagreed with most of Reagan's issue positions in the 1984 election, but went ahead and voted for him anyway because he was a popular, amiable leader.

Citizens suffered no lack of information on the 1984 candidates. Ronald Reagan brought to mind personal style, patriotism, Reaganomics, optimism, conservatism, and military strength. Citizens were informed by the media of Walter Mondale's frontrunner status for the Democratic nomination, his ties to special interests, his dullness, his decency, and his wimp problem. The media informed citizens that Reverend Jesse Jackson was black, he liked Farrakan, he disliked Jews, and he was a great speaker, among other things. The media explained to citizens that Gary Hart had new ideas and that he had a chance for the nomination after winning New Hampshire in a big political upset.

Then the media began to discredit Hart by informing voters about Hart's name change from Hartpence and that he had let a campaign biography go out from his staff that under reported his age by one year. These were widely reported as character problems. Citizens were informed of Geraldine Ferraro's political ability and competence when she was nominated for vice-presidency on the Democratic ticket. The media informed citizens that she had financial problems, that her husband had financial problems, and that as a Catholic woman, she had problems with her position on abortion. Moreover, the male-dominated media wondered if she was tough enough to be president. Throughout this bizarre cast of characters in the selection process, the media informed citizens about the positives and negatives of the candidates.

In the 1988 general campaign, citizens learned that Boston Harbor was polluted, that Dukakis had a problem with forcing people to say the Pledge of Allegiance, and that he never should have let Willie Horton out for a weekend furlough from a Massachusetts prison. The media pack said Bush was no longer a wimp but that he was a leader. He had been involved in Iran-contra but so what, and that he was no A.C.L.U. man. Bush was now likeable and popular, while Dukakis was still too unemotional, boring, and now he had become the "wimp" that they said George Bush once had been. The pack informed voters that Bush had the election wrapped up and that Dukakis was a hopeless campaigner. Of course, the "new George Bush" (perhaps Roger Ailes's finest image creation since the "new Nixon" of 1968) won in an Electoral College landslide. There was no lack of information communicated to voters in the 1988 elections by the mass media.

CONCLUSION

Voters cannot blame the media for being uninformative. With the emphasis on personal characteristics, viability, horse-race issues, and symbolic politics and drama, the media might be too informative for their own good. With respect to substantive issue stands of candidates, citizens can easily search these out in detail in the print media. Therefore, it is sad indeed when some studies reveal that the American electorate is basically uninformed about specific issue stands of all candidates. The fault lies in the inability of citizens to focus in on issues when the media are putting emphasis on other characteristics. Citizens get the kind of presidential selection system that they deserve. We have met the enemy and it certainly is not the media. The media provide the kind of information that we demand and the kind of information that candidates are intent on supplying. Before we ask the media to make dramatic changes in the way they cover the race for the presidency, we must make dramatic changes in our own behavior. As citizens we must be more aggressive in demanding and searching for substantive information to inform our vote choice, if that in fact is truly what we want.

Part 2

NO—
The Media Do Not Inform

Kant Patel

> *Campaignland is a fun-house version of America, in which relatively trivial things loom large and large things are barely visible.*[1]

Many Americans are unhappy with the way we choose our president. A Newsweek Poll during the 1988 presidential election found that two-thirds of the people surveyed think that better qualified candidates should have been selected. Seventy-four percent believe that candidates are not giving honest views on the issues and are saying what they need to say to get elected. The same poll also found that while 54 percent believe that news organizations are doing a good job providing important information about the candidates, a sizable number of voters (41 percent) disagreed.[2]

One of the most important shortcomings in the modern system of electing presidents is its dependence on the news media. Today the news media have come to play a major role in organizing public opinion. The news media have always been an important part of the American electoral landscape. In the past, news media, while important, were not as decisive in the presidential selection process as today. The contemporary role of the media in the presidential election process differs significantly from their past role. Today the news media play the role of agenda-setting— that is, the media influence the perceived salience of key political elements in presidential elections.[3] Modern presidential campaigns are essentially mass media campaigns. This is not to suggest that the mass media determine what happens in a campaign, but rather that for the large majority of voters the campaign has little reality apart from its media version. As Peter Hart, pollster for Democratic presidential nominee Walter Mondale during the 1984 campaign, explains, "A campaign is not played out anymore so much for people or voters; it's played out for the media."[4]

All modern presidential campaigns are dominated by the importance of mass media and particularly television. Campaign events, speeches, and candidates' appearances are shaped and scheduled with an eye for visual impact and what will play well on television. Although television news coverage started in the 1940s and had barely reached maturity in the 1960s, by the 1980s presidential elections were driven by television. This has significantly changed the nature of the campaigns themselves. As David Broder argues:

> The biggest effect television has had on our politics has been to lessen the substance of the campaign itself. And its consequences are not less serious because they are inadvertent.[5]

Why have the news media come to play such an important role in presidential campaigns? What factors have contributed to their significant and often decisive influence in presidential elections? How effectively do the news media perform their role in informing the public?

There are two major reasons why the news media have come to play an important role in modern presidential elections. The first reason is the decline in popularity of political parties in American politics in general and elections in particular. The decline in the influence of the political parties is reflected in the decline in party affiliation among voters, increased split-ticket voting, increased number of voters calling themselves independents, and less reliance by candidates on party machinery for the purposes of volunteer activism and fund-raising. Electoral reforms, political party reforms, and an increase in the number of presidential primaries have significantly lessened the influence of party leaders and party activists in the nomination and the general election process, and have increasingly led to candidate-centered campaigns. The void left by the declining role of political parties has been filled by the news media in general and television in particular. Today the news media have become the principal intermediary between presidential candidates and the voters.

Whether the rise in prominence of news media in general and television in particular led to the decline of political parties or vice versa is open to debate. It is an age-old chicken and egg question as to which came first. Some, including well-known and respected television journalists such as Roger Mudd, have argued that television killed the party structure and replaced old bosses with media consultants, which has made a candidate's image at least as important as his position.[6] Whether the news media have come to fill the void left, consciously or inadvertently, by the decline of political parties, is open to debate. But the fact remains that the decline of political parties has contributed significantly to the enlarged role of the news media in presidential elections. This in turn has changed the very nature of the presidential selection process.

The second reason why the news media have gained importance is because voters have come to rely more heavily on the information they provide. The mass media have become the major source of information about election campaigns for a majority of voters. The major source from which most voters derive information about presidential campaigns are the mass media rather than friends, family members, work associates, other personal contacts, or the work of political parties. Moreover, among the different news media, television has become the most trusted source of information, international and national, for most voters. This places a high premium on television in presidential elections. A credibility study commissioned by the American Society of Newspaper Editors found that even among frequent newspaper readers, television is the preferred medium for most types of news. For national and international news, 65 percent of newspaper readers and 68 percent of all respondents said television was more reliable. The same study found that if frequent newspaper readers had to choose just one source for their news, they would select television or radio by 56 percent to 44 percent over newspapers. The margin was even greater among all respondents. Sixty-four percent chose television broadcasts over newspapers.[7]

This brings us to the point of this article. Given the tremendous influence of the mass media, particularly television, in modern presidential campaigns, one is obliged to examine whether or not the media are in fact effectively informing and educating the general public about the important issues and choices confronting voters during the course of the presidential selection process. After carefully reviewing the body of evidence regarding the informational utility of the media, I have come to the conclusion that the media have seriously failed in their responsibility to inform the American public. The remainder of this chapter explores and discusses the reasons why the media have failed to inform voters, as well as other factors that limit the ability to properly inform the American electorate. These factors or reasons are closely intertwined and interact with one another to produce an overall picture.

OVEREMPHASIS ON THE "HORSE RACE" ASPECTS OF ELECTIONS

> The thing that bothers me the most is that we are too much into the horse race aspect of a campaign. As a political editor of *U.S. News* I am trying to avoid that, but you get swept up and you have to say who wins and who loses. I think getting into the horse race aspect way ahead of Iowa is a mistake.[8]

The news media can easily be faulted for making too much of a horse race out of a primary campaign. During the primary campaign the news media's attention is more likely to be focused on the horse race aspect of the campaign rather than an analysis of issues or issue positions of the candidates. In their need to simplify and condense the news, the media seem fascinated with only the horse race aspects of the election. Of course, it is necessary for the media to cover the horse race, who is winning and who is losing; that is partly what elections are about. Nevertheless, when the horse race becomes the operational definition of what is news in presidential elections,[9] many negative consequences arise. Several studies of social scientists, which have systematically measured the patterns of news coverage, agree that a very high percentage of news coverage is normally devoted to stories about the horse race aspects of primary elections.[10] Moreover, there is an increase in such reporting.

A study by Doris Graber of the campaign news coverage content from 1968 to 1976 found that the proportion of campaign news dealing with horse race aspects—strategies of contenders, who is winning and who is losing, contenders' campaign mistakes—was on the increase in both television and newspapers.[11]

Another study, which measured how well the network news (CBS) and the national wires (UPI) covered the 1980 campaign, concluded that "all national media, regardless of their prestige or financial well-being, emphasize competitiveness—the horse race."[12] A study of the news coverage of the 1984 elections also found that media reporters and editors were more interested in the horse race than in using the campaign as a platform for discussion of issues.[13] The media engaged in their typical horse race brand of coverage also in the 1988 campaign.

Another aspect of the media fascination with the horse race aspect of elections is that election news becomes mainly about the campaign itself—that is, candidates' strategic game plans, what the candidates are saying about themselves and their opponents, their prospects for winning and losing, their appearances, scheduled campaign events, and mistakes. The candidates' image, personality, and staff relations become the main focus of reporting. One study found that election competition and the candidates' campaign styles and quarrels accounted for more than half the news reported in *Time* and *Newsweek*.[14] Anthony Lewis criticized the medias' performance in the 1988 campaign as superficial in its coverage and fascinated primarily with process rather than substance:

> There were times in this campaign when we looked like theater critics—critics interested only in the artfulness of the scenery, not in the message of the play.[15]

This is generally true of newspapers and magazines as well as television, but the problem is more acute with television. For example, during much of the fall 1988 campaign, most of the media portrayed Dukakis's image as an "iceman." But surprisingly, this was never a news theme during the primary elections. How a candidate comes across on television often becomes a news story. The first televised Democratic debate in the 1988 campaign turned out to be a disaster for Bruce Babbitt. As he writes,

> Most of my reviewers looked to the animal kingdom for analogies. *Time* said I looked "as comfortable on television as a moose being pelted with buckshots." The *New Republic* asked, "Is this man about to bite the head off a live chicken?"[16]

The problem is more acute in television because here the story is accompanied by pictures, and good visuals often become the story. When a correspondent draws a parallel between the candidates and the animals at the zoo it has more chance of getting on the air because it is entertaining. As Albert Hunt reports:

> For the most part television journalism in the early primaries . . . alternates between the horse race, a video version of *People Magazine,* and follow-ups on negative newspaper stories.[17]

All these may produce entertaining news but they do not inform or educate voters about the significant choices they face. One of the negative consequences of such coverage is that too much time is spent on the horse race aspect of the campaign, leaving less time for analysis of more substantive issues. An excellent example of the medias' preoccupation with the horse race and campaign issues can be seen shortly before the March 8 Super Tuesday round of primaries in the 1988 elections. A content analysis of the three networks' evening newscasts indicated that horse race news out-spaced issue news twenty to one in the period just before Super Tuesday.[18] The second negative aspect of the overemphasis on horse race aspects is that when the media see a candidate going nowhere, they become a self-fulfilling prophecy. A candidate who is a back-runner struggling to break out of the pack has a much more difficult time getting media exposure to get the voters to take his candidacy seriously.

OVEREMPHASIS ON THE EARLY PRIMARIES

Inasmuch as early caucuses and primary results are the first direct tests of the candidates' strengths and popularity with the voters, the news media come to put a heavy premium on these early results. In fact, even before the caucuses and primaries begin, the news media start to label certain candidates as front-runners and others as long odds for winning their party's nomination. The consensus in the news media as to who the front-runners are is often based on factors such as preprimary polls, interviews with party officials and activists, candidates' organization, fund-raising, and name recognition. The fact that the news media preprimary predictions have often proven to be wrong does not seem to deter them from engaging in this exercise every four years. For example, George McGovern in 1972 and Jimmy Carter in 1976 were considered by the collective wisdom of the media to have had very little chance of winning their party's nomination during the preprimary stage of the campaign.

The news media face a different reporting situation during the primary stage of the presidential election compared with the general election, because there are many more candidates to cover and report on. Given time and space constraints, the media must decide how much coverage to give various candidates. Here again, the news media priority in allocation of coverage time is largely determined by the horse race aspect of the campaign. This often has significant consequences for candidates because it has an impact on their campaign and their chances for winning the nomination. Candidates who are not considered serious challengers by the media are likely to get less news coverage, making their task of getting public attention much more difficult. The perceived front-runners have an advantage because they get more coverage. For example, the Conference on Issues and Media, Inc., a research organization that measures media coverage and impact, found that in the 1984 Democratic primaries, two weeks preceding New Hampshire, Gary Hart received approximately 20 percent of the media coverage accorded Walter Mondale and only half as much of that given to John Glenn.[19] It has been suggested that in modern elections the press has come to perform the partys' traditional role of screening the potential nominees for the presidency.

The tendency of the media to concentrate on the perceived front-runners becomes even more pronounced after the very early caucuses and primaries, especially the Iowa caucuses and New Hampshire primary. The media devote the majority of their coverage to the winners of these early contests even though Iowa and New Hampshire are low-population states and not truly representative of the nation as a whole. After Jimmy Carter won in Iowa and then in New Hampshire, he was on the cover of news magazines, dominated network news, and received more coverage from major newspapers than all the other candidates combined.[20] Similarly, in the 1984 Democratic primary, Gary Hart had received much less media coverage prior to the New Hampshire primary, but his coverage increased tenfold in the first two weeks of March after New Hampshire.[21] Reporters and journalists also tend to project these outcomes onto the nation as a whole. After Bush came in third behind Dole and Robertson in the 1988 Iowa caucus, one NBA correspondent declared Bush's candidacy dead; Dole went ahead of Bush in news coverage for the first and only time.[22]

The news media concentration on front-runners and early winners is partly understandable to the extent that they operate within the constraint of time and space, and winners are legitimate news stories. However, it is the overemphasis on the results of these early caucuses and primaries—the medias' tendency to generalize the result to the nation as a whole, and concentrate on the horse race aspects that give advantage to some candidates while placing others at a disadvantage—that the news media can be faulted for. The amount of coverage given to front-runners and early winners by the media inadvertently ends up promoting their candidacies, thus becoming self-fulfilling prophecies that leave voters uninformed and unable to evaluate all the candidates, for not all candidates get the same amount and type of exposure. Television in particular does not look kindly upon candidates who do not perform well in front of the cameras.

OVEREMPHASIS ON CHARACTER ISSUES

Journalists are not trained in character assessment; one wonders what kind of character marks untrained journalists might have given Jefferson or Lincoln or Franklin Roosevelt.[23]

Another way in which the news media fail to inform voters on significant issues of an election is by placing too much emphasis on a candidate's character. One of the ways in which the medias' role in covering presidential elections has changed since the 1960s and 70s is the way in which journalists and reporters today act as spies snooping into the personal lives of candidates. This was not the case in the past. When John Kennedy was president there were rumors of extramarital affairs, but the news media never reported them. Emphasizing aspects of candidates' personal lives, which have very little to do with their ability to govern and lead the nation, does disservice to the voters and candidates alike. According to a poll by *Editor and Publisher*, only 9 percent chose personal character as the most important issue on which the media should concentrate, while 86 percent said the press should pay most attention to candidates' experience, qualifications, and stand on issues. In the same survey a majority approved of the press reporting that candidates were gay, cheated on their income taxes, or had exaggerated their academic or military record, but less than half approved of reporting on extramarital affairs or past possession and use of marijuana.[24]

The news medias' tendency to overemphasize such matters at the expense of more significant aspects of elections was abundantly demonstrated during the 1988 campaign. Before the Iowa caucuses, election news that dominated the media was Hart's weekend affair with model Donna Rice and Biden's plagiarism of a speech by a British Labour Party leader. In fact, no policy issue at any time received headlines as bold as the ones that accompanied these more sensational items. The story about vice-presidential nominee Dan Quayle having pulled strings to avoid the Vietnam draft dominated the news for several weeks. Similarly, in the 1976 election Jimmy Carter's admission in a Playboy interview about having lusted in his heart for other women received heavy coverage. Certainly, the media need to report on issues of dishonesty of candidates and the voters have a right to know and make their own judgment about candidates. It is when the media overemphasize aspects of candidates' private lives that have very little to do with their ability to lead the nation, at the expense of their qualifications, experience, issue positions, and their proposed solutions to the problems facing the country, that the news media do disservice to the voters and leave them less informed or misinformed.

OVEREMPHASIS ON POLLS

I have been very bearish on polling, which I think has been very much overdone. It's a very handy journalistic device because it has a sort of scientific cast to it, and it reduces complicated questions to numerical quantities. They are things that journalists find easy, and are attracted to.[25]

Another important trend we have witnessed in the last few years in the news medias' election reporting is its overemphasis on polls and their results. Until recently, only a few major private polling firms (Gallup, Harris) conducted polls and sold the results to the news media. But today major newspapers and networks have begun to conduct their own polls and report on them as if they were events over which they had no control. This raises a serious question of whether the news organizations rather than just reporting news are creating their own news.[26] It also poses the danger that news organizations, having heavily invested their own time and money in conducting such polls, might emphasize their own poll results in their reporting while underemphasizing other poll results.

The news media affinity for reporting on poll results is consistent with their tendency to cover the horse race aspect of a campaign and ignore more substantive issues. While public opinion polls are an important part of the news coverage, the danger is that poll results can easily be distorted or misinterpreted by reporters and journalists not trained in scientific polling techniques. There is an additional danger of generalizing too much from a limited poll. Very rarely do the media use poll results to engage in issue analysis. James Stovall in his study of the 1984 campaign concluded that news organizations paid more attention to public opinion polls and less attention to issue positions of the candidates.[27] Journalists are often less cautious in their use of poll numbers even when many polls contradict each other. Today most news organizations do report sample size and sampling errors in their polls, but they rarely consider these factors in interpreting the results. "Polls are as credible as their users; the search for excitement carries within it the danger of distortion."[28] Voters are often inundated with weekly poll results and are misled by the trivial aspects of the campaign. This leaves many voters more confused than informed.

UNDEREMPHASIS

The media's preoccupation with reporting the horse race aspect of the campaign leaves little time for reporting on various candidates' positions on issues. A candidate's statements on public policy issues are more likely to be reported if they represent a change from a previous position or if the statements are inconsistent with previous positions taken by a candidate. The media also pay more attention to issue positions of candidates whose chances for nomination improve. The lack of issue coverage is one of the very legitimate criticisms of the news medias' role in covering presidential elections.

Even when the media cover issues, they are often not the issues that candidates stress most heavily.[29] Thomas Patterson, in his year-long study of the 1976 election, concluded that the issues candidates stressed most heavily were not the same as those reported most prominently in the news, and thus the news reflected the interest of the press more than candidates' interests.[30] Journalists, reporters, and editors exercise significant discretion in choosing certain issues to emphasize over a period of time. This has the effect of influencing voters' perceptions of what they think are the important issues of the day. The type of issue information that appears in news coverage does little to inform voters about the similarities and differences of major issues among candidates. Another study of CBS and UPI news coverage of 1980 elections concluded that both news agencies were superficial in their reporting, concentrating on covering events and persons rather than the questions of public policy.[31] In the 1988 campaign, Dukakis's alleged responsibility for pollution of Boston harbor, escape of prisoner Willie Horton, his position on the pledge of allegiance, and his membership in the A.C.L.U. were made into news items by the media because of Bush's television ads. These were hardly the issues that the new incoming president was likely to face in the office. More complex issues such as balancing the budget and the trade deficit, among others, were largely ignored and the media failed to examine in depth candidates' proposed solutions and their potential consequences. The election coverage focused instead on the vague catch words and phrases such as flexible freeze, revenue enhancement, "read my lips," the "L" word, patriotism, and the flag-waving contest.

Television in particular is more susceptible to charges of lack of issue analysis and for turning complex issues into simplistic slogans and sound bites due to the constraints of time as well as the visual pictures that accompany the story. In fact, television has changed the nature of issue communication in modern campaigns from formal speeches on issues given by candidates to large audiences, as was the case in the past, to the current practice of candidates' communicating their issue messages through brief paid television commercials or to compressing their messages into a brief format in a staged television setting assured to make the evening news.[32] The reason that commercial television networks are more guilty of this than other news media is the fact that as profit-making private corporations, detailed discussions of complicated public policy issues are perceived as having low production value and not entertaining, thus harmful to the ratings game.[33] As Anthony Lewis has suggested in his criticism of the medias' performance in the 1988 elections, the media participated in the degradation of the democratic process by taking up nonissues invented by the candidates to distract voters from the hard problems facing the country—as if they were real issues.[34]

CONCLUSIONS

Unquestionably the news media have become a very important player in modern presidential campaigns. In many respects they have come to play the role that political parties performed in the past: screening potential nominees and informing voters of the candidates' and parties' positions on issues. The increased role of the media has significantly changed the very nature of presidential elections and the manner in which campaigns are conducted. The news media power to inform the voters has become very critical to our democratic system and it influences the manner in which voters make their choices. The news media are increasingly influencing and shaping the agenda of presidential elections in ways that even the media do not understand. The fact that the news media have come to play such a crucial role, inadvertently or by default, with the decline of political parties does not change the fact that in their coverage of presidential elections they have failed to inform the voters of important and substantial choices facing them in electing the nation's highest leader.

The news media fail to inform the voters for two reasons. One reason is that as private profit-making corporations operating within the constraints of time and space, the medias' priorities in election news coverage are often determined by the need for increased audience or readership. The second reason is that even though the media could do a more effective job of informing the voters, they fail to do so because of their overemphasis on the trivial and unimportant aspects of the campaign, which submerges more important issues the voters need to be aware of in making well-informed choices. However, there are exceptions. For example, some of the major national newspapers often do a profile of all the candidates, which include the candidates' background, education, military service record, political qualifications, and stands on issues. Unfortunately, such coverage is done during the preprimary stage, when most voters are not tuned in and not paying serious attention to the political coverage. Doing such profiles of candidates at a later time when voters are attentive to the campaign could better inform the public. Similarly, television programs such as "Nightline" do a fine job of examining substantive issues in a comprehensive fashion and serve as a useful mechanism for informing the voters. Also television programs on PBS such as the MacNeil-Lehrer Newshour, less constrained by advertising revenue, do an excellent job examining the issues by placing less emphasis on the horse race aspects of the campaign. As the above examples illustrate, commercial television could do a more effective job of informing the voters by changing their emphasis in election news coverage, creating more informative programs during the campaign, and by paying less attention to the almighty dollar.

The news media on the one hand, and candidates and their campaign staffers on the other, blame one another for the lack of issue content in presidential elections. The fact that both are probably correct does not help the fact that if the voters are to be well informed what is presented to them must be reality, not fantasy.

CHAPTER FIVE

Should Campaign Commercials be Regulated?

This chapter examines the controversial issue of campaign commercial regulation. The 1988 presidential election was marked, or perhaps marred, by the extensive reliance of both presidential candidates on negative advertisements. The preponderance of negative advertisements in 1988, as well as the use of negative commercials in previous elections, has resulted in a recommendation by observers of American politics and federal legislators to impose regulations on campaign commercials.

Curtis Gans argues in favor of a federal law to regulate the manner in which campaign commercials are conducted. In Gans's view federal regulation is desirable due to the deleterious consequences that negative campaign commercials have had on the fabric of the American electoral process. Gans cites declining voter turnout, the rising cost of campaigns, the decline of political parties, and the lack of candidate accountability as unfortunate by-products of negative campaign commercials. Gans also points to the disturbing trend toward distortion and demagoguery in modern presidential elections as additional consequences of negative campaign commercials. Gans concludes his argument by recommending a specific federal law that would require the purchaser of a negative advertisement to appear before the camera and speak to the camera for the duration of the commercial. In Gans's view, legal regulation of campaign commercials will restore integrity and meaningful debate to the American presidential selection process.

Marion Just questions the rationale of campaign commercial regulation. According to Just, negative campaigning is not a new phenomenon in American politics and the empirical evidence clearly sheds doubt on the claim that negative advertising has profound and unfortunate consequences for rational American voting behavior. Just also argues that regulation of campaign advertisements would decrease the flow of political information to the electorate, which would be quite unfortunate, and legal regulation would do little to improve the tone and quality of presidential campaigns. Moreover, of great concern to Just, is that laws that would place regulations on campaign commercials would conflict directly with the right of free speech as protected under the First Amendment of the United States Constitution. Regulatory legislation in Just's view would present a threat to individual liberty and democratic government.

Part 1

YES—
Campaign Commercials Should be Regulated

Curtis B. Gans

The 1988 presidential election will be remembered without fondness for its low quality and even lower turnout. Faced with a barrage of nattering nastiness on its television screens, candidates unable to say an unprogramed word, and seven-second sound bites substituting for substantive discussion, the public responded appropriately: it voted with its bottom. Half the eligible electorate stayed home, sinking turnout to its lowest level in 64 years and, outside the states of the old Confederacy, its lowest level in 164 years.

The most odious aspects of the modern campaign and its spiraling cost stem from a singe source—the demagogic and distorted television spot advertising, which now occupies more than 80 percent of major campaign budgets, propels unprincipled political consultants to a decisive campaign role, and makes a mockery of rational debate.

The 1988 presidential campaign was neither our dirtiest nor most negative. Lyndon Johnson's campaign against Barry Goldwater, Richard Nixon's against George McGovern and most mid-nineteenth century campaigns were all more negative. Nor is negativism necessarily bad. An opponent's character, record, issue positions, and principal advisors are all legitimate subjects of campaign debate.

But what the American public witnessed in both 1986 and 1988 was far removed from debate. Both campaigns represented the triumph of the demagogic commercial, which at its best tends to be oversimplified and misleading, and which at its worst is distorted and downright dishonest. These campaigns were also a triumph for irresponsible political consultants who have increasingly found no tactic too low or trivial in their effort to lower turnout for the opposition candidate.

The commercials make the American public captive in two respects. Since they occur in the midst of regular programing, they cannot be readily shut off. And since their primary appeal is not to reason but rather to emotions, they are virtually unanswerable. The danger posed by televised political advertising, and especially in its present and most effective manifestations in demagogic and negative advertising, cannot be overstated. The danger, however, can be categorized.[1]

TURNOUT AND TURNOFF

My committee was established in 1976 to look into the problem of low and declining turnout in America. It is hardly a secret that the United States has the lowest voter turnout of any advanced democracy in the world, with the possible and occasional exceptions of Switzerland and India. It is also no secret that with the exception of the highly polarized elections of 1982 and 1984, voter turnout has been declining steadily since 1960, at precisely the time when we have engaged in major reforms to make it easier for people to vote. It is also no coincidence that voters have been tuning out and turning off during precisely the time when television has become a central element in American lives and television advertising has become a central tool in the conduct of political campaigns.

During the last two decades twenty million Americans have ceased voting, attitudes toward politics and political leaders have grown more cynical, and political institutions ranging from precinct committee to national political parties have been atrophying.

Much of this could not be surprising, because the impact of television as an institution is to make of the American public spectators and consumers rather than active participants with a stake in the outcome of our politics.

In its application to politics, the impact of television has been more pernicious. For in those campaigns where television can be made a relevant factor, average campaign budgets are allocating 55 percent to television, which coupled with at least 30 percent allocated to fund-raising means that only 10-15 percent is available for staff and candidate travel, and almost nothing is left for activities involving the citizen. Is it any wonder that we are witnessing a silent spring in American politics in which buttons, bumperstickers, billboards, and any other sign of citizen involvement have vanished as an extinct species?

In its stead is increasingly demagogic use of commercial advertising on television. On the evidence of the consultants alone, they are producing more and more scurrilous ads because they are effective in discouraging voters. In a study conducted by Daniel Yankelovich's Public Agenda Foundation on the question of campaign advertising, those interviewed indicated that what they objected to was not how much was being spent on political campaigns, but how much was going into "air pollution"—the thirty-second and sixty-second demagogic ads.[2] Not by the elected official's performance in office, but by the nature of the campaign, the public is getting a dim view of political enterprise as a whole and the character of public officials. The public is tuning out, turning out, turning off, and staying home. The question, "What if we held an election and nobody came?" may become more than a rhetorical gimmick in the not too distant future.

Cost

Nothing in the foregoing should suggest that the issue of campaign cost is unimportant. For as the cost of campaigns rises, access to the political process by those without money wanes, and public policy becomes increasingly adjudicated by and on behalf of those who contribute. In the three decades since 1960, or roughly the time in which television has assumed the centrality it enjoys in American lives and in the conduct of campaigns, the cost of campaigns has been escalating. In constant dollars, the cost of campaigning has tripled since 1960, doubled since 1972.

There is little question that it is the use and cost of television advertising that is most responsible for driving the costs of campaigns up. In the period between 1952 (when television was first used in political campaigns) and 1972, according to FCC figures, the amount spent on political advertising increased five times, while overall campaign spending doubled.

Since 1974, the part of the campaign budget allocated to television has increased from 30 percent to 55 percent. In the five most expensive senatorial campaigns in 1974, overall campaign costs averaged $1 million or $.67 a vote; by 1984, the five most expensive campaigns averaged $10 million or $7.74 a vote. In 1974 the amount spent on media was $350,000 or $.12 cents a vote; in 1984 the five top spenders spent more than $5 million on television or $3.54 a vote. This increase in the top spending campaigns is also reflected in spending for all competitive senatorial campaigns. Overall costs have gone up twelvefold since 1974, 600 percent in constant dollars; media costs have gone up thirtyfold, fifteenfold in constant dollars.[3] There is little question that it is the fuel of media spending and reliance on television ads (a reliance and cost that far exceed the escalation in the price of such ads) that is propelling campaign costs out of sight.

Institutions

The rise of televised political advertising also coincides with the continuing decline of the central political institutions of the American polity, most notably the political party. This should not be surprising.

Once a candidate was nurtured by the party, trained by its leadership to lead, dependent on local party organization for electoral success, and beholden to the party once in office in such a way that made some discipline on principle and program possible. Now a candidate seeks money and a media advisor, and arrives in Washington dependent only on polls and constituent service for continuance in office.

This transcendence of party in favor of media consultants enhances the centrifugal force of special interest, weakens the forces of popular mobilization, both within parties and among other organizations, and lessens what little stability and cohesion exist in the American political system.

Accountability

The increased dependence on televised advertising that enhances the influence of media consultants weakens the accountability of officeholders and candidates.

Media consultants are by nature not accountable to the electorate. They make their living and insure their future by winning elections for the clients they are hired by. They can and do use whatever techniques and stratagems are likely to benefit their candidate, whether those strategies and tactics are ethical or not.

By using techniques such as actors playing parts, demagogic scene settings, impersonal voice-overs, anonymous commentators, emotional music, and the like, they can, and increasingly frequently do, establish the terms of debate in such a way that their client and principal escapes responsibility for what is conveyed, and in terms that are unanswerable by the opposition, except by resorting to precisely the same techniques.

So what has developed in these United States is competition, not between leaders, not between parties, not between principles and proposals, but between media advisors who compete with each other to see who can outslick the other to win. And the public has no one to hold accountable.

Distortion, Demagoguery, and Political Decline

What this in turn has led to has been increasingly scurrilous campaigning. This, of course, is not a new phenomenon. Mudslinging has been with us for some time. Nor is it a new phenomenon on television, as Senator Goldwater can testify to from his sad experience in 1964. But it appears that it has been elevated to a high art.

The campaign of 1980 was noted for the extreme, demagogic, and negative commercials done by the National Conservative Political Action Committee (N.C.P.A.C.). Subsequent presidential and congressional campaigns in 1982, 1984, and 1988 have been noted by the degree to which these campaign excesses have been practiced, not by independent expenditure groups, but by the majority of political campaigns. As Jill Buckley, a political consultant, suggested at a seminar of the American Bar Association, "We do it because it works," admitting in the process that she had produced about as many scurrilous ads as any other consultant.

The problem of scurrilous ads on television is that they are not effectively answerable by rational debate. Senator Goldwater cannot correct the image that he is an irresponsible bomb thrower as he was portrayed by the famous ad of the little girl with the daisies. Speaker Thomas (Tip) O'Neill cannot correct the image of the fat buffoon the Republican National Committee portrayed him as (with the aid of an actor.) Senator Walter Huddleston cannot correct the emotional effect of a trained bloodhound by rationally citing his 95 percent attendance record. Governor Dukakis cannot correct the image that he willfully and nonchalantly paroled a dangerous convict, Willy Horton, who later committed a heinous crime.

To be more specific with regard to negative advertising, there are five things that need to be noted:

1. Negative, trivial, and scurrilous ads are not a new phenomenon, nor are present versions necessarily more outrageous than those from other elections. What is different is not the type but the volume. Where such ads were once limited to the occasional campaign and accompanied by howls of outrage or put on largely by independent expenditure groups, they are now the staple of all campaigns for which television can be used as a primary medium of communication.

2. Each of these ads and the thousands like them that disgrace the airwaves each election are at best oversimplified and misleading, at worst and often distorted and downright dishonest. Because of this they present a necessarily false picture of the issues, the character of the candidate, and, to a captive public—since these ads are designed to be shown in the midst of programing the public likes—a negative image of the political enterprise as a whole.

3. They have become the staple of campaigns because the independent, nonresponsible, and increasingly irresponsible political consultants who today run American campaigns say they work to win elections. But if truth were told, they work for only 50 percent of the consultants and candidates who win, while 100 percent of the electorate, which has to view these ads, becomes the loser.

4. These ads emerge from the same technological development, the tracking poll. When the consultant for candidate A finds through the tracking poll that the candidate for whom he or she works is substantially behind candidate B, a set of demagogic attack ads is ordered up to cast doubts about the opponent, loosen candidate B's hold on the electorate, and reduce the impulse to vote for B. What happens, as a consequence, is that the consultant for candidate B notes through tracking polls that the gap between the two candidates is closing, has closed, or that A has overtaken B. And in order to restore B's primacy, a dose of the same medicine is ordered up. This is done because the nature of the ads used against B are virtually unanswerable, appealing, as they are intended, to the emotions rather than reason. The only recourse is to

respond in kind. The result is an escalating arms race of attack ads that becomes the equivalent of airwave pollution. And the impression that the electorate gets is that all politicians and the political process as a whole are not worthy of their respect and trust.

5. These ads in turn determine the nature of the entire campaign, for they establish the themes around which the campaign is conducted. If we have campaigns that are increasingly 30-second and 60-second spot advertising, seven-second bites, and candidates who seem unable to say an unprogramed word, it stems from a single source: campaigns that are run almost exclusively on television by irresponsible political consultants who, in the pursuit of winning, know of no tactic too low or trivial to besmirch their opposition and drive down the opponent's turnout. The themes these consultants use for their ads become the themes for the seven-second bites, and the program for candidate speeches by candidates who increasingly seem to be unable to utter an unprogramed word. Does anyone seriously believe that the 1988 presidential election was or should have been about the pledges of allegiance, "good jobs for good wages, prison furlough programs, or competence?"

This is not a self-regulating phenomenon. There are occasions—such as when Governor Roy Roemer chooses a month and half before an election to eschew attack advertising or when candidate John Vinich will air an ad that is patently unfair—that the public, having a clear choice, will, in turn, make one. But for the overwhelming majority of campaigns, what the public sees is a set of virtually indistinguishable (in type) ads that cast aspersions on all candidates and invite the response the public is increasingly resorting to, declaring a pox on all houses and taking a furlough from political participation.

Demogoguery and distortion have always been with us, but television has created a new, dangerous, and destructive playing field. In debate or in print, one can answer one's opposition on relatively equal terms. But it is precisely this sense of debate, of joining issues, of rational discourse, that, I believe, the framers of the First Amendment had in mind that is being determined by the images put forward in the contemporary political campaign.

Independent Campaigns

Some years ago, the Supreme Court in *Buckley v. Valeo*, (424 U.S. 1, 1976) ruled, I believe rightly, that organizations independent of party and candidate had a right to participate in the political dialogue. It did not, however, rule that these organizations had a right to dominate the dialogue. Yet in recent presidential and congressional elections, and perhaps again sometime in the future because of the skill of their demagogic advertisements, one organization has the ability to dominate the political debate.

While not denying these independent organizations the right to participate in the debate, their participation should be in the nature of debate or it is possible that our polity will be dominated not by candidates and parties, but by fringe and splinter groups with the wherewithal to buy time and create demagogic commercials to the detriment of the national dialogue.

Turnover

Finally, it should be noted that our system depends both on continuity and orderly change. Officeholders discharging their duties in office in a responsible manner, should not be put out to pasture, unless or until their views on the major issues of the day differ from the constituency that elected them (or, of course they engage in acts that tend to bring disgrace upon either their person or the office they hold). When there were great issues confronting our society—Vietnam, Watergate, the state of the economy (as in 1982)—there was no difficulty bringing about change, without resort to televised political advertising.

But the present state of affairs is that all officeholders, all careers, are subject to swift political termination, not by the quality of their work, but by the skill and demagoguery of a campaign consultant and the resulting political advertisements. Created images, distorted facts, demagogic film treatment can effectively wreck a lifetime of loyal, effective public service, and with it the stability upon which American democracy depends.

The sad situation we face is that talking cows have replaced talking candidates, demagoguery has replaced debate, and the political system has suffered in the process.

My committee commissioned Austin Ranney and Howard Penniman to do a study of whether and how other other democracies regulated television advertising during their political campaigns. That study found that every other democracy in the world has established some regulation over the use, timing, or format of political televised advertising. All these democracies either allocate free time, limit the amount that can be spent or the amount of total time for political advertising, or apply restrictions as to the format of political advertising on television.

In view of the adverse effects of televised political advertising, the unlikelihood that there will be any self-regulation, the distortion of the constitutional intent of free debate that these ads cause, the United States cannot and should not continue to be the only democracy in the world whose laws stand silent on this issue. I therefore propose that campaign commercials on television be subject to regulation.

THE PROPOSAL

The law I propose, in its simplest terms, provides that the purchaser or any advertisement of ten minutes duration or less, intended to influence the outcome of an election (whether that purchaser be candidate, candidate committee, party, or independent expenditure group)—that purchaser or an identified designee must appear before the camera, speaking to the camera for the duration of the advertisement. It permits some variation in backgrounds provided they are live and taken with the same lens as the speaker, mandates written material identifying the speaker and purchaser of the ad, and permits such written material as will identify the candidate if the speaker is not a candidate, the party of the speaker, whether it is an ad-endorsing election for the first time or reelection, a solicitation of funds, and such material as may aid the hearing impaired. It provides injunction relief to get ads that violate the standards in the legislation off the air, punitive relief in the form of civil penalties, and uses the structure of the Federal Election Commission and the U.S. judiciary for enforcement. It is intended to restore debate by establishing a uniform and verbal format for all ads of a certain length.

Although I am not a lawyer, I would like to say a few words about the constitutionality of legislating in this area, because inevitably the question of free speech is raised when legislating in this area. I do not believe that the framers of our Constitution envisaged freedom of speech for talking cows or for actors playing Fidel Castro or for bloodhounds trailing officeholders. When we moved into the television age, we took a quantum leap into technology. For television is not simply another means of communication. It is to conventional communications what nuclear weaponry is to conventional weaponry. It adds a whole new and destructive dimension of the issue of communication, through the manipulation of emotions. And to carry the analogy one step further, as it is desirable to regulate the use of conventional weaponry and essential to regulate the use of nuclear weaponry, it may or may not be desirable to regulate other forms of speech (and I believe it is not), but it is essential to regulate televised political advertising.

The proposal I offer is not to undercut free expression of views but to liberate that free expression from the cloud of image-making, distortion, and demogoguery that is the current method of communication. It is to restore debate, civility, answerability, and discussion to the presidential campaign process in television, without limiting either how much an individual or group can advertise or what they may want to say.

If we can, as the court has so ruled, demand by law truth in commercial advertising on television; if we can zone pornography, as courts have ruled we can, to certain areas in cities to protect minors; if we can be rid of liquor and cigarette advertising on the air, then I think it should be possible to restore debate and control the deleterious effects of political advertising on television, especially in view of their negative impact on the political process.

CONCLUSION

The issue before us is a part of the fundamental issue of our age. Technology and science grow like topsy, but not all of that growth constitutes progress. The fact that children today now spend their summers freed from the fear of polio attest to the fact that science and technology can produce progress. The fact that our air is foul, our cities are decaying and congested, and the incidence of cancer keeps increasing is testimony to the fact that not all products of technology are benign.

The task of government is to sort out what constitutes progress, what is beneficial for society, and to encourage its growth; and conversely to determine what may pose hazards for that society, and control or stop its growth. Televised political advertisements as they are currently being practiced constitute a technological development not in the interests of the citizenry or polity. They can and must be regulated.

Part 2

NO—
Campaign Commercials Should Not be Regulated

Marion R. Just

After a war, the losers champion disarmament or at least a ban on the weapons that defeated them. To blunt their humiliation, the losing side labels the winners' tactics unfair and their weapons uncivilized. The cries for campaign reform may be seen in that light. Democrats have lost three presidential elections in a row, and believe that they were outgunned by Republican advertising. Democrats have made political spots their chief target, casting their efforts as an attempt to "clean up" political campaigns. One proposal, the Hollings-Danforth bill (S. 999), would penalize broadcasters for airing "negative" ads.

The Hollings (D, SC) and Danforth (R, MO) bill was originally introduced in 1985. "The Clean Campaign Act of 1989," however, is doomed to the same fate as the 1985 bill: a lot of talk and no action. The hearings may be necessary to relieve the Democrats' dissatisfaction with Republican campaign tactics, but the bill will not pass, because campaign advertising regulation is unnecessary—even harmful—and certainly unconstitutional.

By way of reassurance we should note that "dirty politics" has been around at least since the birth of the republic, and the republic still stands. A chronicle of the "negative campaign" does not begin with 1988, or 1986, or even with 1964—the first "year of the negative ad."[1] Historians document that patently false and indisputably negative campaigning took place in the first partisan presidential contest, between John Adams and Thomas Jefferson.[2]

Perhaps we should not be so surprised that election campaigns involve strong language and ad hominem arguments. Chairman Mao tells us that "a revolution is not a dinner party," and neither is a presidential campaign. Serious issues are at stake. In election campaigns the fate of millions may hang in the balance. Shall the country have war or peace? Should we tax the middle classes to help the poor, or should we "read my lips"? Campaign rhetoric is never abstract, but necessarily redounds against persons and parties. Was the previous government corrupt? wrongheaded? weak-kneed? out of touch? Is the alternative smarter, tougher, and more decisive?

The function of the presidential campaign is to provide information about the candidate and their platforms that the voters can use. The ups and downs of the long presidential campaign give the electorate an opportunity to see the candidates under pressure, including the stress of false, offensive, and unsupported criticism. This is not some irrelevant rite of passage. The rigors of the campaign are nothing compared to the presidency itself. Presidents have to be able to endure painful criticism and still have enough mental and emotional reserve left over to lead the country. Is the next president going to handle criticism of his foreign policy as Kennedy did, by canceling his subscription to the newspaper that dared?[3] Will the president misuse the power of the office to spy on and harass political opponents as Nixon did? Or will he be able to turn aside charges of international conspiracy, stupidity, and treason, with a light touch, and direct the complainants to his "little dog Fala," as Franklin Roosevelt did?

The public needs to know what kind of person and what kind of leader they can expect in the White House. How the candidates manage themselves and their campaign constitute essential information for the electorate. It is a laudable goal to raise the tone of political discourse in America, but not at the expense of an informed electorate. Before passing legislation that restricts political speech, we should be convinced that regulation is necessary.

Nearly everyone can point to some ad that is so patently misleading or offensive that it ought to be banned, but an anecdote is not evidence. Regulators should be convinced that the class of offending ads represents a pattern of abuse. There is no point in regulating exceptions that can be dealt with by public ridicule.

The main impetus for regulation appears to be the fear that the false allegations in a spot advertisement could defeat a worthy candidate. There is no convincing evidence, however, that political advertising causes any significant number of people to switch their votes.

During campaigns one hears a great deal about the power of advertising—but mostly from the people who get paid to do it. In 1980, for example, the "Tuesday Team" produced an ad featuring a hirsute Oregonian, that went like this: "There is a bear in the woods. Some people say the bear is tame. Others say it's vicious and dangerous. Since no one can really be sure who's right, isn't it smart to be as strong as the bear?"

We cannot rely on the word of the "Tuesday Team," that "the bear in the woods" spot helped to elect Ronald Reagan in 1980. The Tuesday Team, after all, produced the ad. Their careers depend on making people believe that what they did was effective. In the business of political advertising, whatever the winning candidate did "worked"; and whatever the loser did, did not work. In the case of the "bear in the woods," the ad had a high recall rate, but most people did not get the point that the bear symbolized the Soviet Union (the Russian bear).[4] Was the ad effective anyhow?

It is no use asking the electorate whether it worked, because people do not want to admit that their voting decisions were affected by advertising. Research on voting continually confirms that the most important factor in electoral choice is not campaign advertising, but party affiliation and candidate assessment. In fact, most voters make up their minds by Labor Day, before political advertising gets underway. As a rule, campaign communications, include advertising, primarily serve to reinforce rather than to change voting preferences.

Restricting Political Advertisements Would Decrease the Information Available to the Electorate

The cumulative evidence is that political advertising rarely persuades, but often informs. Most political spot advertisements focus on the issues and the candidates. As a result, researchers generally credit campaign ads with helping to inform the electorate.

While the purpose of political commercials is to influence the audience, most ads go about it by providing information about the candidates and their positions. It might sound like a good idea to require ads to speak only to the issues, but it is virtually impossible to do so, since candidate image is inextricably bound up with the presentation of information. In fact, it is difficult to get an audience to agree whether a particular spot is about images or issues. A classification experiment found that some people thought a series of ads contained information about both issues and images of the candidates, while another group of subjects thought the ads contained only images (and negative ones at that). The researchers concluded that "there was no clear cut dichotomy between issue and image aspects as perceived by the respondents."[5] A fair interpretation of the literature is that the nature of the ad is in the eye of the beholder.[6] While it is difficult to separate out images from issues, it is still possible to quantify the number of times an issue is mentioned in an advertisement. Content analysis of television advertisements provides objective evidence that political spots comprise an important source of information about the issues.

In their study of the 1972 presidential election campaign, Patterson and McClure found that 42 percent of all commercials primarily focused on campaign issues and another 27 percent contained some information about issues, so that almost 70 percent of all ads in the campaign discussed issues to some extent. Two studies of advertising in the next presidential campaign (a study of five hundred political ads by Joslyn and another by Patterson) concluded that in 1976 the candidates' advertising focused on the substance of the campaign: "issues and policies, traits, and records."[7]

Of course that was then and this is now. We have all heard of the Reagan media magic—the "feel good" campaign. Perhaps substance went out the window when "feel good" came in? The evidence, however, does not support a cynical view of advertising. In fact after completing a content analysis of 140 political ads aired in the 1980 campaign, Shyles found the ratio of issues to images in political advertisements was two to one.[8] He writes: "One may question from an empirical standpoint . . . the harsh judgment of some critics that political commercials emphasize image-making while ignoring political issues."

Conceivably the electorate could do without the biased information in advertisements if it could rely on a neutral alternative. The need for campaign spots is made more pressing, however, by the unfortunate paucity of policy information in the news. The reason for issue scarcity is that the news media, particularly television news, are preoccupied with reporting the "horse race" aspect of the presidential campaign. By concentrating on who's ahead and who's behind, the news media tend to ignore the reason for the campaign. In 1972 Patterson and McClure showed for the first time that political advertising on television contained four times as much information about the issues than television news. More than a decade later, Kerns found exactly the same ratio of information in ads vs. television news—the ads had it 4:1. In the last six weeks of the campaign, when voter interest is at its height and when the crucial undecided voters make up their minds, Kerns concluded that "Americans obtain the overwhelming majority of their information about the election from ads." It is not surprising that one of the few direct studies of the information impact of television advertising found that the more people watched television commercials, the more they knew about the campaign.[9]

It seems that the call for regulation is meant less to protect the electorate from disinformation than to protect the candidates from one another. Some critics of campaign advertising assert their most stringent objections to graphics and voice-overs. They want the law to require candidates to be "on camera" in their ads. The Hollings-Danforth bill, for example, requires the candidate to appear in any spot that mentions another candidate.

It is unnecessary to force the point, however, since most ads naturally focus on the candidate running for office. In an exhaustive study of spot advertisements in the 1980 campaign, one researcher found that half the time the voice in television advertising was the candidate's own, and that half of the live action footage was of the candidate talking, with slightly more than half of that time devoted to the candidate looking directly at the camera while delivering the pitch. Another study found similar results for 1982 Senate races. Half of the challenger ads used the candidate's own voice, and about a quarter of both the incumbents and the challengers ads were "introspective" (i.e., head into the camera) ads.[10] The evidence is, therefore, that candidates are not a phantom presence in political advertisements. Inasmuch as advertising aims to persuade the voter to choose a candidate, most advertising involves positive images of the candidate rather than negative images of the opponent.

Historically, political advertisers have shied away from nasty attacks on their opponents, out of concern for audience reaction. The traditional reluctance to emphasize the negative side of the opponent is based on an accurate reading of the audience response. The empirical evidence is that negative ads are more likely to boomerang on the sponsor than to adhere to the victim. The people who are most likely to remember the ad are the ones who support the target and who believe that the charges are false. It is not surprising, therefore, that after viewing an attack on a candidate, three times as many people become more negative to the sponsor of the ad than to the target.[11] Although negative advertising is having a peculiar currency at the moment, the impact will be self-limiting. As negative campaigners lose elections, political consultants will look for a new "magic bullet."

Even if regulators thought it was in the public interest to excise negative remarks from political ads, they would have to know what they were looking for. As the director of the Fair Campaign Practices Committee tells us: "One man's meat tends to be another man's poison; an attack may seem perfectly fair to one observer and utterly foul to another."[12] Is it dirty politics to criticize an incumbent or is that useful information? There is good reason to give the electorate an opportunity to hear the negative version of the incumbent's record, in the face of the incumbent's considerable advantages in self-puffery. It seems fair to conclude that regulating or banning political advertising might make some politicians feel good, but only at the expense of decreasing the information available to the electorate.

Regulating Political Advertising Would not "Clean up" Politics

Even if the electorate were willing to forego the information conveyed by political advertising, regulation of one kind of political speech would not by itself elevate the tone of political campaigns, and might make it worse. Nowadays political advertising is just one part of a presidential candidate's media strategy, which typically includes the uses of surrogates, "narrowcasting" (as opposed to broadcasting), and news manipulation to get across the candidate's message. We can be sure that whatever is regulated out of political advertisements will reappear in other campaign media.

If we penalize negative campaigning by candidates, as the Hollings-Danforth bill does, surrogates will do the dirty work instead. It is an established campaign strategy to insulate the candidate from actions or allegations that might backfire. Perhaps the ultimate surrogate in the world of advertising is the "independent" campaign committee. Like-minded activists can spend any amount of money on a candidate's behalf as long as the expenditures are not intentionally coordinated with the official campaign committee. In 1988, for example, while the Bush campaign was airing its "revolving door" ad about Massachusetts prison furloughs, an independent group sponsored the "Willie Horton" spots. Bush could deny that his campaign was engaged in racist innuendo, because he did not actually pay for the Willie Horton ads.

Dirty politics will persist whether or not political advertising remains on the air. Other campaign communication techniques can narrowcast vicious, racist, or extremist views so that only people sympathetic with the message actually receive it. People might think that the advent of a national press corps and coast-to-coast broadcasting would prevent candidates from saying one thing in Boston and another in Dubuque. But television is not the only new technology of campaigns. Computers have helped to make narrowcasting an effective alternative to broadcasting. When a candidate knows that some voters would find a particular message obnoxious, while others might be enthusiastic, the candidate uses computer-assisted-dialing and computer-generated personalized letters to make sure the material is communicated to receptive audiences.

Candidates use direct mail with relative impunity because the messages are private. The press rarely reports the content of campaign mailings. With zip-coding of mail, a campaign can play to the base fears of any city neighborhood and keep that communication secret from the rest of the state or nation. Computers and the mail banks make it possible today for candidates to target even very small groups for particularistic appeals. Greek-Americans or gun owners can be targeted to receive personalized messages that candidates would not want broadcast to Irish-Americans, or to crime victims. If campaign advertising were restricted, there is no doubt that negative appeals would be narrowcast. Campaign hardball, however, is not solely a function of the "paid" media.

Distortions of the opposing candidate's record are more credible when reported on the news than when they are published in an advertisement. Broadcasting an attack on television news media not only makes the charge more believable, it makes it free. And when the news anchor previews the attack, the author gets double exposure.

Simple economics and the desire to harness the power of the press drives candidates to make the most of "free media." In 1988, for example, the Republicans decided it was important to take the environmental issue away from the Democrats. So the Bush campaign went to Boston harbor and the candidate made a speech at the water's edge. The "death watch" television cameras, trained on the candidate throughout the campaign, did the job of positioning the candidate for the pitch. Bush's message, that Dukakis could not even clean up the environment in his own state, was carried live and repeated all evening long on television news. According to one observer, what we are now seeing in the high-powered world of the presidential media campaign is "news staged according to advertising principles."[13] If candidates were penalized for negative campaigning in advertisements, the message would reappear where it is even more damaging—in campaign news.

Regulating Political Advertising Would be Unconstitutional

Some people are willing to risk the consequences of staged news or a less informed electorate if they could put a stop to the most annoying or scurrilous campaign advertisements; but any action to restrict the content of campaign advertisements would certainly be unconstitutional. First Amendment protection is no where so jealously guarded as in the area of political speech. The right so say unpopular things is so essential to a free society, and the Supreme Court has accorded the First Amendment priority when other rights or interests are in conflict.

In defense of free speech the court has allowed broadcast speech that is blatantly offensive, even racist. There are limited grounds for restricting speech in general, but the grounds for limiting political speech are especially narrow. The "clear and present danger test," which might be held to proscribe speech that could incite a riot, is not sufficient grounds to prevent the desecration of the flag, neo-Nazi marches, or racist rhetoric. In 1972, for example, a Georgia Democratic Senate candidate purchased air time to broadcast the following spot announcement:

> I am J. B. Stoner. I am the only candidate for U.S. Senator who is for the white people. I am the only candidate who is against integration. All of the other candidates are race mixers to one degree or another. I say we must repeal Gambrell's civil rights law. Gambrell's law takes jobs from us whites and gives those jobs to the niggers. The main reason why niggers want integration is because the niggers want our white

women. I am for law and order with the knowledge that you cannot have law and order and niggers too. Vote white. This time vote your convictions by voting white racist J. B. Stoner into the run-off election for U.S. Senator. Thank you. [14]

The political advertisement above was the basis for the Red Lion case, which provided relief to the plaintiffs only in the form of time for reply. One might think that the Hollings-Danforth bill, which requires broadcasters to provide equal time for response to negative ads, would fall under the Red Lion precedent, but that is not likely.

First of all, broadcasters have been mounting more and more strident objections to the equal time provision, which, they argue, unfairly discriminates against one class of publication. (Newspapers, for example, are not required to provide space for reply.) The court has held, in defense of equal time, that the airwaves are a limited resource. Such a claim made sense when there were no more than five or six VHF stations available in a given metropolitan area. The argument became less credible, however, when the UHF stations came along, and is now highly untenable with the advent of fifty-channel cable television. The Federal Communications Commission was sufficiently convinced that equal time could no longer be defended on the grounds of public scarcity that it sought to eliminate the provision from its regulations. Congress objected and the regulation is still in effect; however, it is not clear that it will withstand a serious court challenge. The cost to broadcasters of the Hollings-Danforth bill, which insists on the right to reply whenever a candidate's name is mentioned, might be just the extravagant straw that breaks the back of equal time.

Where the equal time provision of the Hollings-Danforth bill might survive a First Amendment test, the specification of exactly how the candidate must broadcast the message—that is, squarely facing the camera—appears to be such an invasion of free speech that it cannot withstand a challenge. There would have to be some compelling state interest, some balance of rights, for the courts to constrain the exercise of free speech in a national election.

The court, however, is extremely reluctant to restrain political speech even when a genuine state interest can be demonstrated. In the case of the Federal Election Commission Act, for example, the Supreme Court would not permit the Congress to set limits on the amount of private funds spent on an individual's own behalf or to further the cause of another person. The court struck down the provision even when the government argued for need to prevent undue influence over elected officials and to control the cost of electoral competition. If the court could not find compelling state interests in the limitation of campaign expenditures, or in the prevention of riot from racist speech, or even in the burning of the American flag, it certainly will not find compelling state interest in a talking head.

As for the balancing of rights, it is hard to see an argument that the diminished popularity or hurt feelings of a candidate is sufficient grounds to restrict the free flow of ideas in an election campaign, which is at the heart of the democratic process. In a related area, the court has set a very difficult test for libel of public figures. In the case of New York Times v. Sullivan, (376 U.S. 254, 1964) the Supreme Court articulated a new standard—that false and damaging reports about a public figure could be considered libelous only if malicious intent or reckless disregard of truth could be demonstrated. The reason for this exceptional standard is to make sure that officials do not use their position to stifle criticism of public policies in their own interest.

It is hard to imagine that the courts will look any more favorably on the attempt to limit criticism of candidates for public office, many of whom are incumbent public officials. It is overwhelmingly likely that any candidate running against the incumbent president would feel obliged to criticize some aspect of the administration's foreign or domestic policy. After all, if challengers have nothing negative to say about the way the incumbent is managing the presidency, they might as well join the incumbent's reelection campaign.

Any attempt to regulate criticism of the opponent in political advertising, such as the Hollings-Danforth bill, would restrict, for example, what any Democratic candidate could say about President Bush in 1992. On what grounds would the Supreme Court limit that kind of political speech? The principal rights in an election campaign are the candidate's right to speak and the public's right to listen. While we may feel saddened about the hurt feelings of a candidate whose reputation is besmirched in a campaign advertisement, we cannot right that wrong by denying freedom of speech to the opponent. What it comes down to is that regulating campaign speech puts at jeopardy the fundamental liberties essential to democratic government.

CONCLUSION

Limiting political speech by regulating campaign advertisement is not in the public interest. The great majority of political advertisements are positive statements by a candidate, for a candidate. Requiring all campaign spots to comply with that format, however, is unnecessary and potentially harmful. The electorate, particularly those voters with a moderate interest in public affairs, gains a considerable amount of campaign information from advertisements. If the criticism of incumbents were eliminated from campaign spots, some of the most essential voting data would go with it.

We have to ask in whose interest, then, should political advertising be regulated? If the public would not be served, who would? The answer is that some politicians would feel a lot better if they did not have to endure the indignities of negative campaign advertising. To this we should say with Harry Truman: if you can't stand the heat, get out of the kitchen. Campaign spots are nothing compared to a hostile press corps, recalcitrant congressional leaders, international terrorists, and all the other afflictions that presidents have to face. The public has a right to expect that a candidate for president can handle an opponent and the opponent's advertisements.

Regulation of political advertising will not clean up politics. But the major reason that political advertising should not, and will not, be regulated lies in the First Amendment—"Congress shall make no law . . . abridging the freedom of speech."

CHAPTER SIX

Is Public Financing a Desirable Policy?

Provisions for public financing in presidential elections were enacted by Congress in 1974 for the express purpose of promoting economic equality among candidates for the American presidency. Such a measure emerged from the more general democratic reform movement that swept Capitol Hill during the early part of the 1970s. Beginning with the presidential election of 1976 and extending through the 1988 presidential contest, every nominee of the two major parties has chosen to accept the provisions of public funding. Public funds are available not only to the presidential nominees of the two major parties but also to other presidential candidates.

Professor Herbert Alexander, the nation's foremost authority on campaign finance, argues that public funding is a desirable policy and needs to be maintained as the method of financing presidential elections. According to Alexander, the system of public funding, while flawed in some respects, has largely corrected the abuses associated with private contributions, most notably "fat cats" and special-interest donations. At the same time, public funding has encouraged competition among presidential candidates and has created a mechanism for citizen participation. Public funding, in Alexander's view, is good for the health of American democracy and should be extended to congressional elections as well.

United States Senator Mitch McConnell, a Republican from Kentucky and the leading critic on Capitol Hill of the public

funding policy, believes that public funding in presidential elec-
tions is seriously deficient in several respects. McConnell points
to the rampant cheating by presidential candidates and their ac-
countants in order to technically comply with the complex legal-
ities of the public funding policy, the relationship between such
cheating and public cynicism toward the presidential selection
process, the emergence of a welfare system for presidential candi-
dates—all, of course, at the expense of the American taxpayer—
the new brand of corruption in presidential campaigns including
the failure to maintain spending limits, the growth of "soft
money" and the return of the fat cat, and the very unfortunate
impact public funding has had on grassroots democracy. McCo-
nnell includes the findings of a report issued by the Kennedy
School of Government to support his criticisms and concludes his
argument by urging legislative repeal of public funding in presi-
dential elections.

Part 1

YES—
Public Financing is a Desirable Policy

Herbert E. Alexander

Public financing of political campaigns is a form of government assistance that remains controversial despite its implementation in the past four presidential elections, and in a number of state elections.[1]

Underlying the concept of public funding is the assumption that new or alternative sources of campaign funding are desirable. The public funds are intended to help provide, or—in the presidential general election period—to supply in entirety, the money serious candidates need to present themselves and their ideas to the electorate. The public funds also are meant to diminish or to eliminate the need for money from wealthy donors and interest groups, and thereby minimize opportunities for political contributor influence on officeholders. In the presidential prenomination period, public funding is designed to make the contest for nomination more competitive and to encourage candidates to broaden their bases of support by seeking out large numbers of relatively small, matchable contributions.

In a sense, public funding was conceived and has been designed to help equalize inequalities in economic resources and to open up the political system to candidates without ready access to personal funds or wealthy contributors. It is an alternative funding system designed to enable candidates and parties to avoid obligations, tacit or expressed, that may adversely affect the operation of government in the best interests of the common good.

Since the earliest days of the Republic, money has played a major role in American political life.[2] In the Federalist and Jacksonian periods, assessing government employees to cover campaign costs and "spoils system" politics were the rule rather than the exception in presidential election. After the Civil War, wealthy industrialists such as Astor, Vanderbilt, Gould, and Frick, began to pay a major share of campaign costs. Ulysses S. Grant, for example, is said to have entered office in 1869 more heavily indebted to wealthy contributors than any previous president. Corporations also played a major role, and President McKinley's 1896 campaign was the first to set quotas and determine contributions based on the donor's ability to pay. Banks were asked to give one quarter of one percent of their capital. Life insurance companies and other types of businesses contributed, but it was not until 1907 that direct corporate contributions to federal campaigns were prohibited.

The $100 per plate dinner first appeared during Franklin D. Roosevelt's 1936 campaign for the presidency and the idea spread quickly and widely. Increasing campaign costs caused higher-priced affairs to become common at all levels of the political system, and big contributors continued to play a major role throughout the campaigns of the 1940s, 50s, and 60s. It was not, however, always easy to ascertain a great deal of information about who they were or how much they gave. Before 1972 federal law required disclosure of campaign funds, but only by political committees admitting they were interstate; many campaign committees therefore were legally established intrastate in states with no disclosure law.

In 1968, Nixon, McCarthy, and Robert E. Kennedy are each believed to have had at least one $500,000 donor in their prenomination campaign. Nixon received almost 2.8 million, an unprecedented sum in modern times, from insurance executive W. Clement Stone for his nomination and general election campaigns that year.

Public reaction to the level of individual contributions and the call for full disclosure of campaign money were instrumental in the adoption of the Federal Election Campaign Act (F.E.C.A.) in 1971, when primary and runoff as well as general election campaigns were all included under coverage of the law. It also required disclosure by any committee, even an intrastate one, raising or spending in excess of $1,000 in presidential or congressional contests. The massive amounts of data in these reports have provided scholars and journalists with a welcome opportunity to study and analyze campaign finance practices in greater detail and with greater certainty than ever before.

Donors of large contributions reached their highest level of participation in the 1972 presidential election. The information about these largest of donors ($10,000 or more) indicated that they donated money to the candidates in extraordinary amounts. Just 1,254 individuals contributed a total of $51.3 million. The top 153 contributors to Nixon's campaign accounted for $20 million of this total.[3]

Public concern over the large increase in big individual contributions and the discovery during the Watergate investigations that corporations and foreign nationals had made illegal transfers to the Nixon campaign (and others), brought new pressures for reform. As finally passed by Congress in 1974, a bill amending the 1971 legislation limited contributions by an individual to $1,000 for each primary, runoff, and general election, and placed an annual aggregate contribution limit of $25,000 for individuals for all federal candidates and committees. The law also provided for public financing—but only for presidential elections. Twice, in 1973 and in 1974, the Senate passed bills to extend the provisions for public financing to cover congressional campaigns as well, but the House has never done so.

Most of the proposals for federal funding of campaigns for the U.S. Senate and House call for mixed private and public financing of general election campaigns only. To qualify for public funds under such a system, each candidate would be required to raise a threshold amount of small contributions from individuals (perhaps $10,000 or $1000,000 for the House, amounts varying according to state population size, from $150,000 to $650,000 for the Senate) in order to demonstrate viability as a candidate. With the threshold reached, some proposals call for flat grants and some for matching funds. Most proposals, like the presidential financing system, would impose an overall spending limit on those accepting public funds, and candidates opting into the system would be limited in the amounts of personal money they could spend or contribute.

Since its enactment in 1971 and 1974, the presidential public financing system has been operated with a minimum of difficulty or controversy. All serious candidates with the exception of John Connally in 1980 have accepted it. Connally rejected the program because he perceived the only way he could compete with front-runner Ronald Reagan was to spend beyond the limitations in states he thought he had a chance of winning. The objection appears to have been to the spending limit, not to public financing as such.

The most positive aspect of public financing has been the opportunity it has given certain candidates to compete in the political system. Since the presidential matching system was first employed in 1976, matching funds have provided potential candidates who lacked name recognition or access to large amounts of private campaign funds the opportunity to effectively contend for presidential nomination. If it were not for the combination of contribution limits and public funding, Jimmy Carter, who lacked access to the traditional sources of large Democratic contributions, probably would have lost out early in the 1976 primary season to those candidates such as Senator Henry M. Jackson, who enjoyed such access. In 1980 public funds helped George Bush establish himself as Ronald Reagan's major competitor and stay the course of the primaries and the caucuses. Public funds also helped John Anderson become an influential force in some early Republican primaries and start building the name recognition and national organization he needed to mount his independent candidacy for the presidency.

In 1984 matching funds helped Senator Gary Hart refill his depleted campaign treasury following his unexpected New Hampshire primary victory and the subsequent upsurge in contributions helped carry his campaign to the convention. In the 1984 general election campaign, public funds kept Walter Mondale's campaign afloat against formidable odds against front-runner incumbent President Ronald Reagan.

Matching funds helped keep Jesse Jackson's underfinanced but nevertheless well-publicized campaigns competitive in both 1984 and 1988. In all these cases the matching funds provisions of the F.E.C.A. opened up the electoral process to some candidates whose campaign otherwise might not have been able to survive.

PUBLIC FUNDING AND THE 1988 ELECTION

With no incumbent president running in 1988, the election was wide open for the first time in twenty years. The costs to the voters, the tax-payers, and the candidates campaigns were considerable.

Taking the three phases—prenomination, convention, and general election—the cost of electing a president in 1988 was $500 million. This represents a 54 percent increase from the 1984 cost ($325 million).[4]

The competition for nomination in both parties combined cost about $212 million, twice that of 1984, when there was no Republican challenge to President Reagan's renomination, but a competitive Democratic contest. Inflation and entitlements for eligible candidates and parties in the 1988 convention and general election also began to eat up the balance of the Presidential Election Campaign Fund, which was, in turn, being supplied by dwindling income-tax checkoffs. The public funding system, which served four presidential elections, was not in jeopardy, but many new problems occurred that need to be remedied.

The Prenomination Campaign

The major problems manifested in the 1988 prenomination phase of the presidential selection process was the inflexibility of the law to respond to highly competitive campaigns in both parties and events such as Super Tuesday. March 8 was almost half a national primary—twenty states for the Democrats and seventeen for the Republicans. The candidates could not spend the $5 million minimum that most experts said was necessary in order to campaign effectively in those numbers of states, or to purchase spot announcements in the fifty or more media markets. The candidates had to be selective in marshaling and allocating their resources in order not to leave themselves too short for the rest of the long presidential campaign season.

If Pat Robertson (who received $10.4 million in matching funds, making him the all-time leader in this category) or Bob Dole had remained competitive with George Bush through the California primary and until the Republican convention, the leading spenders would have been unable to allocate enough overall expenditure limits that the law imposed—$23.1 million plus a 20 percent supplement of $4.6 million for fund-raising costs (totaling $27.7 million per candidate). Even without such competition, Bush had to curtail his schedule a month before the convention in order to conserve his spending sufficiently to avoid violating the election law. In contrast, Michael Dukakis's opposition in seeking nomination was mainly Jesse Jackson, whose middling spending did not push toward the upper limits as the Bush, Dole, and Robertson competition raised the ante for the Republicans.[5] In the prenomination period, the main problem was in the expenditure limitation, not in public funding as such.

Financing the National Conventions

The second phase of the presidential selection process, the national nominating conventions, was financed by public funds provided to the two major parties—$9.2 million each. But the Atlanta convention cost more than twice as much—$22.4 million—with the remainder provided by the city and host committees. Atlanta assembled a financial package to attract the convention to the city. The Atlanta city government dedicated a special tax levied on hotel guests for the purpose. This enabled the host committee, the Atlanta 88 Committee, to borrow $5 million from two Atlanta banks, which have been the largest creditors. The loans are being paid off by revenues from the tax.

The Republican convention in New Orleans cost at least $19.7 million, composed of receipts of $9.2 million in federal subsidy, $6.5 million from New Orleans, and $4 million in host committee support, mainly corporate in source.

The Republicans held their 1984 convention in Dallas. State law and long-standing local tradition prevented tax revenue from being used to finance convention-related cost. Accordingly, the city sought and received a Federal Election Commission (F.E.C.) ruling that it could establish and administer a nonprofit convention fund to finance facilities and services for the convention, provided the fund pay for such items and services at their fair market value. The ruling stated that payments made to the city-administered fund for convention facilities and services, and donations made to the fund, would not constitute contributions to the Republican National Committee and would not count against the committee's convention spending ceiling.[6]

Consequently the convention fund was able to collect donations in unlimited amounts from individual, associations, businesses, and corporations, and did not have to disclose the names of contributors. The Internal Revenue Service also ruled that donations to the Dallas convention fund would be fully tax-deductible.

The 1988 conventions were similarly financed in part by corporate and other large contributions, which went along with the grants of federal public funds supplemented by Atlanta and New Orleans public funds. The F.E.C. gave General Motors and other automobile manufacturers permission to lend through local dealership fleets of autos for transporting important and elected officials at the conventions.[7] Both parties also were able to arrange reduced-cost services by agreeing to designate airlines and others as "official suppliers" for conventions.

To date the mix of public and private financing (including tax-exempt funding) of the nominating conventions satisfies the parties because it provides sufficient funding and involves local participation. But the development every four years of new means of introducing private money clouds the premise in the 1974 law that public money would essentially replace private funds. The F.E.C. has permitted, year by year, more avenues for private—often corporate and labor—funds until, in 1984 and 1988, the amounts matched or exceeded the public funds. The infusion of large amounts of private funds made the accompanying expenditure limits meaningless.

The General Election Campaigns

The Democratic nomination went to Dukakis in mid-July, giving him an extra month before Bush's nomination in mid-August. Dukakis had to spread out the use of his money over a longer time until the November election, but Bush was able to concentrate his general election spending over a shorter period. Bush's major media spending did not begin until mid-September, after he took the lead in the public opinion polls from Dukakis, who had been the preconvention front-runner.

In the general election phase of the presidential selection process, the most notable financial phenomenon was the search for soft money. Soft money is raised and spent outside the restraints of federal law and is determined by state laws, many of whom are less stringent. Efforts by the campaigns to raise soft money became as competitive and high-profile as the search for votes on November 8.

Soft money was sanctioned by the 1979 amendments to the Federal Election Campaign Act. It had been raised and spent in the 1980 and 1984 presidential campaigns, but the money was raised in low-key efforts, not the high-profile competitive ways as in 1988.

Both parties at the national level sought, through parallel fund-raising efforts, carried on by the candidates' prenomination campaign operatives, some $40–50 million in contributions to supplement the public funds each presidential and vice-presidential ticket received; $46.1 million plus $8.3 million the national parties could spend on behalf of the ticket, to be supplemented by however much hard and soft money the parties raised and spent. Money was raised centrally at a frantic pace as if no public funding or expenditure limits existed. It was raised not by the parties, but by the same Bush and Dukakis finance people who raised the candidates' prenomination funds. And it was raised in large individual contributions—some as much as $100,000 each; the Republicans claimed 267 contributors of $100,000 or more, while the Democrats counted 130 individuals who gave or raised $100,000.[8]

Michael Dukakis put a $100,000 limit on amounts of soft money that would be accepted, and refused to take funds from corporations, PACs, or labor unions. However, before Dukakis was nominated, the Democrats accepted soft money from corporate and labor sources for help in funding the Democratic National Convention. Most Republican soft money contributions were from individuals—one disclosed as high as $503,263 was contributed by former ambassador Nicholas Salgo—but some were corporate.[9] Some Republican soft money was raised in amounts as low as $1,000 for tickets to the gala luncheon at the Republican convention. The costs of the gala were part of the Republican soft money expenditures.

The 1988 general election period, in which candidate spending limits were set by law at $46.1 million, found more than twice as much spent, mainly by combinations of candidate and party committees at the state and local levels. The erosion of the effectiveness of the contribution and expenditure limits represents a return to big money—public and private, hard and soft, candidate and party. It threatens the general election public funding concept, that full public funding would be provided, with minimal national party participation and effective expenditure limitations. Public funds were intended to help provide or supply in entirety the money that serious candidates need to present themselves and their ideas to the electorate. Such public money also was meant to diminish or eliminate the need for financing from wealthy donors and interest groups, thereby minimizing the influence contributors possibly could exert on officeholders. And, of course, public funding was designed to relieve candidates of the need to engage in fund-raising; instead, they helped to raise soft money. If soft money expenditures do violence to the rationale for public funding, the whole election law framework is open to doubt.

Public funding may not work perfectly and may not have solved all the problems of presidential campaigns, but it has corrected many of the abuses that occurred whenever candidates became obligated to wealthy persons or to interest groups in order to run increasingly costly campaigns.

Some special interests and wealthy contributors give money to candidates out of public spiritedness, but some do not. They want something in return: favors, access, tax loopholes, ambassadorships, and other "special considerations." If this type of influence can be lessened or eliminated, the candidates are more likely to be concerned with policy options and consensus-building in the best long-term interests of the nation.

Public funding also encourages competition and underscores the traditional American belief that any person can become president—not if he or she can acquire enough money to do so, but because he or she is the best person with the best ideas. If it can continue to succeed in this, it will help to renew faith in the integrity of the government. Although Congress did not intend to fund hopeless presidential candidates with large sums at taxpayer expense, encouraging many candidates provides the voters with a wider choice of candidates.

THE TAX CHECKOFF

The feasibility of public financing has depended on the taxpayers' willingness to earmark a small portion of their tax liabilities—one dollar for individuals and two dollars for married persons filing jointly—for the presidential election campaign fund by using the federal income tax checkoff. In operation since 1972, this system has provided more than enough money to cover the public funds certified to presidential prenomination and general election candidates, and to major parties for their national nominating conventions. Certifications by the Federal Election Commission totaled $70.9 million in 1976, $100.6 million in 1980,

$133.1 million in 1984, and approximately $177.8 million in 1988. There have been surpluses after each presidential election year.

However, the high rate of growth in spending has resulted in a level of government payouts that is likely to exceed the amount of revenue generated by the system. From 1976 through 1987, the approximate percentage of tax returns checking off money for the presidential election campaign fund has ranged from a high of 28.7 percent in 1980 to a low of 21 percent in 1987. Based on estimates of future spending and revenue collection, the F.E.C. projects that the 1992 campaign will have to use more than half of the surplus fund available in order to meet costs, resulting in a $71 million deficit. If 1992 were to be highly competitive, existing surpluses could be used up earlier.

Increases in the amount of the tax checkoff (one dollar per taxpayer since 1972), in the amounts of public funding allocations, and in the overall expenditure limits may be necessary if the presidential system is to remain viable.

Political scientists have considered the checkoff a form of citizen participation. While its rate, like voting, has been declining, the thirty three million or more persons checking off constitutes a large body of support compared with numbers of those who contribute money, who give service to parties and candidates, or who vote in congressional election years.

PUBLIC FUNDING IN CONGRESSIONAL CAMPAIGNS

In congressional campaigns, in particular, the political rationale for public funding arises from parallel approaches to a related problem. Some candidates, especially incumbents, attract more money than others and this creates imbalances in candidate spending. The remedy proposed is to limit spending and contributions and provide public funds—thus holding the advantaged down and helping the disadvantaged up: the result, presumably, it to make elections more competitive. These public policies, however, have differential impacts, as political scientist Gary Jacobson has shown.[10] Jacobson, whose findings have been widely accepted, starts with the view that simply being known and remembered by voters is a very important factor in an electoral success. The average incumbent, provided with the resources of office, already enjoys an advantage in voter recognition prior to the campaign. The dissemination of additional information about the incumbent during the campaign, therefore, may often be superfluous even though it helps reinforce voter opinion. On the other hand, the challenger not so well known to most voters, has everything to gain from an extensive and expensive effort to acquire voter awareness.

Translated into financial terms, this means that because Senators and Representatives are generally better known, they usually need less campaign money—but are able to raise more. The challengers, while they may need more money, have difficulty getting it. But when they do, either through providing it to their own campaigns out of their own wealth, or by attracting it, they become better known and are more likely to win. If the incumbent then raises money to meet the threat, spending money helps him or her less per dollar spent than additional dollars spent by the challenger. In summary, those voters who change as a result of increased campaign spending generally tend to benefit challengers.

Jacobson concludes that public subsidies would increase spending for both incumbent and challenger, but would work to the benefit of the latter, thus making elections more competitive. On the other hand, any policy that attempts to equalize the financial positions of candidates by limiting campaign spending would benefit incumbents, thus lessening electoral competition.

FLOORS WITHOUT CEILINGS

Some supporters of public funding, including this author, advocate public funding floors without spending limit ceilings. This concept is favored by many of the mature democracies in western Europe, where government subsidies are given to political parties with no limits on receiving and spending private contributions. The idea is that partial public funding, or a floor, gives candidates (or parties) at least minimal access to the electorate and provides alternative funds so that candidates (or parties) can reject undesirable private contributions.

At the same time, if this approach were accepted in the United States, the absence of spending limits would avoid the constitutional issues raised in the case of *Buckley v. Valeo* (424 U.S. 1, 1976); while this system appears to favor incumbents who have an advantage in raising funds, the floors actually assist challengers by providing them with money enabling minimal access to the electorate. The Jacobson findings reinforce the concept of floors without ceilings.

Floors without ceilings are what was actually experienced in the presidential general elections of 1988, when public funds provided the floors, but the ceilings or expenditure limits were not effective, because of substantial soft money spending. It took from 1976 to 1988 for soft money to break out significantly, but the lesson is that as the system evolves, ceilings eventually collapse.

Ensuring that all serious contenders have a reasonable minimum is more important than limiting how much candidates can spend. The bigger problem is how to provide money to candidates, not unduly restrict it. Public funding is designed to ease fundraising problems.

Despite objections, public funding remains the approach of choice for those who believe that the current system of financing congressional campaigns with private contributions from individuals and groups causes problems that can be remedied only by use of public funds to pay for at least some portion of campaign costs.

Part 2

NO—
Public Financing is Not a Desirable Policy

Mitch McConnell

During the debate over congressional campaign finance reform in Congress, the presidential election system regularly was touted as an ideal of regulatory perfection—where spending limits and public financing of political campaigns had brought order and integrity in comparison to the private campaign financing system of Congress.

If one examines presidential campaign financing practices more carefully, however, one finds that the expenditure limits and public financing imposed by the Federal Election Campaign Act of 1974 have created a regulatory disaster, where grassroots volunteers have been replaced by lawyers and accountants, candidates break the law with impunity, and wealthy contributors feed millions of dollars through innumerable backdoor accounts.

The essential reason for the failure of spending limits and public financing is that it seeks to accomplish the impossible: to squeeze all private money out of politics. Limits on private money in politics work like a rock placed on Jello: the rock sinks down and everything oozes out the sides. Private money is inextricably linked to politics, and laws that separate the two will invariably result in endless, ineffective red tape that restrains legitimate political activity while doing nothing about more questionable practices. That is what has happened in the presidential election system.

UNINTENDED CONSEQUENCES

Cheat to Compete

After 1974, when spending limits and public financing were instituted in the presidential system, every single major candidate has been cited by the Federal Election Commission for substantial violations of the election laws. Compare these rampant—and largely unpunished—abuses with the rare election law citations that occur in the congressional system. Fewer than 5 percent of the thousands of candidates who run for Congress each year are cited by the F.E.C. for violations of the congressional campaign finance laws—where, incidentally there are no spending limits or public financing.

One obvious reason for all the "cheating" among presidential candidates is that the law itself is too complicated to follow. In fact, presidential candidates allocate one of every four campaign dollars for lawyers and accountants, to examine the law, attempt to comply with it, and find ingenious ways around it. In 1988 the George Bush for president campaign processed every contribution it received through over one hundred steps to ensure compliance with a maze of F.E.C. regulations.

Yet even with the most painstaking procedures, the law becomes stretched far beyond its confining bounds, and the F.E.C. steps in with citation in hand, to the embarrassment of the candidate. Very few of these legal violations involve issues of corruption or cloak-and-dagger transactions. Rather, they usually concern whether a rental car procured in Massachusetts may be driven in New Hampshire, or whether volunteers working in Iowa may be bunked in a neighboring state. The presidential election laws waste a huge amount of candidate and F.E.C. time preventing these petty accounting mishaps, while ignoring the wholesale invasion of the system by wealthy contributors and political organizations.

In 1980 total spending by all candidates on accountants and lawyers alone was $21.4 million, as much as was spent in total on the most expensive Senate race in history. In 1984 Ronald Reagan and Walter Mondale each budgeted a million dollars for "compliance costs," which translates to teams of campaign finance legal experts developing new loopholes and creative accounting schemes. Robert Beckel, a senior Mondale campaign staffer and respected consultant, puts it best when he says, "If you're not finding every loophole that's available, you're not doing your job."

In fact, there are thousands of ways of getting around the restrictive limits imposed on presidential campaigns. In such circumstances, legality becomes merely a matter of degree. There are limits, for example, on what presidential campaigns may spend in each state. At least that is what the law says. Nevertheless, most candidates spend money on television ads in Massachusetts to reach voters in New Hampshire. The mail for Iowa's voters is sent from New York and charged against New York's limit.

In 1984 the Democratic nominee spent about $2 million in New Hampshire alone, even though the legal limit for the state was only $400,000. The campaign finally got caught when it charged $56,000 to its Massachusetts and Minnesota budgets for rental cars that never left Iowa or New Hampshire. Meanwhile, the Republican nominee was being cited for using his primary election funds to run for the general election.

Candidates also cheat on their overall spending limits by using "delegate committees": political committees that are supposed to select favorable state delegates. In 1984 one campaign used its delegation selection committees to circumvent both contributions and spending limits. Campaign lawyers found that delegate committees were a "loophole big enough to drive a truck through." Overall, the campaign's delegate committees processed $750,000, including several contributions from "maxed-out" donors.

Candidates also cheat on spending limits with "precandidacy committees," designed to test the waters before initiating a formal presidential bid. From 1981 to 1984 one such committee raised and spent $15 million, partly to buy political favors—through donations to other politicians—and to spread the candidate's name across the country, all outside the legal spending limits.

Other popular ways of cheating in the presidential system include: having labor organizations pay the deposit costs for phone banks; sharing office space with special interest groups in order to save on rent; and getting friendly banks and corporations to extend very generous credit accounts. All of these have been tried, with varying measures of success, by both Democrats and Republicans.

Erosion of Public Faith in the System

The effect of these abuses has been to erode the public's faith in the integrity of presidential candidates and campaign laws. The

Kennedy School of Government at Harvard University warned that "the creative accounting spawned under the presidential system is stimulating overwhelming cynicism about campaign reforms."

Hardened campaign staffers admit that one of the top planning priorities for a campaign is to identify in advance ways to circumvent the limits and rules—not deciding what you stand for, not articulating what you believe in, but amassing an army of lawyers and accountants who can tell you how to get around the law.

WELFARE FOR POLITICIANS

Further, there is the cost of the public financing system—which is born by *all* taxpayers, whether or not they participate in the fictional volunteerism of the dollar "checkoff" on their tax returns. For the money that is appropriated through the checkoff is taken out of the general revenues, which might otherwise be used for veterans' programs, elderly benefits, early childhood vaccinations, or education.

The last three presidential elections have consumed a total of half a billion dollars of the taxpayers money. In 1988 the two party primaries alone cost $40 million. Following that, each party spent several million more on lavish convention events—all on the taxpayers' tab.

Now that public financing has become an entitlement program for politicians, fringe candidates are sprouting like mushrooms to get their share. Extremist candidates squander taxpayers' dollars to spread views that most Americans do not agree with and are not particularly interested in supporting with their hard-earned money. In 1984 Lyndon LaRouche received half a million dollars from the American taxpayers. LaRouche received another half-million in 1988, even though the candidate was under investigation for credit card fraud.

Then there is Lenora Fulani, a New York psychologist/social worker who considers herself to be presidential material. Although she is not exactly a household word in American politics, Lenora Fulani eventually received almost a million dollars from the federal government to run her presidential campaign. Pop artist Andy Warhol once predicted that, in the future, everyone would be famous for fifteen minutes. Even he, however, did not imagine that

American taxpayers would be subsidizing everyone's fifteen minutes in the spotlight.

Certainly, everyone has a right to run for president in this country. No American would argue with that, but few would say that we should be forced to pay for each person's political ambitions, however quixotic or vain. Moreover, if the presidential system has encouraged a proliferation of fringe candidates, can one not imagine the field of candidates who would emerge if we extended free public financing to congressional races? All who looked in the mirror and fancied themself a Senator or Congressman would be lining up to pick up a government check to run for office.

THE NEW CORRUPTION: SPENDING AROUND THE SYSTEM

The Failure of Spending Limits

Between the last two presidential elections, overall spending increased by over 50 percent—despite the presence of spending limits and public financing. By comparison, between the last two congressional cycles—where there are no spending limits or public financing—total campaign spending remained virtually flat.

Spending limits and public financing have *not* reduced overall spending in presidential elections. Professor Arterton of Yale University has said that, "Trying to put a dollar figure on the money spent in presidential contests is akin to figuring out how much the outlaws carried away from a train robbery. There are just too many pockets to add up."

The John F. Kennedy School of Government at Harvard University found that expenditure limits and public financing in presidential elections have not stopped the exponential growth of spending in campaigns. After a brief slowdown in spending in 1976, the money flowing into presidential politics has increased at about the same rate as before spending limits and public financing were instituted. In fact, we cannot even measure for certain how spending is growing, because the spending limits have forced millions of dollars into undisclosed, unreported, unlimited channels.

The Growth of Soft Money

In 1980 organized labor provided an estimated $11.1 million in "soft money" to presidential candidates, all unreported and all unlimited, completely outside the spending limits that exist in the presidential system. In 1984 labor and other special interests spent $30.4 million in soft money to support the Democratic nominee. This money went for organized telephone banks, political leaflets, voter registration efforts, and targeted get-out-the-vote drives.

In Ohio alone, the AFL-CIO set up eighty phone banks and paid unemployed members $4 an hour to make ten thousand calls per day—criticizing the Republican administration's policies but without advocating a specific candidate. The teamsters spent $2 million and provided political services worth another $6 million to benefit the Republican candidate, Ronald Reagan.

After the 1976 election, the first time these presidential "reforms" were in place, political scientist Michael Malbin wrote:

> The biggest winner of the Presidential system was organized labor. Public financing shut off private contributions.... Party contributions also were limited.... In contrast, labor could spend as much as it wanted in communicating with union members, registering them to vote, and getting them to the polls.

Malbin went on to say:

> When labor unites behind one candidate, as it did in 1976, a system in which private contributions are prohibited leaves it in a position no other groups can match. Little wonder that labor calls the campaign finance experiment a success.

Since special interest soft money is under the table, no one knows for certain how much is spent. But the rate of increase for soft money spending is about—as best we can tell—400 percent each election cycle.

In 1984 special interests reported spending $4.7 million on political communications to members. Many analysts say this is only "the tip of the iceberg," since loopholes let most communications go completely unreported. About $6.7 million was spent by 85 tax-exempt organizations to conduct "nonpartisan" voter drives. All these operations were undisclosed and outside the legal limits, yet the funds raised and spent by these organizations were carefully directed by operatives in the political parties and the presidential campaigns.

In sum, before spending limits and taxpayer financing, outside spending constituted less than 10 percent of overall spending. In 1980 and after, special interest spending to influence elections has represented at least one-quarter of all money spent on behalf of candidates. If political party spending is added in, then about one-third of all expenditures now made in presidential elections are outside the control of the two candidates.

Return of the "Fat Cats"

Under the presidential system, we also have seen a return of the "fat cats." These are the huge contributors, who can ante up hundreds of thousands of dollars for their favorite candidate, often in exchange for an ambassadorship or a cushy administrative job. They have disappeared in congressional elections, where contributors are held to a strict $1,000 per person limit. The fat cats are back and flourishing, however, under the "reformed" presidential system.

In 1983 veteran political activist Stewart Mott bailed out a struggling Democratic contender by allowing him to charge $131,000 to his direct mail fund, and then holding a $500-a-person fund-raiser to help him pay the bill. Stewart Mott did the same thing in 1980, by extending half a million dollars worth of credit to independent candidate John Anderson. This enabled Mott to boast, "I figured out how to be a fat cat again."

The Kennedy School of Government concluded in 1982:

> A serious consequence of the growth of money in presidential elections has been the effort by political forces to expand the flow of money outside the constricted budgets of the actual contenders. These funding sources are all less accountable to the electorate than are the candidates. This constitutes a failure of the act's original purpose.

VOTER TURNOUT AND GRASSROOTS DEMOCRACY

Because of all these discouraging developments, voter turnout has stagnated in presidential elections. Voter turnout was at 55 percent in 1972—before we passed this law—and it dropped to just above 50 percent in 1988.

Finally, grassroots politics has suffered the most under the "reformed" presidential system of expenditure limits and taxpayer financing. David Broder, probably the most respected political reporter in America, wrote in the *Washington Post:*

> There is a cost to public financing. Public financing in presidential campaigns has meant a virtual shutdown of local headquarters financed by small contributions. Grassroots democracy has died.

Grassroots democracy has died. Killed by excessive regulation, intrusive government, armies of lawyers, volumes of accounting rules, and self-serving special interest groups that are taking over.

We should not be trying to put an arbitrary clamp on voluntary citizen participation in politics. That is all a spending limit is. It tells the candidate that he or she cannot amass any support above a certain arbitrary limit. It tells the voluntary small donor that he or she cannot contribute to a particular candidate, because that candidate's limit on private support already had been reached.

REPORTS OF THE KENNEDY SCHOOL

The Kennedy School of Government at Harvard University has been intimately involved in the process of implementing expenditure limits and public financing in presidential elections. When these measures were being considered, the House Administration Committee requested a study from the school regarding the policy implications of such "reforms." The school released its report in 1979, and then was asked to perform a follow-up report in 1982, by the Senate Rules and Administration Committee. In both instances, the school found rampant abuses and other evidence of the system's total breakdown.

In its 1982 report to the Senate Rules Committee, the school underscored the problems with unduly restricting the flow of money in politics:

> Among the problems of the post-Watergate reforms are related to the attempt to restrict the money spent in Presidential

campaigns. Candidates are not allowed to spend enough money. The expenditure limits have spawned a whole series of serious problems of definition, allocation, and enforcement.

The Kennedy School report continued:

On the other hand, the effort to control total spending has not succeeded. Those involved in Presidential politics are able to raise and spend unlimited amounts of money through conduits other than the candidates' campaign committees. To make matters worse, most of the other means through which money is now being poured into Presidential politics are inherently less accountable to the electorate and should not be encouraged by the campaign laws.

Finally, this report concluded:

Thus, our most important recommendation is to eliminate the limitations on expenditures made by candidates.

According to the Kennedy School report, spending limits have proven to be a total failure. They have failed to curtail spending in presidential politics; they have failed to shorten the overall lengths of campaigns; they have interfered excessively with campaign strategies; and they have frustrated enforcement by spawning a host of arbitrary definitions and creative accounting practices.

Perhaps of greatest concern, the public financing and spending limits in the presidential system have fostered disrespect for the law among candidates, consultants, the public, and even those who are charged with the duty of enforcing the law. As one respected campaign and media consultant puts it, "I think this whole F.E.C. thing is a sham."

KEEPING IT SIMPLE; A SUCCESS STORY TO REMEMBER

In comparison, the simple, straightforward campaign finance regulation system that governs Congress has worked quite well since its enactment in 1971. The law provides that no individual may contribute more than $1,000 to a candidate in any election, and no political action committee (PAC) may contribute more than $5,000. It sets strict limits on what individuals and PACs may contribute to political parties, and requires all contributions to be disclosed to the public.

Few campaign finance experts would dispute that the act has been a success: fat cat contributors have been pushed out of congressional campaign financing, as candidates are compelled to reach out to thousands of small donors all across their states or districts for support. Public disclosure lets the voters decide whether a candidate's integrity is compromised by special interest PAC contributions, thereby helping to deter even the appearance of impropriety.

The reason why the act has been such a success is that it respects one immutable fact that seems to elude the proponents of public financing and spending limits: private money always will be in politics, regardless of any limits or taxpayer subsidies or the Federal Election Commission. Because of that immutable fact, a spending limit merely squeezes money out of monitored, controlled channels, and diverts it into unregulated, invisible channels.

Rather than squeeze money out of accountable channels, the law regulating congressional races *encourages* as much money as possible to flow through its system of limits and reporting requirements. Candidates and contributors would rather follow the law than figure ways around it, because it is fairly simple, clear-cut, and—most importantly—unrestrictive. That is also why few congressional candidates ever break the law. By comparison, under the spending limits in presidential races, candidates have to cheat to compete.

CONCLUSION

The presidential system of public financing and spending limits was enacted to control spending, remove special interest influence, increase public faith in the integrity of the system, promote voter turnout, and improve accountability of funds spent in presidential elections. It has achieved none of these objectives; in fact, this system has severely aggravated these problems in recent years.

The only solution to the systemic breakdown of presidential campaign finance regulation is to repeal spending limits and public financing, and replace these failed programs with regulations based on the simple and successful congressional campaign finance system. If we do not act quickly, the way we elect presidents—and the very institution of the presidency—may fall quickly into disrepute.

CHAPTER SEVEN

Should Presidential
Debates be Required?

With presidential debates now an institutionalized feature of the American presidential selection process, it is perhaps wise to examine whether or not debates do in fact enhance the quality of the selection process. More importantly, we need to examine the arguments for and against the mandatory requirement of presidential debates.

William Carroll argues that debates should be required. Carroll provides the reader with a substantive discussion regarding the positive impact of presidential debates conducted in 1960, 1976, 1980, 1984, and 1988. In Carroll's view previous presidential debates have enhanced responsible voting behavior and, in the event a presidential incumbent is nominated for reelection, the debates require the president to publicly defend his record. Carroll also stresses the utility of debates as mechanisms that educate voters on issues and provide important clues to the character and leadership qualities of presidential candidates.

James I. Lengle and Dianne C. Lambert argue there is very little reason to require presidential debates. In systematic fashion, the authors address serious questions regarding the fairness of debates, the ability of debates to produce rational voting behavior, enlighten voters about the character of candidates, test the qualifications of candidates, reach large audiences, and increase political interest. According to Lengle and Lambert, debates fail in every respect and such an exercise does little to enhance the quality of the presidential selection process. In their view presidential debates need not be required.

Part 1

YES—
Presidential Debates Should be Required

William Carroll

To ask whether presidential debates should be required is in some sense an academic question, for televised debates are now probably a permanent feature of presidential elections. Every presidential election since 1976 has witnessed some form of debate, and public expectations and media pressure virtually guarantee that debates will take place in all future elections. But still the question is raised whether they *should* take place at all. Although the author is cognizant of the current shortcomings of modern presidential debates, and that revisions in the debate format would substantially enhance the quality and utility of debates, the argument will nevertheless be presented that debates must remain an integral component of the presidential selection process.

It is this author's view that presidential debates should be required, either in a revised form or even as they are currently conducted. To present a compelling case in favor of required presidential debates, it is first necessary to review our experience with the "great debates" of 1960, the absence of debates in 1964, 1968, and 1972, and those debates that have taken place during every presidential election year since 1976.

The Great Debates of 1960: Nixon v. Kennedy

The first televised presidential debates occurred in 1960, four in all, between Richard Nixon and John F. Kennedy. The debates themselves were held as a result of network pressure on Congress to ammend, temporarily, federal regulations regarding equal time, which had up to then prevented televised debates.[1] It is now part of American political folklore that these debates, especially the first, provided the winning difference for Kennedy. According to most analysts then and since, the debates were a disaster for Nixon, destroying the distinction he was hoping to draw between his maturity and experience, and his opponent's youthfulness and lack of experience. Nixon's unease before the cameras contrasted with Kennedy's coolness, while Kennedy demonstrated a firm grasp of the issues, which belied the image of playboy and political dilitente many may have had of him, and on which Nixon was hoping to capitalize. By the end of the debates, Kennedy held a slight lead over Nixon in public opinion polls. Many previously undecided voters cited the debates as playing an important part in making up their minds, with nearly three million voters attributing to the debates alone their final decisions to vote for Kennedy.[2] Kennedy went on to win the election, by only 112,000 votes. The presidential debates therefore were a determining factor in the final outcome of the 1960 presidential election. Voter perceptions of the two candidates appear to have been conditioned and several million voting decisions were affected by the debates.

1964, 1968, and 1972: The Absence of Debates

Presidential debates were not present in the elections of 1964, 1968, and 1972. A fair question is whether or not debates would have made any difference in the three presidential elections. In all probability, it is unlikely that debates would have changed the outcome of either the 1964 or 1972 elections.

Lyndon Johnson held a substantial lead over Barry Goldwater throughout the entire 1964 campaign, finally winning a landslide victory in the election. The 1972 election was another landslide, with the now incumbent Nixon demolishing the Democratic candidate George McGovern, whose name has come to be emblematic of the supposedly hopeless fate of liberal Democratic presidential candidates. As in 1964, it is unlikely that a debate would have made any difference. However, unlike the 1964 and 1972 presidential elections, the 1968 election was extremely competitive, with Hubert Humphrey still closing the gap on Richard Nixon until election day. One debate or series of debates might very well have helped push Humphrey into the lead. Certainly Humphrey wanted a debate, baiting Nixon with calls of "Sir Richard the Chicken Hearted."[3] Nixon, ahead in the polls, felt no need to debate and, due to unpleasant memories of the 1960 election, had little fondness for presidential debates.

Regardless of whether the three elections were landslide or competitive, what was lost in these elections by not having debates was the opportunity of comparing the candidates directly. The candidates themselves, especially the challengers, lost the opportunity of directly confronting their opponents. Neither Johnson in 1968 nor Nixon in 1972 was obliged to explain or defend his policies in a public debate against his opponent. As it was, in the 1972 campaign, in the words of Hunter S. Thompson, "everyone was grilled but Nixon."[4]

Debates provide the only formal means of forcing the candidates to confront each other, and to address *directly* critical and probing questions. It may be that this is most important when an incumbent president is running for reelection, who otherwise might adopt a "Rose Garden" strategy, or appear only before enthusiastic crowds of supporters who cheer everything he says. Only in the debates is a candidate obliged to confront his opponent and respond to his questions and those of the panel. We should also recall that presidents in our system are not obliged to explain and defend their policies on the floor of Congress, directly confronting the opposition, as the British Prime Minister must do. Press conferences are then the only opportunity of questioning the president directly, but these are held entirely at the president's discretion and can only be a substitute for direct confrontation by a political opponent. Perhaps this is one reason the press has adopted an increasingly adversarial role.

1976: Ford v. Carter

In 1976 both the incumbent Gerald Ford and his Democratic challenger Jimmy Carter hoped to benefit from their planned three debates. Ford, who in fact had challenged Carter to debate in his acceptance speech at the Republican convention, looked forward to the opportunity to appear presidential. For his part, Carter hoped to demonstrate his depth of knowledge and seriousness as a candidate.

In fact, both candidates performed well enough in the three debates, although at first it appeared Ford was the principal beneficiary.[5] But Ford was ultimately damaged in the second debate by an apparent gaffe in reference to eastern Europe's degree of independence from the Soviet Union, although this did not show up until after the play given it by the media over the next several days. Indeed, immediate postdebate polls showed people thought Ford won even this second debate, in some cases by a two to one margin. But several days later, following all the commentary on Ford's "blunder," Carter was now perceived winner by an identical two to one margin.[6] Carter went on to win a fairly close election, quite possibly due to the three presidential debates.

The 1976 election also saw the first vice-presidential debate, between Ford's running mate Robert Dole and Carter's running mate Walter Mondale. Mondale was easily the perceived winner, but the debate does not appear to have significantly affected the election.

1980: Carter v. Reagan

Four years later President Carter, now the incumbent, was hoping to use a debate with his Republican challenger Ronald Reagan to highlight the latter's alleged extremism and ignorance of the issues, while again demonstrating his own depth of knowledge and accentuating his status as incumbent president. After considerable delay, a single debate was held, which challenger Reagan used successfully to dispel doubts about his capabilities by appearing calm, reasonable, and adequately versed on the issues. It was Carter who appeared to be on the defensive, and Reagan wound up the debate with a telling, rhetorical question asking people if they thought themselves better off today than four years ago. The American economy at the time was suffering from high unemployment, high inflation, and rising interest rates.

Reagan's relatively narrow lead over Carter before the debate grew wider after the debate, and again public perception of who won the debate was significantly affected by subsequent analysis in the media.[7] Carter went down to a crushing defeat in the election one week later. It is apparent that the presidential debate in 1980 conditioned voter perceptions of the two candidates.

1984: Reagan v. Mondale

Before his first debate with the Democratic challenger Walter Mondale in 1984, Ronald Reagan held a huge 21 point lead in the polls.[8] The first debate was watched by an impressive 84 percent of registered voters, who saw Reagan turn in a weak performance, appearing confused at times and rambling in his closing statement. Mondale was seen as the winner by a 9 point margin immediately after the debate, but over the next several days, again after all the media discussion of Reagan's weak performance, this grew to a 49 point margin.[9] Despite Mondale's win, he still trailed Reagan by 13 points in the voter preference polls going into their second debate.

In the second debate Mondale was substantively strong, but Reagan had regained his confidence and in typical, one-liner fashion put the age issue to rest by stating in response to a question about his age that he would not hold his opponent's youth and inexperience against him. Reagan was given the slight edge in immediate postdebate polls, which grew in the days following. If this second debate was Mondale's last chance to overcome Reagan and reduce his big lead in the polls, he clearly had failed to do so. Given his already huge lead over Mondale, Reagan might still have coasted to reelection in any event. But at least he was obliged to confront his challenger and respond to direct questioning from his challenger and from the panelists. It was only through the debate that President Reagan was forced to confront Democratic challenger Walter Mondale.

The 1984 election saw another vice-presidential debate, between Vice-President George Bush and Geraldine Ferraro; Bush was the apparent winner.

1988: Bush v. Dukakis

Our most recent experience with presidential debates was the 1988 election, with two presidential debates between the Republican nominee Bush and the Democratic candidate Michael Dukakis, and one between the vice-presidential candidates Dan Quayle and Lloyd Bentsen. Some have argued that the presidential debates in 1988 were crucial, given the volatility of public opinion, with dramatic shifts before and after the conventions, and with a third of the voters still undecided.[10] Furthermore, if candidate image has become of primary importance in voter choice, especially in presidential elections, the candidates' performance in televised debates becomes all the more important to the outcome of the election.

Bush overcame a large deficit in the polls immediately after the Democratic convention to hold a lead over Dukakis going into the first debate. In the immediate postdebate polls the first debate was seen as a draw, with Dukakis then emerging as the winner in later polls after the press and media discussion of the debate. But Dukakis derived no lasting benefit from the debate, as Bush still held his lead in the voter preference polls.[11] Dukakis therefore needed the second debate to regain the momentum he had been losing since the nominating conventions. However, his performance was not strong enough, in particular again failing to make emotional contact with voters; and again failing to defend his liberalism and offer strong rebuttals to the Bush campaign's negative attacks. Pundits immediately declared the race over, which for all intents and purposes it was.

It seems safe to conclude that debates can have an impact in close elections, particularly when large numbers of voters remain undecided at the time of the debates, as in 1960, 1976, 1980, and 1988—elections that appear to have hinged on the outcome of presidential debates. The debates can especially help the challenger, as in 1960 and 1980—or fail to, as in 1984 and 1988.

VOTER PERCEPTIONS, EDUCATION, AND ISSUES

There are academic studies indicating that perceptions about who won or lost a presidential debate are largely determined by predebate candidate preferences, as are perceptions of the positions taken by the candidates in the debate, with people supporting the positions of their chosen candidate.[12] For already committed voters, then, the debates serve mainly to solidify their support. However, for weak partisans, independents, and undecided voters, the debates may increase their interest in the election and their understanding of the issues; even their perceptions of the candidates could be changed.[13]

Debates also allow for a comparison of information, not only between the candidates but between what the candidates say in the debates and what is received from the candidates' paid advertisements. As such, presidential debates provide *added* information as the candidates react and respond spontaneously to the questions asked them during the debates.[14] Moreover, not only are the debates watched by millions of voters, but research discovers that they are widely discussed by the American public, as well as by the media.[15] American presidential debates, therefore, are not tangential to the election process, but rather constitute one of the highlights of the presidential campaign.

Are *issues* really presented and debated in presidential debates? Numerous analyses of the content of the debates clearly indicate that they are.[16] The candidates do present their positions on a range of issues, as they are forced to respond to substantive questions raised by panelists or by their opponent. Content analysis of the debates further reveals that the candidates *differ* on the issues, and that they stress different issues and symbols. Thus in both debates in 1988, Dukakis stressed domestic policy issues and the themes of leadership, family, and opportunity, while Bush tried to stress his education theme and repeatedly raised the "issues" of Dukakis's membership in the A.C.L.U. and his liberalism.[17] Issues also "evolve" over time, with the salient issues varying from one election to the next. Thus foreign policy issues and the Soviet threat were more prominent in the Kennedy-Nixon debates in 1960 than in the Carter-Ford debates in 1976, when domestic issues were prominent.[18] Certainly Vietnam would have figured prominently in debates in 1964, 1968, and 1972 if they had been held. Issues are in fact raised and the candidates are obliged to state their position on important domestic and foreign policy questions. As such, "political choice," one of the fundamental tenets of democratic philosophy, is promoted through the presidential debate.

Nor is the criticism that debates are nothing but opportunities for the candidates to deliver one-liners entirely valid. As I have just indicated, issues are indeed raised and debated, so that debates are not just about images. If the emphasis in debate coverage by the media has been on who won or lost, who looked nervous or unemotional, who delivered a telling one-liner or committed a gaffe, then the fault lies with the media, the candidates, or even the public, but certainly not with the debates themselves. The media may indeed help to shape public reactions to the debates; but the media help to shape public perceptions on many things, and media influence, even possible media distortion, cannot be used as an excuse for doing away with presidential debates.

One could, then, ask if voters themselves find the debates useful, for understanding the issues and learning the candidates' positions on the issues. Again there are studies indicating that a majority of the public does think the debates are useful, and that the debates even influence their evaluations of the candidates.[19] We know that these evaluations are also greatly influenced by pre-debate expectations and postdebate media coverage, but that does not necessarily detract from the influence or usefulness of debates.

DEBATES AND PRESIDENTIAL LEADERSHIP

Do presidential debates provide meaningful clues with re-spect to the ability of a candidate to effectively serve as the American president? Do presidential debates offer special insight regarding presidential character? Of course it is difficult to tell just from debates how effectively a candidate could manage the executive branch, work with the United States Congress, or serve as the nation's Commander-in-Chief, activity that all presidents must assume. No one has the ability to predict with 100 percent certainty exactly what the true capacity of a presidential candidate is to serve as the nation's top executive. Nevertheless, debates at least can give us a clearer sense of candidates' priorities, and we can also get some indication of how each candidate responds to pres-sure. In both regards, performance in debates may indeed reveal something about how a candidate would behave or perform as pres-ident. Moreover, how a candidate handles the debates may offer a clue to one's character. If one or the other candidate appears ideo-logically inflexible or gratuitously negative, this should serve to raise some doubts about that candidate. Even manner and bearing are not irrelevant, for they may be indicators of self-confidence and poise, traits requisite for effectively leading the nation. Certainly, communicative skills are tested in debates that, in the media age, are absolutely essential for mobilizing public support for legisla-tive agendas. How a president communicates deeply impacts on his ability to work with the United States Congress and world leaders.

A debate becomes a test of a candidate's poise, ability to withstand pressure, communicative skills, and the ability to gen-erate public support. There are several ways that debates may offer clues about how a candidate would perform as president. Moreover, given the preponderence of campaign commercials produced by media consultants trained in the art of manufacturing images, and given the increasing number of staged and orchestrated campaign events, it would be tragic to deny the American people the rich opportunity of evaluating presidential character during the heat of a nationally televised, live, and competitive debate.

CONCLUSION

What has been demonstrated in this argument is that presidential debates are a very important component of the American presidential selection process. Indeed, in some respects, the debates are the energizing elements of the presidential campaign. Debates appear to be very useful to voters, informing them of the candidates' stand on the issues. Debates appear to be particularly important with respect to helping undecided voters arrive at a voting decision. In this age of weak partisanship and subsequent voter volatility, the presidential debates clearly take on a very special significance. Presidential debates serve to increase the flow of information from candidate to voter; information that is neither filtered nor screened. The check against packaged campaign commercials is quite relevant here.

Presidential debates are also watched by millions of voters, thereby linking the American people directly to the election process, and debates appear to be appreciated by voters and widely discussed. At the same time, the American public is afforded the opportunity to assess, to some extent, the poise, confidence, and general character of presidential candidates—information that contributes to responsible voting behavior. It is apparent that presidential debates were the deciding factors in certain presidential elections. Had debates been required in the 1968 presidential election, they might very well have produced a different outcome. As a means of bringing presidential candidates together, to confront one another directly before the watching eyes of the American public, no other forum equals that which is provided by the presidential debate.

While I recognize that presidential debates as they are currently conducted are somewhat imperfect, particularly with respect to spontaneity, choice of sponsors, panel participants, and the conduct of moderators, and that reforms are clearly needed to improve upon the format of debates, especially allowing for more follow-up questions, the argument still holds that the disadvantages of debates are quite minor compared to the advantages presidential debates offer to the presidential selection process. Not only are presidential debates central to the selection process, but the debates are also central to our democracy. Presidential debates perform a legitimizing function in presidential elections. So long as debates are perceived to give the candidates a fair and equal opportunity to present their positions on foreign and domestic policies, and to adequately challenge the policies of the opposition candidate, then the more confidence and respect the American people will have toward the election outcome.

In some respects, the presidential debates lend themselves to the principle of democracy known as "due process." The debates also serve to strengthen the claim that the victor is the legitimately chosen representative of the American people. Such a claim is absolutely essential to effective governing. If democracy is not about free and open debate with all the attendant risks and shortcomings, then it is about nothing. In the end, one might say that to lose faith in presidential debates is to lose faith in the possibility of democracy. Presidential debates are therefore necessary, definitely advantageous, and directly conducive to the sustenance of the democratic state. Debates must be required.

Part 2

NO—
Presidential Debates Should Not be Required

James I. Lengle
Dianne C. Lambert

Since the time of the Greek city states and republican Rome, debate has been regarded as an essential element of good government. Socrates sought to define the best regime by exploring the concept of justice in a dialogue, antiquity's word for debate.[1] Democratic thinkers from Locke to Tocqueville advocated the vigorous exchange of ideas.[2] Influenced by democratic thought, Thomas Jefferson noted that "truth . . . will prevail . . . unless . . . disarmed of her natural weapons, free argument and debate."[3] The founding fathers designed a political system of competing institutions to promote a clash between opposing ideas and interests.[4]

When the great debates of American history are recalled, the constitutional convention comes first to mind. The notes of James Madison reveal the deep divisions surrounding the adoption of the Constitution.[5] Later, debaters such as Henry Clay, Daniel Webster, John C. Calhoun, and Robert Hayne dominated American political discourse. Divisive issues such as slavery, the tariff, the League of Nations, civil rights, and the Vietnam war polarized the country into opposing camps. If debates did not always reveal the "truth" in a policy area, at least they generated a middle ground, which a majority could support.

While the genus, "debates," can be traced back to influential thinkers and to dramatic and consequential political confrontations, the species, "presidential," is a relatively new breed of political communication. The great debates in America's past usually took place in legislative chambers. Until recently, debates have seldom been associated with campaigning, least of all presidential campaigning.

In our early republic, custom prescribed that the "office seek the man," not vice versa.[6] Thus, personal campaigning by candidates was taboo. Campaigns began to assume some of their more contemporary aspects during the Jacksonian period, as large public rallies and patriotic speeches became commonplace, and as issues and images joined character and public service as important components of a candidate's persona.

It was not until the twentieth century, however, that most presidential candidates took to the campaign trail to personally solicit votes.[7] Nevertheless, debates between candidates were rare. From colonial times to the advent of television, only one election debate is remembered—the senatorial debates between Abraham Lincoln and Stephen Douglas.

The arrival of television provided the catalyst for campaign debates. The first nationally televised debate between presidential candidates occurred in 1960. For four one-hour sessions, in what were billed as "the great debates," Senator John F. Kennedy and Vice-President Richard M. Nixon faced each other and the nation in this novel experiment in presidential campaigning.[8]

Sixteen years elapsed before the next set of debates in 1976 between President Gerald Ford and challenger Jimmy Carter, an interval caused by the simple political maxim that front-runners see no advantage in debating. Since 1976, however, debates have been a central feature of each campaign. In 1984 the decision by President Ronald Reagan to accept Walter Mondale's invitation to debate is credited with institutionalizing debates—front-runner Reagan ignored precedent and political expediency by accepting Mondale's challenge.

The era of presidential debates is here to stay. The public expects them, the press promotes them, and candidates dare not avoid them.

Let there be no mistake, however; today's presidential debates are not akin to the great debates of deliberative bodies, or to the Lincoln-Douglas debates, or to debates at all. They are joint press conferences governed by rigid formats and gag rules that stifle spontaneity and interaction, and limit responses and rebuttals. Moreover, debates exaggerate some of the worst tendencies of our electoral politics while delivering few of the presumed benefits. Thus, before reformers rush blindly to legislate televised debates every four years, we believe it is important to debate the value of debates so that performance can be distinguished from promise.

Debates are Fair?

Debates are appealing for a variety of reasons. First and foremost, they appear to conform to American notions of fair play. Because both candidates face the same setting, lighting, questions, time constraints, panel, and audience, it is believed that neither candidate derives any tactical, political advantage from debates.

Nothing could be further from the truth. Different settings highlight different strengths. In sports, for instance, marathons reward endurance; sprints reward speed. In debates a bias also exists; candidates with "game show host" qualities—the attractive face, pleasing voice, quick wit, and congenial disposition—have a natural advantage over candidates treated less kindly by the television lens. To institutionalize debates is to perpetuate this bias and to elevate personality as the key to success in the electoral arena. This prospect is fraught with hidden dangers, for style may be unrelated to other important political skills and experiences. Some of the nation's most talented politicians, such as Senators Robert Dole (R-KS), Bill Bradley (D-NJ), and Sam Nunn (D-GA), are generally regarded as average to poor performers on television, while many politicians skilled in the arts of television lack substance and credentials. As a result, debates skew the presidential selection process from substance to style and from the work horses to the show horses of American politics.

Debates Produce Rational Voters?

According to conventional wisdom, debates enhance the democratic process by educating the public about issue differences between the candidates.[9] Two assumptions underlie this argument: first, that debates are substantive discussions about the issues; and second, that voters are sufficiently interested and open-minded to recognize, assimilate, and act on these differences. Neither condition receives much support from the historical or empirical record.

Debates are excellent opportunities for candidates to delineate their policies and programs. Unfortunately, candidates waste the opportunity. Even a sophisticated observer of American poli-

tics would have difficulty remembering one major policy pro-
nouncement or one detailed substantive exchange from the nine
televised presidential debates. The reason for this substantive void
is obvious: in debates, ambiguity is an asset; clarity, a liability.
Taking specific positions on issues needlessly alienates those with
opposing views. Moreover, clear positions are hard to defend and,
once announced, difficult to abandon.

This does not mean that candidates are always ambiguous.
When pressed, they manage to offer a few "painless" solutions for
achieving "peace" and "prosperity." In the 1988 presidential debate, George Bush and Michael Dukakis opted for this strategy
when questioned about one of the most important problems facing
the country, the budget deficit. Bush proposed his "flexible freeze,"
and Dukakis argued for more vigilant tax collection. Neither response was honest or edifying. And unfortunately such responses
are the rule, not the exception.

The failure of debates as educational forums does not entirely
lie with the candidates. The public must also assume some of the
blame. Empirical studies generally show the public to be uninterested and uninformed about public affairs.[10] Even if debates were
substantive in nature, viewing is distinct from learning. Moreover,
much of the audience may have missed the earlier phases of the
campaign where issues were first articulated; these people have no
reference from which to make informed decisions. At best, the
viewer who is educated by the debates on issues, who does learn
slightly more, is the politically interested and educated. Those
with ample information, a small group indeed, increase their
hoard, while those with meager information remain impoverished.

But this does not mean that even for the political elite debates play a crucial role in the vote decision. Studies show that
debates simply reinforce preexisting partisan and candidate
predispositions.[11]

From yet a third perspective, the electronic media are also to
blame for the failure of debates to live up to their promise. While
it is true that debates are unfiltered, once the debate is concluded,
the news twisters take over. It is to these spinners that the public
turns for an explanation of what they just heard. A drift-
in-sentiment phenomenon has been documented—public opinion
immediately after a debate is noticeably different several days later
when the media have had ample opportunity to focus on bloopers,

assess the "presidential" demeanor and look, and discuss who won and who lost.[12] Media analyses condense debates to snippets, sacrificing whatever richness, substance, and gravity existed. It is to this kind of instant analyses that the public ultimately looks for its education.

In addition, the media cover debates as a horse race, not as a seminar. Of immediate importance to them is who won and who lost, and not the information being conveyed. Historically, debates are generally won on style, not substance; and nothing appeals to network news editors more than a snappy thirty-second sound-bite.

Ronald Reagan salvaged his career on numerous occasions with one-liners that dominated postdebate news coverage. His quote, "I'm paying for this microphone, Mr. Green," from a 1980 New Hampshire presidential primary debate, is single-handedly credited for turning around his faltering campaign for the 1980 Republican presidential nomination.[13] His repeated response, "There you go again," to President Carter in the 1980 presidential debates came to symbolize Carter's alleged misrepresentation of Reagan's positions on the issues.[14] Reagan's response in the second debate in 1984 with Walter Mondale, "I will not make age an issue in this campaign; I am not going to exploit, for political purposes, my opponent's youth and inexperience," laid to rest the "age" question arising from the first debate.[15]

Sound-bites from other debates have had similar impact. Walter Mondale's question, "Where's the beef?," directed at Gary Hart during a primary debate in 1984, derailed Hart's candidacy.[16] And Lloyd Bentsen's comment to Dan Quayle, "Senator, I served with Jack Kennedy. I knew Jack Kennedy. Jack Kennedy was a friend of mine. Senator, you're no Jack Kennedy," during the 1988 vice-presidential debate had Democrats around the country wishing that the Dukakis/Bentsen ticket had been reversed.[17]

In the medias' eye, bloopers, or thirty-second misstatements are sure ways to lose a debate. An entire hour and a half discussion of the issues could be destroyed by one error or gaffe, which commentators put on display like a fine trophy. Press coverage of President Ford's misstatement about an absence of Soviet domination in eastern Europe stalled his dramatic comeback against Jimmy Carter in 1976.[18] When the definitive history of presidential debates is written, sound-bites and bloopers, not substance, will be the lead line.

In sum, debates do not elevate the electorate to rational voters. This premise is a myth. Candidates do not produce substantive choices; the viewers are barely interested at best, apathetic at worst; and the media rewrite the debate encounter.

Debates Educate about Character?

Even if debates by and large do not create enlightened voters, they still might be valued for their insights into character, which James David Barber persuasively argues is the key to presidential success.[19] Uncovering character, however, is a dicey operation. For Barber, it involves a thorough study of an aspirant's childhood, early adulthood, and first political encounters—no easy task for even the best trained social scientist. Nevertheless, debates are touted for their potential to reveal character, and Americans are encouraged to practice armchair psychology.

This proposition is full of land mines. Images projected on television are unrelated to a candidate's character. Charismatic candidates can easily hide personal flaws behind an engaging smile and sense of humor. The public persona of John F. Kennedy at the time of his debate with Richard Nixon certainly gave no indication of private weaknesses since revealed.[20] At the other extreme, some qualified candidates, such as Walter Mondale, have had difficulty projecting their true identities in televised debates. In both cases, appearances were deceiving, and debates did little to distinguish private realities from public perceptions.

That debates provide a window to observe the candidates' characters is problematic from a second perspective: what appear as character weaknesses may be character strengths. Media criticism of Michael Dukakis for his performance during the second debate with George Bush in 1988 is a perfect example:

> The media consensus was that Dukakis would need a decisive victory in the [second] debate . . . But a "decisive victory" would evidently have to involve more than a superior substantive performance. After all, Dukakis had been regarded as the winner on substance in the first debate, and it had not helped him greatly in the polls. Now, Dukakis would have to reach his audience on an emotional and visceral level: *to teach them something new about his character.* [emphasis added]

The debate's first question, though brutal, gave him a chance to do just that. CNN anchorman Bernard Shaw asked Dukakis, "If Kitty Dukakis were raped and murdered, would you favor an irrevocable death penalty for the killer?" Dukakis might have used his response to express his horror of crime, his love for his family, and his desire for vengeance, as well as his fervent belief in the rule of a humane law. Instead, he calmly, almost passively, reaffirmed his opposition to the death penalty. The debate could have ended at that point.[21]

This widely held predebate expectation and postdebate interpretation dominated news coverage. Yet what are the pop psychologists in the media and academia trying to tell us about character? That it can be revealed through the answer to one question? That controlling one's emotions is a character flaw? That being consistent on an issue is a character flaw? That not trumpeting an issue is a character flaw? That maintaining some degree of detachment when asked a hypothetical question about a personal tragedy is a character flaw? That all of the above add up to something disturbing about Michael Dukakis that makes him unfit to be president? Debates encourage this kind of psychological gibberish and personal caricaturing, as candidates become patients and network analysts play Sigmund Freud, scrutinizing body language and answers for their "deep" insights into candidate makeup.

Debates Test Qualifications?

Perhaps it is altogether impossible to know the inner person from the sum total of one campaign, debates included. If we aim lower, we might find that debates are a useful gauge to measure and compare presidential qualifications. It is believed that candidates who can take the heat afforded by ninety minutes of so-called grilling by a panel of journalists can handle the pressures of the Oval Office and face-to-face encounters with world leaders. If a candidate does not sweat, mop his brow, dart his eyes, appear ill at ease, or read from index cards, all the better. Avoiding gaffes, misstatements, or bloopers is also a plus. But is this the stuff of presidential timber?

The plain truth about debates is that they reveal very little about presidential qualifications, because the skills they test and the conditions they simulate are irrelevant to presidential performance. Good campaign debaters may make good presidential debaters, but the nation will never know, because, once elected, presidents need not debate ever again. Also, debates give no clue whether a candidate can choose and motivate an honest and capable cabinet; whether a candidate can oversee a huge bureaucracy; whether a candidate accepts critical advice and, just as importantly, is able to synthesize and evaluate the advice; whether a candidate can mobilize public opinion, organized interests, and national, state, and local party leaders in support of his programs; and whether a candidate can work responsibly with Congressional leaders. These and other presidential qualifications are best uncovered by examining careers, not by watching debates. As Daniel Boorstin has argued:

> A man's ability, while standing under kleig lights, without notes, to answer in two and one half minutes a question kept secret until that moment has only the most dubious relevance, if at all, to his qualifications to make deliberate presidential decisions of long-standing public questions after being instructed by a corp of advisors.[22]

Debates Reach Large Audiences?

There is no doubt that a nationally televised presidential debate reaches a larger audience of prospective voters than any other mode of presidential campaigning. As Table 6 shows, 59 percent of American households with televisions were tuned into the first Kennedy/Nixon debate. Over the last three elections, however, ratings have dropped dramatically, from 58.9 percent of households in 1980 to 36.4 percent in 1988. As Table 6 also shows, only 35.9 percent of American households watched the second debate between George Bush and Michael Dukakis, the lowest rating in the history of presidential debates.

What explains the decline in ratings? Perhaps debates have lost their novelty or are viewed more cynically. Perhaps the ratings underestimate the audience due to the "tape and playback later" capability of VCRs. Perhaps the potential audience is siphoned off by the availability of alternative programing on cable television.

Reaching a large but declining audience, however, does involve a trade-off: the more that candidates rely on television to communicate with the electorate, the less they have "flesh to

TABLE 6
Nielsen Average Household Rating Percent for Televised
Presidential Debates

	1960	1976	1980	1984	1988
Debate #1	59.1%	53.5%	58.9%	45.3%	36.8%
Debate #2	59.1	52.4		46.0	35.9
Debate #3	61.0	47.8			
Debate #4	57.8				
Average	59.3	51.2	58.9	45.7	36.4

press" personally with the public. Old-fashioned "retail" (i.e., face-to-face) campaigning has many virtues. First, daily interaction with the public educates the candidate about problems, issues, and opinions that may not be reflected in quick and dirty polls or in the advice of cynical old "pros." That the cost of educating the public through debates comes at the expense of educating candidates about the public is one of the ironies of presidential debates.

Second, unlike video campaigning, which is a "one-man act," retail campaigning involves a huge supporting cast, including state and local parties, organized interest groups, and grassroots activists. Relying primarily on televised debates to spread the message and energize support limits opportunities for mass involvement, and threatens the participatory foundation of democracy.

Debates Increase Political Interest?

It is also thought that debates provide good advertising for presidential elections and increase public interest in campaigns. Survey and turnout data, however, show otherwise. Public interest in presidential elections is low. Over the last ten elections, an average of only 36 percent of the country claimed to be "very much" interested in campaigns, and the difference in levels of interest between debate years and nondebate years was negligible.[23] Furthermore, the 1988 campaign set a record for disinterest: only 28 percent of the public claimed to be "very much" interested in the race. This is the lowest level of interest since the inception of academic polling in 1940.[24]

Moreover, increased interest, if present but undetectable in polls, should manifest itself in increased turnout. Since the inception of presidential debates, however, turnout has steadily dropped from 63 percent in 1960 to 50 percent in 1988. Despite the pomp and circumstance of two debates in 1988, turnout dropped to a 64-year low. Clearly, presidential debates do not generate greater interest or greater turnout.

CONCLUSION

If one looks to presidential debates to cure the problems of American democracy, one is looking in the wrong place. Debates do not raise interest or turnout, and do not educate the public about issues, character, or qualifications. To solve these problems, we need to look elsewhere.

Yet presidential debates have become a fixture on the American political scene. At times they serve the candidates' needs, the consultants' needs, and the media's needs even if they offer the public and political parties very little. No illusion is harbored that an attempt to disband them would not be accompanied by a tremendous hue and cry both from the few who might profit from them and those who never watch at all. We propose no such ban.

What we do propose is an assault on all the efforts to institutionalize debates. Debates are just one of many forms of political communication, no better or worse than commercials, speeches, addresses, press conferences, or campaign pamphlets. Because we see few inherent virtues or advantages in debates, we see no compelling reason to require them. If candidates want to debate, then debates should be held, but no candidate should be forced to debate. Mandatory debates would monopolize the candidate's time and attention, and would dominate electoral discourse by forcing out diverse information that emanates from different sources through different channels. By limiting other forms of information flow and candidate contact, legislated debates artificially constrict the dynamics of the electoral marketplace. In an exalted effort to enhance democracy, institutionalized debates indeed might diminish democracy. It is our view that debates should be left alone.

CHAPTER EIGHT

Should the
Electoral College be Abolished?

*The existence of the Electoral College, a constitutional insti-
tution constructed by the founding fathers over two hundred years
ago, is perhaps the oldest controversy facing the presidential selection process. The issue was fiercely debated at the constitutional
convention and debate continues to this day.*

*Lawrence D. Longley argues that the Electoral College
should be abolished primarily because the institution is inherently undemocratic. Longley clearly outlines the flaws of the Electoral College, which include the faithless elector, the winner-take-
all system, the "constant two" electoral votes, the contingency
election procedure, and the uncertainty of the winner winning.
Longley firmly believes that the legitimacy of the American presidency is deeply threatened by the maintenance of the Electoral
College.*

*Denny Pilant views the Electoral College as an imperfect, yet
essential, mechanism for presidential selection. Pilant systematically refutes several of the arguments raised by critics of the Electoral College and argues that the Electoral College as it has
functioned over the past two hundred years has maintained the
principle of federalism and has provided an important element of
stability to the presidential selection process and American democracy. Pilant believes the record of achievement must be
weighed against potential flaws; to abolish the Electoral College
could prove detrimental to the larger political system.*

*Both Pilant and Longley provide the reader with substantive
discussions regarding the formation of the Electoral College and
the intent of the framers.*

Part 1

YES—
The Electoral College Should be Abolished

Lawrence D. Longley

The American Electoral College is a curious political institution. Obscure and even unknown to the ordinary U.S. citizen, it nevertheless serves as a crucial mechanism for transforming popular votes cast for president into electoral votes that actually elect the president. If the Electoral College operated only as a neutral and sure means for counting and aggregating votes, it would be the subject of little controversy. The Electoral College, however, is neither certain in its operations nor neutral in its effects. It may fail to produce a winner, in which case an extraordinarily awkward contingency procedure comes into play. Even when it operates relatively smoothly, it does not just tabulate popular votes in the form of electoral votes. Rather, it is an institution that works with noteworthy inequality—it favors some interests and hurts other. In short, the Electoral College is a flawed means of determining the presidency. Its workings at best are neither sure nor smooth, and at worse contain the potential for constitutional crisis. Yet it continues to exist as the constitutional mechanism for electing the people's president.

HOW IT CAME TO BE

The founding fathers wrote the Electoral College system into the U.S. Constitution at the constitutional convention in 1787 not because they saw it as a particularly desirable means of electing the president, but rather because they viewed it as an acceptable compromise; it was the second choice of many delegates, though the first choice of few. The Philadelphia delegates had been torn and divided, but had finally reached painful agreements on the monumental issues of national-state powers, presidential-congressional relationships, and most of all the issue of equal state representation versus representation based on population for the new national legislature. Having weathered these storms, the founding fathers were determined not to let the constitutional convention split anew over the means of presidential election. Some delegates, however, favored election of the president by Congress; others strongly favored a direct popular election by the people. Even more crucially, each proposal had adamant opponents; adoption of either might mean a breakdown of the emerging convention consensus on the draft Constitution. These concerns resulted in a compromise plan providing for an intermediate electoral body to be called an Electoral College.

Under this plan, each state legislature would choose a method to select "electors" equal in number to the total of the state's congressional representatives and senators. The electors would meet in their states on a day chosen by Congress to cast ballots for the presidential candidate of their choice; they would then transmit the record of the vote to the president of the United States Senate, who would tabulate the votes for all the states. In the event of a tie, or the failure of any candidate to gain a majority of the electoral votes, the House of Representatives would immediately make the choice, with each state delegation having a single vote. Central to this complex arrangement was the idea that the Electoral College, made up of prominent individuals from each state, would act independently and with deliberation in electing the president. Alternatively, should no majority be forthcoming in the Electoral College, the determination of the president would devolve upon the House.

This Electoral College arrangement, awkward as it might appear, had several apparent virtues: it was widely acceptable, it seemed unlikely to give rise to any immediate problem (it was clear to all that George Washington was going to be president, whatever the electoral system), and it appeared—incorrectly, it turned out—to incorporate a certain balance between state and popular interest. Most of all, this compromise plan got the constitutional convention over yet another hurdle in its immensely difficult process of making a constitution. The result, however, was the creation of a complex and unwieldy multistage mechanism for electing the president. It has been alleged that a camel resulted from the deliberations of a committee; so the Electoral College can be viewed as born out of immediate political necessity at the constitutional convention. As one noted commentator on this period, John Roche, has put it:

> The electoral college was neither an exercise in applied Platonism nor an experiment in indirect government based on elitist distrust of the masses. It was merely a jerry-rigged improvisation which has subsequently been endowed with a high theoretical content. . . . The vital aspect of the electoral college was that it got the Convention over the hurdle and protected everybody's interests. The future was left to cope with the problem of what to do with this . . . mechanism.

To the extent that the founding fathers attempted to anticipate how the Electoral College would work, they were wrong. They had assumed that the electors chosen would, in effect, *nominate* a number of prominent individuals, with no one person—because of diverse state and regional interests—usually receiving the specified absolute *majority* of electoral votes. At times a George Washington might be the unanimous Electoral College choice, but as George Mason of Virginia argued in Philadelphia, nineteen times out of twenty, the final choice of president among the three top contenders would be made not by the Electoral College itself, but by the House of Representatives voting by states, with one vote per state.

Inherent in this system, then, was a mechanism for electing the people's president that has not, in fact, operated as the founders assumed. What was not foreseen was the rise of national political parties able to aggregate and focus national support on two, or occasionally three, candidates. Only in 1800 and 1824 did no contender receive an electoral vote majority. The House contingency system as the usual means of presidential election has fallen into disuse; rather the president has come to be chosen by the electors meeting in state-by-state gatherings. Moreover, the electors themselves are now selected by the voters in a popular election on the basis of which major candidate they are expected to support. In effect, popular election of the president has replaced a system originally based on presidential selection by independent electors. The structure of the original process remains, however, with potentially chaotic consequences, should necessity force its utilization.

Another aspect of the system has also failed to work as its creators had intended. Under the assumption of the founding fathers, the Electoral College—reflecting roughly the varying population sizes of the states—would favor the large states at the expense of the small states (or, more accurately, population rather than equally weighed individual states). When the House contingency procedure went into effect—as it usually would—the voting would be one vote per state delegation, thus representing individual states regardless of population. This system, then, was a compromise between the principles of *population* and *state interest*—but a balance that rested on the assumption that the House contingency election procedure would normally be used. Since 1824, however, this has not occurred, and the original balance of interests foreseen by the founders has been destroyed in favor of a representation of population—albeit, at best, a distorted representation.

The historical facts, then, are that the original Electoral College system has not, for over one hundred sixty years, worked at all as assumed by its creators. It was replaced as a nominating mechanism by national political parties, and it has not provided a balance between state interests and population interest. In addition, the Electoral College has had a number of crucial changes introduced into its operations since its conception. Among these are the Twelfth Amendment to the Constitution, ratified in 1804, which sought to ensure that the Electoral College would elect a president and vice-president of the same party; the development of universal popular election of electors early in the nineteenth century; the emergence of electors pledged to particular parties or candidates; the occurrence, albeit rare, of the curious phenomenon of "faithless electors" who break their pledge or violate expectations by their vote for president; and the emergence of a winner-take-all system for determining each state's bloc of electoral votes. Together, these changes constitute major modifications of the system contemplated and created by the Philadelphia delegates. From an assembly of independently thinking statesmen usually serving to nominate three top contenders for a final decision by the House of Representatives, there has rather developed an Electoral College made up of unknown individuals whose only virtue is an automatic voting for their party's nominee, and an Electoral College whose only function is to confirm a popular electoral verdict handed down six weeks earlier.

FLAWS OF THE CONTEMPORARY ELECTORAL COLLEGE

The shortcomings of the contemporary electoral college are many, but five major flaws stand out. These are the faithless elector, the winner-take-all system, the "constant two" electoral votes, the contingency election procedure, and the uncertainty of the winner winning.

The Faithless Elector

The first of these flaws or problems of the contemporary Electoral College arises out of the fact that today it is not the assembly of wise and learned elders as assumed by its creators, but is rather little more than a state by state collection of political hacks and fat cats usually selected because of their past loyalty and support for the party. Neither in the quality of the electors nor in law is there any assurance that the electors will vote as expected by those who voted for them. State laws requiring electors to vote as they have pledged are in practice unenforceable and almost certainly unconstitutional. The language of the Constitution directs that "the electors shall vote"—which suggests that they must have discretion as to how they cast their votes. As a result, personal pledges—along with party and candidate loyalty—can be seen as the only basis of elector voting consistent with the will of a state's electorate.

The problem of the "faithless elector" is neither theoretical nor unimportant. One Republican elector, Doctor Lloyd W. Bailey of North Carolina, decided to vote for George Wallace after the 1968 election rather than for his pledged candidate, Richard Nixon, after deciding that Nixon was a communist. Another Republican elector, Roger MacBride of Virginia, likewise deserted Nixon in 1972 to vote instead for Libertarian Party candidate John Hospers. In the 1976 election, once again there was a faithless elector—and curiously enough, once again a deviant Republican elector. Elector Mike Padden, from the state of Washington, decided, six weeks after the November election, that he preferred not to support Republican nominee Gerald Ford, because he had not been forthright enough in denouncing abortion. Instead Padden cast his electoral vote in that year for Ronald Reagan, four years before Reagan won the Republican nomination and was elected president. Another variant electoral vote was cast in 1988 by a West Virginia Democratic elector who cast his presidential vote not for nominee Michael Dukakis but for Democratic vice-presidential nominee Lloyd Bentsen as a protest against the Electoral College system. Other defections from voter expectations also occurred in 1948, 1956, and 1960, or in other words, in seven of the eleven most recent U.S. presidential elections. Even more important is that the likelihood of such deviations occurring on a multiple basis would be greatly heightened should an electoral vote majority rest on only one or two votes, a real possibility in any close presidential election.

In fact, when one looks at the election return for the most recent close U.S. election, 1976, one can observe that if about 5,560 votes had switched from Jimmy Carter to Ford in Ohio, Carter would have lost that state and thus had 272 electoral votes, only two more than the absolute minimum needed of 270. In that case, two or three Democratic individual electors seeking personal recognition or attention to a pet cause could withhold—or threaten to withhold—their electoral votes from Carter, and thus make the election outcome very uncertain.

Republican vice-presidential nominee Robert Dole provided evidence of the possibilities inherent in such a close electoral vote election as 1976. Testifying before the Senate Judiciary Committee on January 27, 1977, in *favor* of abolishing the Electoral College, Senator Dole remarked that in the course of the 1976 election night election count:

> We were looking around on the theory that maybe Ohio might turn around because they had an automatic recount. We were shopping—not shopping, excuse me. Looking around for electors. Some took a look at Missouri, some were looking at Louisiana, some in Mississippi, because their laws are a little bit different. And we might have picked up one or two in Louisiana. There were allegations of fraud maybe in Mis-

sissippi, and something else in Missouri. We [would] need to pick up three or four after Ohio. So that may happen in any event. But it just seems to me that the temptation is there for that elector in a very tight race to really negotiate quite a bunch.

The Winner-Take-All System

The second problem of the contemporary Electoral College system lies in the almost universal state statutory provisions (the sole exception being the state of Maine) giving *all* of a state's electoral votes to the winner of a state's popular vote plurality (not even a majority). This extraconstitutional practice, gradually adopted by all states during the nineteenth century as a means of enhancing state power, can lead to bizarre results, such as in Arkansas in 1968, where Hubert Humphrey and Richard Nixon together divided slightly over 61 percent of the popular vote, while George Wallace, with less than 39 percent popular support, received 100 percent of the state's electoral votes. Even more significant, however, is the fact that the winner-take-all determination of slates of state electors tends to magnify tremendously the relative voting power of residents of the largest states. Each of their voters may, by their vote, decide not just one vote, but how a bloc of 36 or 47 electoral votes are cast—if electors are faithful.

As a result, the Electoral College has a major impact on candidate strategy—as shown by the concern of Jimmy Carter and Gerald Ford strategists, in the final weeks of the very close and uncertain 1976 campaign, with the nine big electoral vote states that together had 245 of the 270 electoral votes necessary to win. The vote in seven of these nine megastates proved to be exceedingly close, with both candidates receiving at least a 48 percent share. Similarly, presidential candidates George Bush and Michael Dukakis focused their 1988 campaigns on the largest electoral vote states, which were likewise seen as determinant of the presidential contest's outcome.

The Electoral College does not treat voters alike—a thousand voters in Scranton, Pennsylvania, are far more important strategically than a similar number of voters in Wilmington, Delaware. This inequity also places a premium on the support of key political leaders in large electoral vote states—as could be observed in the 1976 election in the candidates' desperate wooing of Mayors

Rizzo of Philadelphia and Daley of Chicago. These political leaders were seen as likely to play a major role in determining the electoral outcome in the large states of Pennsylvania and Illinois, and thus the winner of a large bloc of electoral votes. The Electoral College treats political leaders as well as voters unequally—those in large marginal states are vigorously courted.

The Electoral College also encourages fraud—or at least fear and rumor of fraud. In 1976 New York, which by itself had more than enough electoral votes to determine the winner of the presidential contest, went to Carter by 290,000 popular votes. Claims of voting irregularities and calls for recount were made on election night, but were later withdrawn because of Carter's clear national popular vote win. *If* fraud were present in New York, only 290,000 votes determined the 1976 presidential election. Under a national direct election plan, at least 1.7 million votes would have had to have been irregular in the same election to have changed the outcome.

The Electoral College at times also provides third-party candidates the opportunity to exercise magnified political influence in the election of the president, when they can gather votes in large, closely balanced states. In 1976 third-party candidate Eugene McCarthy, with less than 1 percent of the popular vote, came close to tilting the election through his strength in close pivotal states. In four states (Iowa, Maine, Oklahoma, and Oregon) totaling 26 electoral votes, McCarthy's vote exceeded the margin by which Ford defeated Carter. In those states, McCarthy's candidacy *may* have swung those states to Ford. Even more significantly, had McCarthy been on the New York ballot (he had been ruled off at the last moment on technical grounds), it is likely Ford would have carried that state with its 41 electoral votes, and with it the election—despite Carter's overall national vote majority and lead of well over 1.5 million votes.

The "Constant Two" Electoral Votes

A third feature of the Electoral College system lies in the apportionment of electoral votes among the states. The constitutional formula is simple: one vote per state per Senator and Representative. Another distortion from equality appears here because of "the constant two" electoral votes, regardless of population, which correspond to each state's two Senators. Because of this, inhabitants of the smallest states are advantaged to the extent that they "control" three electoral votes (two for the state's two Senators and one for the Representative), while their small population might otherwise entitle them to but one or two votes. This is weighing by states, not by population—however, the importance of this feature is greatly outweighed by the previously mentioned winner-take-all system. Nevertheless, this feature of the Electoral College—as the preceding one—is yet another distorting factor in the election of the president. This structural feature of the Electoral College ensures that it can never be a neutral counting device and that it inherently contains a variety of biases dependent solely upon the state in which voters cast their ballots. The contemporary Electoral College is not just an archaic mechanism for counting the votes for president; it is also an institution that aggregates popular votes in an inherently imperfect manner.

The Contingency Election Procedure

The fourth feature of the contemporary Electoral College system is the most complex—and probably also the most dangerous for the stability of the political system. The contingency election procedure outlined in the Constitution provides that if no candidate receives an absolute majority of the electoral vote—in recent years, 270 electoral votes—the House of Representatives chooses the president from among the top three candidates. Two questions need to be asked: Is such an electoral college deadlock likely to occur in contemporary politics? And would the consequences be likely to be disastrous? A simple answer to both questions is yes.

In some illustrative examples, in 1960 a switch of less than 9,000 popular votes from John Kennedy to Richard Nixon in Illinois and Missouri would have prevented either candidate from receiving an Electoral College majority. Similarly, in 1968 a 53,000 vote shift in New Jersey, Missouri, and New Hampshire would have resulted in an Electoral College deadlock, with Nixon then receiving 269 votes—one short of a majority. Finally, in the 1976 election, if some 11,950 popular votes in Delaware and Ohio had shifted from Carter to Ford, Ford would have carried these two states. The result of the 1976 election would then have been *an exact tie* in electoral votes: 269 to 269. The presidency would have been decided *not* on election night, but through deals or switches at the Electoral College meetings the following December 13, or alternatively by means of later uncertainties of the House of Representatives.

What specifically might happen in the case of an apparent Electoral College nonmajority or deadlock? A first possibility, of course, would be that a faithless elector or two, pledged to one candidate, might switch at the time of the actual meeting of the Electoral College so as to create a majority for the other presidential candidate. Such an action might resolve the crisis, although it would be sad to think of the president's mandate as based on such a thin reed of legitimacy.

If, however, no deals or actions at the time of the mid-December meetings of the Electoral College were successful in forming a majority, then the action would shift to the House of Representatives, meeting at noon on January 6, only 14 days before the constitutionally scheduled inauguration day for the new president.

The House of Representatives contingency procedure, which would now be followed, is, as discussed earlier, an awkward relic of the compromises of the writing of the new Constitution. Serious problems of equity would exist, certainly, in following the constitutionally perscribed one-vote-per-state procedure. Beyond this problem of fairness lurks an even more serious problem: What if the House itself should deadlock and be unable to agree on a president?

In a two-candidate race, this would be unlikely to be a real problem; however, in a three-candidate contest, such as 1968 or 1980, there might well be enormous difficulties in getting a majority of states behind one candidate, as House members agonized over choosing between partisan labels and support for the candidate (such as George Wallace or John Anderson) who had carried their district. The result, in 1968 or in 1980, might well have been no immediate majority forthcoming of twenty-six states, and political uncertainty and chaos as the nation approached inauguration day uncertain as to who was to be president.

The Uncertainty of the Winner Winning

Under the present system, there is no assurance that the winner of the popular vote will win the presidential election. This problem is a fundamental one: Can an American president operate effectively if he or she has received fewer votes than the loser? I would suggest that the effect upon the legitimacy of a contemporary American presidency would be disastrous if a president were elected by an obscure Electoral College after losing in the popular vote.

An American "divided verdict" election *can* happen, and *has* in fact occurred two or three times in American history, the most recent indisputable case (the election of 1960 being undeterminable) being the election of 1888, when the 100,000 popular vote plurality of Grover Cleveland was turned into a losing 42 percent of the electoral vote. Was there a real possibility of such a divided verdict in the last close U.S. election, 1976? An analysis of the election results shows that if 9,245 votes had shifted to Ford in Ohio and Hawaii, *Ford* would have been elected president with 270 electoral votes, the absolute minimum, despite Carter's 51 percent of the popular vote and margin of 1.7 million votes.

One hesitates to contemplate the political and constitutional consequences had a nonelected president, such as Ford, been inaugurated for four more years despite having been rejected by a majority of the American voters in his only presidential election.

CONCLUSION

The American electoral college has disturbing potential as an institution potentially threatening the certainty of U.S. elections and the legitimacy of the people's president. But even beyond these considerations, the electoral college inherently—by its very nature—is a distorted counting device for turning popular votes into electoral votes. It can never be a faithful reflection of the popular will, and will always stand between the citizen and the president.

It is for these reasons that substantial efforts have been made in recent years to reform or abolish the Electoral College, especially following the close and potentially uncertain presidential elections of 1968 and 1976. These "hairbreadth elections" resulted in a constitutional amendment, which would do away with the Electoral College, overwhelmingly passed by the House of Representatives in 1969, only to be defeated in the U.S. Senate in 1970. Similar constitutional proposals were debated by the Senate once again during the period of 1977 to 1979, prior to failing in that chamber in July 1979 for want of the necessary two-thirds vote. Inertia, institutional conservatism, and the self-interest of Senators from states perceived as advantaged by the existing Electoral College, served to preserve the Electoral College during the debates of the 1970s, despite the concerted efforts of well-organized and persistent electoral reformers.

The politics of Electoral College reform are kindled by close U.S. presidential elections, which demonstrate to many the inadequacies of the Electoral College as a means of electing the people's president. Should the 1992 or subsequent U.S. election prove to be uncertain in outcome or unfairly determined by the special characteristics of the Electoral College, that institution will become again a major target of reformers' efforts. Until that time, the Electoral College will continue as an important aspect of American politics, shaping and in part determining the election of the U.S. president.

Part 2

NO—
The Electoral College Should Not be Abolished

Denny Pilant

After every close presidential election, there is a flurry of criticism directed at the supposedly "dangerous and archaic" Electoral College system of electing the president. Implied in these attacks on the Electoral College is the idea that our presidential selection method today is exactly like the one formulated in 1787 in the original Constitution. In reality this is not the case. Our Electoral College operates quite differently from how the founders envisaged it. It has been changed both by constitutional amendment and by custom and usage. Yet, while it has evolved along with other institutions of American government, it has continued to support the political goals of the founding fathers—even though in ways not anticipated by them.

Many of the criticisms of the Electoral College appear to be based on a misunderstanding of the basic political theory of the American constitutional system, so it is appropriate to begin a defense of the Electoral College with a review of the intention of the founders and the evolution of our presidential selection method.

INTENT OF THE FOUNDERS

How to select the president was one of the most vexing problems the founders faced at Philadelphia in that long, hot summer of 1787. The framers considered numerous ways of selecting the president, including election by the Congress and direct popular election. Congressional selection was rejected because it would have made the president dependent on Congress and thus would violate a basic operative principle of American government—the separation of powers.

The usual interpretation of why direct popular election was rejected hinges on an elitist assumption. Supposedly the framers were fearful of mob democracy and preferred to add a layer of electors as the election authority. There is some truth to this interpretation, but it is overdrawn. The founders did believe that the public was prone to act hastily out of passion and then would often be forced to repent at leisure. Therefore the founders encouraged, in a number of ways, the "filtering" or refining of public opinion in order to reduce incidents of precipitous political action.[1]

But the real reason why direct popular election of the president was rejected was because it violated another fundamental principle of American government—federalism. Our founding fathers were the first to invent a way of dispersing power that today is designated by the term federalism. Of all the institutions of American government, federalism has most often received the supreme compliment from other countries, that of imitation. By creating a *federal* system instead of a *national* one, the states remained the basic political units through a number of constitutional provisions. The states have exclusive and complete control over the selection of presidential electors and national officeholders are forbidden to be electors. Small states also benefited from certain concessions made to them in preference to the large states. Each state was given a minimum of three electoral votes, a majority of states was required to elect the president rather than a plurality of votes, and the president was to be selected by states in the eventuality of a contingent election in the House. In the last analysis, it was not distrust of popular democracy as such that defeated direct election of the president, but rather a genuine commitment to the principle of federalism.

With respect to the election of a president and a vice-president, the founders' solution to the problem of quality in the second office was in every way remarkable. Instead of voting for a president and vice-president, electors would vote for two men as president and force the leading loser to be vice-president. It was a perfect paper plan to get vice-presidents of presidential caliber, but the idea was doomed almost from the beginning due to a development totally unanticipated by the founding fathers—the rise of the modern political party.

Whereas the framers assumed that electors would vote for two men *as* president—not as president and vice-president—the advent of political parties brought with it preferences between the candidates the party specifically wanted for president and for vice-president. With the passage of the Twelfth Amendment in 1804, promulgated as a result of the politics inherent in the election of 1800, electors were required to vote separately for the president and vice-president. Now both the winning president and the winning vice-president had to receive a *majority* of the electoral vote. If no vice-presidential candidate had a majority, then the election would go to the Senate, which would choose from among the *top* two candidates.

The Electoral College, as it has evolved over the years, has given us a president every single presidential election, a president, moreover, who has virtually always been accepted as legitimate. We have had a stable executive who has proved to be adequate to the exegencies of the union. So why do critics want to abolish an institution that has stood the test of time, that has evolved to meet new circumstances, and that continues to meet the goals of the framers of the constitution, albeit by different means than they anticipated? Those in favor of abolishing or reforming the Electoral College normally cite several flaws, which, it is argued, potentially undermine the democratic spirit of the presidential selection process and ultimately the quality of American democracy. Such criticisms, however, tend to exaggerate the alleged dangers of the Electoral College and, for the most part, arouse unnecessary fear. Many criticisms, moreover, are based on an implicit majoritarian theory, which is explicitly rejected by American constitutionalism. The following discussion systematically evaluates the common criticisms of the Electoral College and at the same time should underscore the virtues of this institution as they relate to the presidential selection process and the American political system.

THE RUNNER-UP PRESIDENT POSSIBILITY

The major criticism of the Electoral College is that it is mathematically possible for the winner of the electoral vote to have fewer popular votes than the opponent, creating a "runner-up" president. The reason this is possible is due to the working of the general ticket system, which awards all a state's electoral vote to whomever wins a popular vote plurality. If a candidate wins a few states by a landslide and then loses by a small margin in others, it is possible the winner could have more popular votes than the opponent, and yet still lose the election in the Electoral College—making the opponent a runner-up president.

How often has this happened? The record is really an optimistic one and shows that there is little chance that a runner-up president will be elected. Reformers generally point to three instances of possible "runner-up" presidents. The first instance occurred in the election of 1824. Not all states had popular election of electors at this time (about 1/4 of the states chose electors by the legislature). There were four major candidates for electoral votes (Andrew Jackson, William H. Crawford, John Quincy Adams, and Henry Clay). The number of candidates made it certain that the election would go into the House unless some of the candidates would combine forces beforehand. That proved impossible when Clay refused to join the Crawford group. The election was thrown into the House and due to political maneuvering Clay managed to get John Quincy Adams elected to the presidency over Jackson. Clay was then appointed Secretary of State as a reward for his efforts. However, the popular vote mandate was unclear in this election, so Adams was not, strictly speaking, a runner-up president.[2]

Professor Best points out that the election of 1824 illustrates the necessity for a structured nomination process that can winnow down the number of candidates before the final selection takes place. In 1824 the nominating process was not well developed.[3]

In 1876 the Hayes-Tilden election controversy presents us with one of the most tangled affairs in the history of presidential elections. Rutherford B. Hayes, a Republican, had approximately 250,000 fewer popular votes than Samuel J. Tilden, the Democrat. But Tilden lost by one electoral vote. There was a dispute over the electoral votes in Oregon, South Carolina, Florida, and Louisiana. There was widespread fraud and corruption in the vote-counting on both sides. A Presidential commission composed of five Senators, five Representatives, and five Supreme Court Justices was appointed (without constitutional prescription), to settle the dispute.

There were eight Republicans and seven Democrats on the commission, and they voted 8–7, by a straight party vote, to award the disputed votes to Hayes.[4] Not surprisingly, the Democrats found the result annoying. So to assuage their wounds, the Republicans promised them that they would withdraw federal troops from the south and end Reconstruction in return for the Democrats' acceptance of Hayes as president. So the famous "dirty bargain" was struck. Again, Hayes is not really a runner-up president but one who was put in by political corruption. The election results cannot be attributed to defects in the Electoral College.

In 1888 a true runner-up president was selected by the Electoral College. Grover Cleveland had approximately 100,000 more popular votes, but Benjamin Harrison had a majority of electoral votes and became a runner-up president. However, what Cleveland had done was to run up very large electoral majorities in a few southern states while failing to get pluralities in the others. The Electoral College forces candidates to broaden their appeal in order to get elected. Huge regional majorities by themselves are insufficient for successful election. This is, overall, a net good for our system rather than a liability, because it forces presidential candidates to widen their appeal beyond narrow sectional interests.[5]

The record of the Electoral College, with regard to its actual tendency to produce a runner-up presidency, shows that we have more cause for content than alarm. Only one true runner-up president in the entire history of the Electoral College is a very good record. It shows that the possibilities of a runner-up president are more theoretical than real.

The Shift-in-Votes Critique

Reformers, recognizing that the historical case for change is quite shaky, in many cases rely on a shift-in-votes argument to attack the Electoral College. Opponents of the Electoral College have claimed that a shift of less than 1 percent of the national vote in approximately fifteen elections would have resulted in a runner-up president. The problem with the shift-in-votes critique is that it is based on the manipulation of numerical data without any serious consideration being given to the voters themselves. Election laws, policy positions, and patterns of party strength are ignored by the mathematical manipulators even though such factors are usually decisive in determining election outcomes. Furthermore, if a candidate takes a stand that results in a favorable shift of votes in one state, there is no guarantee that it will also result in a favorable shift elsewhere.[6] In fact, it might have the opposite result. Never has so much been made of so speculative an analysis by the reformers! Not once in this century has a runner-up president been selected.

The Disfranchisement and Inequality of Voting Power Arguments

Because of the general ticket system (winner take all) in the states, some critics maintain that a voter's vote cast for a losing candidate is lost (wasted) and given over to the candidate voted against. (This is the same argument sometimes directed against all single-member district plurality vote systems.) Reformers argue that states should reflect their internal vote division for the separate candidates instead of handing the electoral vote over in a bloc. The reformers are really calling for a system of proportional representation, which in order to be consistent, should be applied to congressional as well as presidential elections. Most reformers are afraid to call for proportional representation for Congress because of the splintering effect it typically has on the political party system. As long as a voter's vote is correctly recorded for the chosen candidate, then no voter's vote can be said to be "wasted" and no one is disfranchised.

Some critics of the Electoral College claim that the system creates great disparities in voting power—that a voter in California, for example, has more than twice the voting power of a voter in Arkansas.[7] Again, this is a criticism of the general ticket system with its winner-take-all rule. This argument assumes that a particular pattern of voting is equally likely to occur in each state. But different states have different voting patterns. Obviously, a large state with a 50–50 split between the parties would attract more attention from the national parties than one that shows a strong preference toward one of the major parties. It is the big states with competitive party systems that benefit under the current system, not just the large states per se.[8] Also one must ask whether or not safe states are totally bereft of political influence under the current system. Both of the major parties find their chances of winning the presidency to be considerably enhanced if they have a safe base to count on. The Democrats used to have such a base in the south and in recent years the Republicans have maintained a safe margin in the mountain states. Because of this, voters in safe states cannot be said to be ignored by the party winners who enjoy their support.

While political scientists disagree over precisely what maintains a two-party system, pointing to a variety of institutional, social, and economic causes, most do agree that the institution of the general ticket system with its winner-take-all feature plays a major role in freezing out minor parties and preserving our two-party system.[9] By awarding all electoral vote to the plurality vote winner, coalition-making and compromise must occur before the election. This gives voters an opportunity to vote on the results of the compromise. In contrast, countries like Israel, with proportional representation as the basis for election to the Parliament, force political coalitions to form in the Parliament itself—*after* the election when the voters no longer have a direct say.

Political Effects of the Electoral College System

Critics of the Electoral College system also maintain that the general ticket system puts a premium on strategically placed interest groups in the big, highly competitive pivotal states, so that ethnic minorities, urban interests, trade unions, and the like, have more influence than their number would otherwise give them. If a state's popular vote is split nearly 50–50 between the two major parties, then a cohesive interest group or ethnic minority, by casting its votes as a bloc, could deliver the election to a particular candidate, enabling that person to win all of the state's electoral vote.

If there are any iron laws in political science, one would have to be that there is no such thing as a politically neutral election scheme. Electoral arrangements are not simple mechanical devices enabling persons to be selected for office. They are complex institutions that have profound consequences for the overall political system, because they all incorporate biases of one kind of another. The Electoral College does create some distortion, but it is distortion that runs in the right direction. The Electoral College forces presidential candidates to pay more attention to minorities and metropolitan interests than would otherwise be the case (this is not necessarily true in the case of landslide elections).[10] However, this bias serves to counteract a bias in favor of rural, more homogeneous interests that predominate in the U.S. Senate and House of Representatives. If a bias-free election scheme is impossible to achieve, then why not have an arrangement that balances out different biases? Although not part of the original checks and balances envisaged by the framers, the dominance of the urban and industrial states, with competitive parties, in the Electoral College scheme represents a weighted federal principle.[11]

Faithless Elector

Over the years there have been a handful of presidential electors who have decided to vote for someone other than the popular vote-winner in the state. It is unclear whether they can be constitutionally obligated to cast their vote as instructed by voters or party. (See, e.g., *Ray* v. *Blair*, 343 U.S. 214, 1952.) If they are constitutionally free agents, then they can potentially frustrate the popular will in the state. On the other hand, if their votes can be mandated by state law or by political party rules, then they are rubber stamps with nothing to do. To put it another way, they are either useless or dangerous. This has led some reformers to call for an "automatic" plan, which would do away with the physical person of the elector and require instead that electoral votes be certified by designated election authorities.

This is technically a flawless plan. But considered collectively, the number of faithless electors is statistically insignificant: they constitute only a half-dozen or so out of over 18,000 persons having served as electors.[12] It would seem that this is not the pressing problem reformers claim it is. Therefore, there appears to be little real need to have a constitutional amendment to correct an extremely rare occurrence. None of the faithless electors have had the slightest effect on election outcomes.

Voter Turnout and Apathy

Critics of the Electoral College system have claimed that the general ticket system discourages voters who are not members of the majority party from voting, because second and third parties, regardless of how many popular votes they get, will receive no electoral votes under a winner-take-all system. Proponents of a direct popular vote claim that their scheme would encourage voter turnout because every vote would be counted. But what the proponents of a direct popular vote forget is that without the Electoral

College, the rules of the political game have changed. No longer will the 50 percent line (with two major parties) be critical in winning elections. Instead, presidential candidates will have to look for that margin of votes that will give them an edge over their opponent. This edge, under a direct popular vote, would come from homogenous one-party states rather than from the urban industrialized states as under the present scheme. Most of the latter are highly competitive two-party states that would not yield significant vote margins to either candidate. Therefore presidential candidates, in the absence of an Electoral College, would concentrate their attention on the one-party homogenous states where they could gain an advantage over their opponent.[13] Big rewards would go to the party leaders in states that could deliver winning blocs of votes. So party leaders in one-party states would have every incentive to maintain the status quo.

The Contingency Election

According to Article II, Section 1 of the Constitution, as amended by the Twelfth Amendment, if no presidential candidate gets a *majority* vote in the Electoral College, then a contingency election is held in the House with each state casting one vote for one of the three highest vote getters. A majority of the states is necessary to select the winner. If no vice-presidential candidate gets a majority, the Senate shall choose from among the top two candidates. Critics are quick to point out that the one-state, one-vote rule is unfair to the large states. There is no vote if a state's delegation is tied and it is possible that a president and vice-president of different parties could be selected. Reformers say that all these problems could be solved with a relatively minor change. Simply have the decision made by a joint session of Congress with each member having one vote. This would solve all the problems mentioned above, plus it would encourage coalition-making in the selection process. However, if the majority party in Congress is not the party of the president, it could cause real problems, for it is unlikely that the majority party in Congress would vote against its own candidate—regardless of the popular vote.[14]

When we look at the record, we do not have much cause for alarm. Ever since the Twelfth Amendment was adopted and the general ticket system became predominant in 1832, the contingency election has become a very remote possibility. It is there if it is ever needed, but it has not been necessary in over 165 years. It is difficult to argue that this is a matter of pressing concern.

What is a matter of concern is the proposal by proponents of direct popular election of the president that a 40 percent plurality be required for election with a runoff between the top two candidates if no one gets the 40 percent. By specifying the 40 percent figure, proponents are tacitly recognizing that direct election will cause a splintering of the party system, making automatic majorities impossible. If runoff elections are required, it might take months to certify the winner in a close election. Is this what the reformers really want?[15]

American Constitutional Theory and the Electoral College

Critics of the Electoral College system, particularly proponents of a direct popular election, seem to assume that the only "democratic" way to elect the president is via a majoritarian national plebiscite. This suggestion ignores the entire political theory of the American Constitution. The founding fathers were not establishing a national democracy but a federal democratic republic.[16] As inheritors of the liberal ideas of men like John Locke, the framers were primarily interested in preserving liberty against potential tyranny. One possible source of tyranny was the tyranny of the majority. A significant part of our Constitution must be understood as an attempt to protect minority rights against the potential tyranny of a plebiscitary democracy.

In the history of political thought, the Constitution of 1787 represents a "mixed" regime in which democratic (U.S. House), aristocratic (U.S. Senate and U.S. Courts), and monarchical (presidency) elements are carefully blended. The framers hoped the Constitution they were writing would embody the best features of these different forms of government, while avoiding their worst excesses. Hence the "democratic" elements in our Constitution (e.g., the popular vote) are tempered by having staggered elections, fixed terms of office, federalism, judicial review, and various checks and balances. We allocate two senators to each state on the basis of geography, not population. We appoint federal judges for life. In fact the existence of a written constitution and a Bill of Rights that places certain liberties beyond the reach of popular majorities illustrate a deliberate rejection of majoritarian democratic ideas. The framers wanted to make sure that the majority will was based on the *reasoned deliberation* of the many rather than on the in-flamed passions of an unreflective mob.

The way the Electoral College actually operates today, presidents are elected by popular vote—but that vote is aggregated by states instead of being aggregated nationally. In other words, the value of federalism is combined with the value of a popular vote. There is nothing particularly undemocratic or undesirable about such a combination. It has served us well for about two centuries.

If we examine the standards we set forth for evaluating the method of electing the president, we see that the Electoral College does in fact contribute to maintaining a two-party system; it keeps the states as the basic political units, thereby supporting the value of federalism. It has produced a president every presidential election with very little actual tendency to elect runner-up presidents or require a contingency or runoff election. The Electoral College contributes to political checks and balances by forcing the president to pay more attention to urban and ethnic interests in competitive industrial states, thus counterbalancing the rural interests that tend to predominate in Congress.

In short, the record of achievement of the Electoral College turns out to be impressive indeed. It is a tried and true system with which we have had much practical experience. It is to be preferred over untested theoretical schemes that could turn out to have devastating effects on our political system. The founding fathers did good work. It is incumbent on our generation that we not inadvertantly destroy both their constitutional accomplishments and the historical development of them by embracing dubious "reforms."

CHAPTER NINE

Is On-Site Voter Registration Desirable?

This chapter examines the debatable proposition to allow eligible voters the opportunity to register as a voter at the polling place on the day of the presidential election. Such a proposal reflects the growing concern among political scientists as well as political practitioners with the low level of voter turnout in American elections.

Peverill Squire argues in favor of on-site voter registration. In Squire's view the mechanical procedure of voter registration currently serves as the major impediment to voter participation in elections and as such should be simplified and standardized to on-site registration across state lines. Squire presents comparative state data to demonstrate that on-site registration facilitates turnout in elections. He also identifies the United States as the only country in which the full burden of voter registration is placed on the individual rather than the government, the end result being an abysmally low level of voter turnout in elections.

David B. Hill argues against on-site voter registration. According to Hill, on-site registration, if implemented in the form of a national policy, would deeply infringe upon the federal tradition of allowing states the opportunity to conduct and manage their own electoral process. At the same time, the integrity of elections would be threatened, due to the increased opportunity for corruption, and the cost of conducting elections in which on-site registration is allowed would impose a heavy financial burden on state governments. Additional points raised by Hill challenge the premise that on-site registration would substantially increase turnout and alter election outcomes. Hill also questions the potential ramifications of on-site voter registration as it relates to the quality of the American polity. The on-site proposal in Hill's view is irresponsible, extreme, and definitely a risk to the republic.

Part 1

YES—
On-Site Voter Registration is Desirable

Peverill Squire

Compared to citizens in other Western de.nocracies, Americans vote at notoriously low rates. Less than 51 percent of the voting age population cast a ballot in the 1988 presidential campaign, a figure only marginally lower than in other recent elections. Voters elsewhere turn out in much larger numbers; in many countries turnouts of 80 to 90 percent are common. With the possible exception of the Swiss, Americans would appear to be the democratic world's least diligent voters.

This phenomenon is distressing because citizens and scholars alike think that voting is important. Having about half of the potential voters in a presidential election actually participating means that the winner is likely to gain office with only a little more the one-quarter of the adult population having voted in his or her favor. Certainly, in this situation doubts can be raised about the legitimacy of those elected to lead. Indeed, the legitimacy of the entire political system can be challenged.

In this chapter I will investigate why Americans are such poor voters. I will assess different explanations and argue that the registration system employed in this country inhibits turnout. This line of argument suggests several possible solutions to the problem of low turnout, the most important of which is the institution of election-day voter registration.

EXPLANATIONS FOR LOW TURNOUT

Why do Americans vote at such embarrassingly low rates? Several explanations can be offered. The most appealing, at least initially, is that Americans do not turn out on election day because they are unhappy with the political system or those holding power in it.[1]

This alienation argument became fashionable in the aftermath of the Vietnam war and the Watergate affair, when public opinion surveys revealed a significant drop in support for American political institutions.[2] The main idea behind this notion is that disgust with the political system manifests itself by withdrawal from the process. Alienated Americans choose not to vote.

Although this explanation has some attraction, it is seriously flawed. Most significantly, no evidence has been presented to show that alienated citizens are less likely to vote than those who are more positive about the system. Indeed, alienated individuals vote at the same rate as others.[3] In the 1980 election, for example, individuals who thought the government was run by a few big interests voted at the same rate as those who said it was run for the benefit of all. Individuals who believed the federal government was doing a poor job actually voted at a *higher* rate than those who said it was doing a good job.[4] Overall, attitudes toward the government do not explain differences in turnout among Americans.

Alienation also fails to explain why Americans vote at such low rates compared to others. Examinations of public attitudes toward the political system in a number of countries reveal that Americans have more confidence in and are prouder of their government that citizens elsewhere.[5] Americans also are "more likely than citizens of any European nation to express interest in politics, to read political stories in their newspapers, and to discuss politics with friends."[6] Americans vote at lower rates than citizens elsewhere, but not because they are less interested in politics or because they lack confidence or pride in their political system.[7]

Another explanation for low turnout in the United States focuses on the party system. Essentially, proponents of this approach claim many Americans fail to cast a ballot because neither the Republicans nor the Democrats represent their interests.[8] In particular, it is argued that the lack of a true labor party lowers turnout among the lower economic classes. Rigorous examination of comparative voter turnout by G. Bingham Powell provides evidence to substantiate the claim that the party structure in this country decreases turnout.[9] Examining industrial democracies, Robert W. Jackman, however, concludes that multiparty systems actually depress turnout.

Although it is not clear whether particular party systems increase or decrease turnout, projecting American turnout based on other party configurations seems problematic. It is well established that the structure of electoral competition in the United States, with single-member districts and the Electoral College, dictates that a two-party system will thrive and any other would falter. Moreover, the American experience with third and fourth parties does not bode well for the notion that more parties, and therefore more choices, will bring more voters to the polls. In 1948, for example, the ballot appearance of Strom Thurmond and the Dixiecrats representing the political right, and Henry Wallace and the Progressives representing the political left, resulted in one of the *lowest* turnouts of the century. Likewise, the candidacies of George Wallace in 1968 and John Anderson in 1980 each brought a lower percentage of voters to the polls than in the preceding presidential election. Finally, given the existence of essentially the same two-party system in each of the fifty states, party structure cannot explain differences in turnout among the states.

If party system and voter attitudes toward government do not explain why Americans vote at low rates, what does? The most significant difference between the American voting system and those employed elsewhere is the registration process. Only in the United States is the full burden of registration placed on the individual citizen. Elsewhere, the government takes the initiative in placing individuals on a roster of eligible voters. That is, when a citizen reaches the age of majority or changes address, the government automatically enters him or her on the voter registration list. The individual is not required to take any action other than to cast a ballot on election day.

In the United States, the registration process works very differently. Control over registration procedures is decentralized; each state adopts its own rules, constrained only by a few national standards imposed by Supreme Court decisions. Except in North Dakota, where no registration is required, Americans must register before being allowed to vote. In most states registration must occur anywhere from at least five to fifty days in advance of the election. Moreover, unlike election day, which is well publicized and virtually impossible not to be aware of, registration deadlines are shrouded in mystery. Learning where and when to register is not easy; in most places such information is not well advertised. Keep in mind that, although Americans evidence greater interest in politics than citizens in other democracies, it is far from central to their lives. A significant number of Americans do not have even the most minimal information about registration requirements. For example, one survey of North Dakota residents following the 1972 election found that a third of those who did not vote said that failure to register was the cause.[10]

The difficulty of registering should not be underestimated. Although a number of states have tried to make it easier, through the use of deputy registrars, post card registration, and other programs, in many places it is still a daunting task for those who are unfamiliar with overcoming bureaucratic obstacles. One study of nonvoters in the 1984 election found that half cited failure to register as the reason for not casting a ballot.[11] When asked why they had not registered, only 17 percent said because they were uninterested in politics. Almost 70 percent gave more mechanical reasons: recently moved and not reregistered (47 percent), work during registration hours (11 percent), do not know how to register (6 percent), have to go too far from home to register (3 percent). Accordingly, a low salience activity, like voter registration, is less likely to be undertaken when doing so is made difficult or burdensome.

Because Americans must take the initiative to register before they can vote, many who would likely cast a ballot are prevented from doing so because they have failed to get their name on the registration rolls. Much of the gap in voter turnout between the United States and the rest of the democratic world is accounted for by differences in registration systems.[12] Indeed, turnout among registered Americans is very high: 85 percent in the 1980 election, for example.[13] Even Americans who profess little interest in politics vote at about a 75 percent rate, if they can get registered.[14] Simply stated, where registration is easy, as it is in much of the world, voter turnout is high. Where registration is difficult, as in the United States, turnout is low. Getting Americans registered is the key to increasing turnout.

The effect of registration requirements on turnout can be seen in differences in participation levels among the states. Table 7 presents voter turnout rates in the 1988 presidential election by

state. The states are arranged by closing date. The closing date—
the last day before an election that voters can put their name on
the registered voter list—has been shown to be the most important
variable in explaining differences in turnout across states.[15]
Although other characteristics of a state's population influence
turnout rates, particularly mean age and education, as Table 7
demonstrates the closer the closing date is to the election, the
higher turnout tends to be.

In particular, North Dakota and the three states where voters
may register the day of the election have substantially higher turnout than other states.[16] These four states had a mean turnout of 63
percent, far better than the national average of 50.2 percent.

INCREASING TURNOUT

It seems intuitively reasonable that election-day registration
would increase turnout. As an election nears and publicity and excitement about it mount, citizens are more likely to become motivated to participate. Making registration and voting essentially a
one-step process removes the former as an inhibition to the latter.
The best estimate is that instituting national election-day registration would increase turnout by about 9 percent.[17]

Several objections can be made to election-day registration.
First, some people believe that registration is an important screening device. They think that people who overcome that hurdle demonstrate interest in politics. The basic notion is, as one Iowa state
representative recently remarked in opposing legislation to ease
registration, "I would rather have fewer people vote and have informed voters."[18] But the idea that bringing more people to the
polls would debase the electorate is not supported by the evidence.
It is wrong to think that all registered voters are interested in politics, and that those who are unregistered are apathetic. Comparisons of actual electorates and ones projected based on easier
registration laws demonstrate that there are few demographic or
attitudinal differences between those who did vote and those who
would have if they had been registered.[19]

A second complaint is that there is too much potential for
abuse and fraud with election-day registration. Certainly the states
with the most election-day registration experience—Maine, Minnesota, and Wisconsin—are among those considered to have

TABLE 7
Voter Turnout and Closing Date, 1988

Closing Date	State	Turnout Percent
None (No registration or election day)	Maine	62
	Minnesota	66
	North Dakota	62
	Wisconsin	62
1–10 days	Alabama	46
	Iowa	59
	New Hampshire	55
	Oklahoma	49
	Utah	60
11–20 days	Arkansas	47
	Idaho	58
	Kansas	54
	Nebraska	57
	South Dakota	62
	Vermont	59
21–30 days	Alaska	52
	California	50
	Colorado	55
	Connecticut	58
	Delaware	51
	Florida	45
	Georgia	39
	Hawaii	43
	Illinois	53
	Indiana	53
	Kentucky	48
	Louisiana	51
	Maryland	49
	Massachusetts	58
	Michigan	54
	Mississippi	51
	Missouri	55
	Montana	63
	Nevada	45
	New Jersey	52
	New Mexico	47
	New York	48
	North Carolina	43
	Ohio	55
	Oregon	59
	Pennsylvania	50
	Rhode Island	53

"clean" politics. Until 1986 Oregon had been considered among that group. But in the general election that year, Oregon voters passed a ballot proposition imposing a 21-day closing date. The move to do away with election-day registration was motivated by abuse of that process by the Bhagwan Rajneesh and his cult followers. A few years earlier, the Bhagwan had established a commune in a small, eastern Oregon community, and his followers soon outnumbered the town's longtime residents. The religious group took control of the town through the ballot box, and threatened to take command of the county. The Bhagwan's devotees exploited the state's election day registration laws by fusing street people from California, registering them to vote, and then sending them back to California after the election. Most of Oregon's voters rebelled against this cynical use of their electoral system.

Certainly, then, election-day registration can be abused—as can any registration system. It would seem reasonable to expect that technological advances in the area of computers will make more difficult the sorts of abuses most feared by election officials. In addition, the ability to register a voter quickly and to report that registration to a central authority eases a final objection to election-day registration: the administrative burden. Dealing with thousands of new registrations on election day is an imposing task in a world of pencils and papers, but a fairly easy one with computers.

Because registration is the key to increasing turnout, any steps that can be taken to make it easier should result in more people coming to the polls. For example, the largest group of chronic nonvoters is not the poor, minorities, or the young—although each of these groups contains many people. Instead, those who have recently moved—about 30 percent of the population over a two-year period—are the largest bloc of light voters, because they have not reregistered to vote at their new address. Proposals to link their reregistration to post office change-of-address-forms suggest a possible 9 percent increase in national turnout.[20] States are pursuing other innovative means of increasing registration, including using state bureaucrats to register those with whom they interact, and registering individuals when they apply for drivers licenses or file their state taxes.

It is clear that registering more people will increase voter turnout, and that election-day registration is the device most likely to maximize registrations. Does it matter if turnout is low?

Surveys suggest that bringing every eligible voter to the polls would not change the outcome of any recent presidential election.[21] Indeed, nonvoting is acceptable in our political system: as Austin Ranney (1983) suggests, it is not a social disease. But the decision not to vote ought to be made by an individual choosing not to go to the polls on election day, not forced on him or her by an earlier failure to surmount a relatively mundane bureaucratic barrier.

Part 2

NO—
On-Site Voter Registration is Not Desirable

David B. Hill

American democracy constantly adjusts to ever-changing tides of political circumstance and popular demand. The process of adjustment has been especially evident in granting of the franchise to citizens. Once the exclusive privilege of propertied white males, the right to cast a ballot in regular elections has become a universal right of every adult American.

The road to this end was neither easy nor quickly traversed. Decades upon decades were spent in the Congress and state legislatures and in the courts sorting through the arguments for and against allowing votes by previously disenfranchised groups, such as women, former black slaves, 18- to 20-year-olds, and so forth.

More subtle restrictions on voting, such as the poll tax, literacy tests, and other practices that were purposefully or unwittingly used to prevent less privileged classes of voters from participating in elections, have been swept away by the forces of change.

While there can be reasonable disagreements about the selflessness of the motives of various proponents of each "reform" in electoral laws, there can be little doubt that the granting of "rights" has been a central motivational factor in the actions of those who encourage change.

Persons who were previously denied any opportunity to vote were given a privilege that was declared a right of American citizens as early as in the Declaration of Independence.

Once most voters were granted the right to vote, however, some reformers did not want to stop. As in other areas, election reformers seem no longer satisfied to establish citizens' rights to voting or other privileges in society. Instead, liberals, intellectuals, and their beneficiary politicians are demanding something that might be referred to as equality of results, a step beyond equality of opportunity to exercise a right.

In the area of registration and voting, the result is that many reformers seem bent on protesting until every age-eligible American citizen is a registered voter, perhaps even if the eligible are not really interested in either registering or casting a ballot.

The reformers have not (typically) gone so far as to suggest that we legally *require* all Americans to vote, something that many have poked fun at socialist regimes for doing for decades, but rather that there be universal registration to vote. In short, most liberals and intellectuals today would like to see some means whereby the roughly one out of three age-eligible adults not registered be somehow added with dispatch to the rolls of eligible voters.

The reasons for asking America to adopt reforms that will bring about this result in voter registration are not always stated or explicit. Some reformers simply prefer to "assume" that voting is such an essential component of democratic government that no one should question motives of persons who are encouraging either registration or voting.

Nevertheless, one cannot help but suspect that the motives for universal registration are mainly political or ideological in nature.[1] Certainly if one examines any empirical evidence regarding the demographic characteristics of nonregistered adult citizens, one cannot help but suspect that these disenfranchised individuals might be inclined to support liberal and Democratic candidacies more than their opposites (even though academic studies do not necessarily support this conclusion[2]).

It is this likely ideological implication of universal registration that must certainly be at the core of motivations driving most reformers to call for reforms such as same-day registration that are likely to bring about universal voting.

The purpose of this essay is to critique some of the motivations and assumptions of persons supporting liberalized voter registration, such as same-day registration, and to point to a plethora of reasons why this is bad public policy, not only unnecessary but potentially disruptive of the democratic political process in this country.

Perhaps the most important accusation to be made by this essay is that reformers seriously confuse voters' *rights* with voters' *obligations*.

Any fair-minded evaluation of the progress made thus far in extending the franchise to new groups of Americans would conclude that the process led to the granting of voting rights to all citizens. Now that those rights have been granted, reformers have discovered to their sure dismay that not everyone wishes to take advantage of every right they posses as citizens. Civic duty, in some quarters, is passé.

Undoubtedly, election reformers are also perplexed that persons who have already availed themselves of the opportunity to register to vote are actually participating in elections in lower and lower numbers. Because of this broad-based decline in Americans' desire to participate in affecting the outcomes of elections, those who have been on the losing end of elections have struck out in a different direction.

Now they attempt to force acceptance of rights, even ones that are not zealously sought by their recipients. Thus, we see proposals for registering voters whenever they are given a driver's license, for example, irrespective of whether the individual really desires to be registered to vote or not.

While it is not within the purview of this essay, and not necessarily a proposal that has been placed on the table thus far, one cannot help but wonder whether reformers, once given the prize of universal voter registration, might press forward in their agenda with efforts to make actual participation in every election a mandated legal responsibility of every voter, punishable by some sanction similar to those in less democratic states.

VOTER REGISTRATION PROPOSALS

While the more narrow topic of this essay is same-day voter registration, it is useful to point out that same-day registration is only one of several techniques that have been proposed in order to encourage registration by the large unregistered adult population.

Some of the other techniques that have been proposed include tying voter registration to some other process, such as obtaining a driver's license or securing public utilities, easing registration by allowing individuals to register by mail or some other technique that does not require presentation of oneself to voter registration officials, and allowing the deputization of persons other than public officials to solicit voter registration away from governmental offices, in homes, the work place, and other places where the unregistered may congregate.[3]

And, of course, these reforms are also part and parcel of the general move not only to register these individuals to vote, but to encourage their participation, as well as to motivate large number of persons who are already registered but choose not to participate.

Proposed reforms designed to encourage nonvoters have included everything from changing the election day to a Saturday, to making election day a national holiday, to keeping polls open for perhaps forty eight consecutive hours rather than the twelve hours that most polling places are typically open.[4]

Same-day registration, or its closely related cousin—doing away with all voter registration requirements for age-eligible adults—is predicated on the assumption that many persons are interested in voting but somehow either forget or find it difficult to get around to registering to vote prior to elections. This contention is raised even in states that allow very liberal voter registration procedures, such as in the writer's home state of Texas, wherein voters are allowed to simply send a state-supplied postcard, readily available in almost every public office, bank, post office, or by request by telephone, wherein one provides a small amount of information and mails it to the voter registration officials of the county. One can thus be placed on the official register of voters without ever having to go to the trouble of formally registering at a government office or even leaving one's own home, for that matter.

A reasonable question is why so many reformers have focused on same-day registration as a proposed solution to the problem. Is it necessarily a better approach than some of the other means designed to ensure that convenience not be a barrier to registration?

It appears that there are two primary motivations for proponents' advocacy of same-day registration over other reforms designed to increase participation: (1) high statistical estimates of the likely efficacy of same-day registration on turnout;[5] and, (2) the likely partisan or political effect of same-day registration.

First, while fewer than a half-dozen states currently allow this practice (or have taken a similar action of doing away with the practice of voter registration— e.g., North Dakota), academics have utilized these outliers as an opportunity to develop mathematical models that predict the likely effects on turnout if all other states were to make similar changes in their registration laws.

These studies have sometimes been limited in that they do not have available comparable data on other, more narrowly adopted, reforms, such as postcard registration, or even other possible reforms that have never been proposed, such as providing some sort of financial or other incentive for persons to register to vote.

These academic studies have generally concluded that, from the testable alternatives (admittedly a small set), the greatest single improvement in voter registration could be brought about by allowing same-day registration. These studies also hold that increased registration of voters will make the greatest contribution to reversing the several-decade decline in voter turnout for national elections—that is, registering more voters is an easier "fix" than getting more of the existing pool of registered voters to participate.[6]

What these researcher reformers fail to recognize, or at least acknowledge, is that same-day registration clearly involves going beyond simply guaranteeing people the right to vote, and has some very real liabilities that could fundamentally undermine much more valuable principles embodied in elections and voter participation.

Dangers of Same-Day Registration

The first argument that can be made against same-day voter registration is that its advocates are attempting to implement it as a national policy that will strip individual states of important traditional powers in the federal system of government.

It is not relevant for reformers to cite issues of federal interference when state policies clearly abridged the constitutional right to vote—that is, when states misused poll taxes or literacy tests. The current situation involves no rights issues; rather it involves administrative issues.

Presently, every state has an opportunity to revise its own laws to allow for election-day registration. Thus far, despite reformers' best efforts, less than a half-dozen states have chosen to undertake this action.

In past movements toward national voter registration policy, reformers would frequently use as an argument for national implementation of reforms that only a few "backwater" and racist southern states were standing in the way of reform, such as those that eliminated the poll tax, literacy test, and so forth.

But with regard to same-day registration, the reformers have a problem. Because so few states have seen the merits of this proposal, it is evident that even some progressive, self-respecting "liberal" state legislatures are not predisposed to adopt this policy.

Not satisfied that they have not made progress at the state level, reformers have pushed ahead with efforts to get congressional legislation that would allow for practices such as same-day registration on the supposed premise that such practices should be implemented in order to mitigate "latent" voter registration discrimination.

Although liberals and intellectuals typically roll their eyes and scoff at pleas to preserve the federal system and its inherent allowance for varying policies across the states so long as federalism does not become a de facto front for implicit discriminatory practices, there is some merit to the federal process.

Allowing individual states to reflect the mores, values, and customs of their individual populations, in a very unique manner among the nations of the world, allows us in this country to experiment with new and different practices of governing, including establishing laws that determine who may register to vote and how.

Out of the variation, and there is significant variation in such practices across the fifty states, comes an opportunity to learn more about what practices are most nurturing of registration and voting, and with that information policy-makers can choose or not choose to make certain changes in view of the preferences of their citizens. After all, the apparent contribution that same-day registration makes to turnout would not have been noted had there been only one uniform national registration policy and procedure.

If same-day registration can be accomplished only through national policy-making by the Congress, it is unnecessarily injurious of the general advantages of our federal system, rendering individual states impotent to fashion registration procedures that meet the needs of their own population.

Election Integrity

While there can be reasonable disagreements about the degree to which same-day registration might contribute to corruption of elections (i.e., because people fraudulently present themselves as age-eligible citizens residing in a particular precinct or precincts, without allowing an opportunity for election administrators to confirm that information), there can be little doubt that the opportunities for corrupting the process are much greater with this system.[7]

At the present time, in order to confirm an individual's eligibility to vote, states require some sort of documentation and other evidence to confirm that the individual is in fact a citizen and resides at the address where he or she claims, and is not registered to vote at some other place. In turn, this information is typically confirmed by the mailing of registration credential to the address supplied by the applicant.

There can be no doubt that if thousands of persons who were not previously registered to vote were suddenly to present themselves at local precinct polling places, this would result in an enormous number of challenges of voters' credentials. This would tie up the electoral process procedurally on election day itself, and in the weeks following threaten to cast a web of suspicion over the outcome of the election itself.

Might widespread corruption actually result from increased participation? If the experiences of the nineteenth century have anything to say about the current age, we cannot be sanguine. In discussing high turnout (75 percent plus) of the period 1848 to 1896, Robert Kuttner quotes a 1929 vote history as charging that "vote early, vote often" was the theme:

> Hoodlums were rounded up and lodged for a night or so in various lodging houses or cheap hotels and then registered from all of them. On the day of the election, gangs of "repeaters" were hauled from precinct to precinct and voted under different names.[8]

The possibility that same-day registration would even increase the perception, if not the reality, that elections are corruptible is an extraordinarily unfavorable consequence of this proposition. Intellectuals have long argued that one of the principal purposes of elections is to legitimate the government (or the "regime," to use another term), and build support for the system of government and a sense of community among individual citizens.[9]

In this regard, it might be argued that the legitimating function of elections is often significantly more important in the larger scheme of things than the more obvious function they serve, that being the choice of elected public officials for a given term of office or the making of decisions about more narrow public policy issues. If government is rendered less legitimate in the course of elections, it matters little that we select suitable leaders or policies. And any leader who has ever been elected under circumstances that are clearly questionable will readily confess that it makes governing more difficult.

Expense

While it might seem inappropriate to speak of the cost of democracy in dollars and cents, state and local governments that are hard pressed to meet the needs for everything from indigent health care to state university funding and economic development programs would end up picking up the tab for reformers' largesse for registering new voters.

While some of the cost of voter registration in elections is relatively fixed and would be unaffected by the influx of voters expected by reformers, there are other costs that would be certain to increase. For example, because droves of unregistered persons might possibly descend upon voting places on election day (remember, one-third of the age-eligible citizens are not presently registered), election officials would have to be prepared by significantly increasing the number of paid poll workers, voting devices or ballots, and so forth, whether the anticipated run on the polls occurs or not. In short, it would add tens of millions of dollars of expense to the administration of elections for uncertain results.

Because election-day registration is especially attractive to those who might fraudulently attempt to vote in multiple locations, it would also increase the burden for cross-jurisdictional checking of voter registration, a task that many states are unprepared to manage.

Because most states presently rely almost exclusively on individual countries to register voters and maintain lists of those who are registered, an entirely new state administered system would have to be undertaken to cross-check lists from each county for multiple entries. In a state such as Texas, with over two hundred and fifty counties, the cost of computing and data management for such a system would be enormous. While some states already perform this task to some extent, in view of the great mobility of Americans today, it would increase the urgency for better, hence more costly, execution of it.

The No-Effect Argument

While intellectuals have been one of the prime moving forces behind calling attention to the possible effects of same-day registration on voter turnout, many of these same intellectuals have consistently included in their reported research that the inclusion of more nonregistered persons in the electorate is not likely to alter significantly the outcome of elections. For example, detailed analyses by Ruy Teixeira[10] conclude that neither Walter Mondale nor Michael Dukakis would have won election in 1984 or 1988 solely by the infusion of all nonregistered persons in the polling place.

While these same sources acknowledge that the Democrats would probably have a net advantage among election-day registrants, there appears to be widespread conclusion in the research literature that the advantage is nowhere near as great as some might believe, based on conventional wisdom.[11] In part, this conclusion is intuitive because of the significant decline in turnout since 1960, resulting in nonvoting not just by the least educated and least affluent segments of the population, but by a more cross-sectional slice of Americans.

The Know-Nothing Problem

Even if we agree that election-day registrants would not introduce a strong partisan bias into the electoral process, favoring the Democrats, there is a much more nefarious outcome that would assuredly result from the addition of nonvoters. By definition, most nonregistrants are going to be less interested and less informed about politics than people who have taken the opportunity to register. Granted, there are individuals who because of recent change of address, work responsibilities, or difficulties in registering because of restrictive state registration practices (limited registration hours, etc.), in the main, anyone who really cares about government and elections should be able to find the simple act of registration a relatively easy act to accomplish in all but a few jurisdictions.

The fact is, nonregistration is more a function of disinterest than a product of structural barriers. This conclusion is borne out by the results of a survey taken several years ago, which found that just under half (49 percent) of those who were not registered to vote expressed any interest in registering to vote when contacted by pollsters.[12] And even those who were "interested" might not be trusted to be avidly so. Anyone familiar with the polling process knows that verbal expressions of interest to an interviewer are most assuredly going to be inflated by a respondent's attempt to appear responsive to civic responsibilities and obligations.

But perhaps more troubling than the lack of interest on the part of registrants is their lack of information about the process. Obviously, if they are not interested enough to make the effort to register to vote, they are probably not going to be interested in most substantive or policy aspects of politics.

If this be the case, we have to ask ourselves, do we find attractive the reformers' contentions that election-day registration would bring more of these persons into the political process? Do we want disinterested and ill-informed persons participating in elections? The same survey discussed above found, for example, that prior to the 1984 election, only 18 percent of persons who were not registered to vote could name any Democratic aspirant for president of the United States in a preelection poll.[13]

Other surveys through the years have shown that significant percentages of all Americans, much less registered voters, are unfamiliar with the basics of government and current events. For example, one study has shown that there is widespread confusion among Americans about the American policies in Central America and which side is favored by the American government.[14] Persons who are less educated, younger, and otherwise fall into categories of persons likely not to be registered to vote, are the most confused about these matters. If these people have no idea whether the Americans favor or oppose the Sandinistas, do we really want them voting in congressional elections, for example, wherein one of the central issues is American policy toward the Sandinista government? If election-day registrants think that Bush is a supporter of the Sandinistas, this may cause them to vote for candidates who also favor the Sandinistas, only to discover later that they had the cowboys and Indians reversed.

Another unwitting consequence of possibly introducing a horde of disinterested voters is that it would raise the stakes in the closing days of an election campaign. Candidates would be tempted to make increasingly dramatic promises and charges against their opponents in an attempt to excite and mobilize a potential voter who is, by definition, not responsive to everyday exhortations to register and vote. Already there are legions of critics of the sensational, negative-style campaign that has become common. Introduce election-day registration and the problem will only worsen. You can bank on it.

There is, of course, great danger in arguing that some voters are too disinterested or ignorant to be justifiably involved in the electoral process. It appears elitist (which I suppose it is) and is also subject to the counterclaim that if persons were registered to vote, this might stimulate their interest in following politics so that they might be prepared to vote in elections. Given the importance and preciousness of elections in a democracy, however, I feel perfectly comfortable in suggesting that in regard to the chicken and egg problem, I would prefer that voters become informed and concerned prior to their becoming involved in the electoral process, not after.

CONCLUSIONS

What seems most ill-advised about election-day registration is that it is better thought of as a "last resort" response to the problems of low registration and low turnout, not a first choice solution. It seems overvulnerable to corruption and other liabilities when there are other, more reasonable and responsible, means of overcoming difficulty in registration, such as through postcard registration up to three or four weeks prior to an election, for example.

To start out by allowing election-day registration is analogous in elections to saying that we should go to postcard elections, or a system of universal absentee voting, in order to deal with the problem of the inconvenience of voting. Until we try some other, more controlled forms to encourage voting, such as extending the election period to two days or moving elections to Saturdays or a special holiday, it seems irresponsible to jump ahead to the most extreme and risky solution to the problem.

The fact that liberals, and particularly liberal intellectuals, are so interested in this proposal, despite its obvious risks, height-

ens the concern that the proposal is not as nonpartisan or nonideo-
logical as claimed. One cannot help but suspect that despite reams
of statistical data indicating that same-day registrants would not
alter the outcome of the election, there beats in the heart of liberals the eternal hope that somehow a wave of similarly predisposed
unregistered liberal ideologues would swoop down on election day
and change the outcome of a key election.

If that be the real motivation, voters of a responsible, conservative stripe should cry foul now before the change comes.

CHAPTER TEN

Should Political Parties Govern the Presidential Selection Process?

Of all the controversial issues that have surfaced during the age of "modern" presidential selection, the issue of political party control is clearly the most controversial and fundamental. Indeed, the vast majority of reforms that have occurred from 1968 to the present have directly affected in one form or another the power and place of parties within the context of the presidential selection process.

W. Wayne Shannon believes that it is very desirable for political parties to control the process by which we select the president. Shannon points to a number of benefits that exist when political parties exert substantial influence throughout the various phases of the presidential selection process. Central to Shannon's position is the relationship of political parties to effective presidential governance. Through influential political parties, presidential candidates and presidents acquire broad support for public policy agendas, governing coalitions are formed and maintained, issues are more clearly defined, citizens are more effectively educated on policy options, voters are linked to the larger political process, and a sense of common purpose is established between presidents and fellow partisans in Congress. According to Shannon, political party control over the presidential selection process manifests itself in a system of effective presidential leadership and vibrant democracy.

Alan J. Cigler takes issue with those who advocate a more dominant and influential role for political parties in the process of selecting the president. Cigler's opposition to those who sub-scribe to a system of responsible party government stems from two perspectives. First, Cigler believes that political conditions in American politics exist to the extent that it is simply unrealistic to advocate party control over the presidential selection process. Cigler identifies the forces of new politics, as well as the constitu-tional dimensions of American government that fundamentally prohibit any movement toward a political process governed by parties. Cigler's second argument against party control is more normative. In this respect, Cigler believes that the virtues of strong political parties have been overglorified by political scien-tists and that deep negative consequences in presidential leader-ship can in fact emerge from a selection process dominated by party organizations. Cigler discusses the potential of political party domination to alienate the American electorate and inten-sify conflict between the executive and legislative branches of government. Cigler discusses how domineering political parties can serve as impediments to effective national leadership. In Cigler's view, party control over the presidential selection process, as witnessed from American history, is more likely to yield presi-dents in the tradition of a Harding rather than a Roosevelt.

The arguments presented by Shannon and Cigler address the fundamental question concerning the type of presidential selec-tion process that best serves the interest of effective presidential leadership and American democracy.

Part 1

YES—
Political Parties Should Govern the Presidential Selection Process

W. Wayne Shannon

How the American nation—a vast, socially heterogeneous republic with a constitution designed to divide and limit the authority of government—can generate national leadership and formulate coherent public policy has always been a difficult question.[1] In his penetrating study of the Washington community in the early 1800s, James Sterling Young reached the conclusion that the capacity of the new nation's institutions for making and enforcing national decisions was "grossly deficient." The Madisonian logic of "ambition against ambition" on which the community was based had checked the power of the national state all too well: it was so divided that it had no way to make coherent decisions. The only hope for the future lay in inventing "a capacity for rulership within a constitutional framework deliberately designed to make rulership difficult." Fortunately, Young concluded, the Jacksonian revolution would soon invent the formula for national leadership on which we would henceforth rely—the strong presidency, backed by vigorous party organizations throughout the great expanse of the country, and an aroused partisan electorate.[2]

Young, it is worth noting, was looking back from the perspective of the mid-1960s, a time when the American formula of presidential government seemed to be working quite well. Lyndon Johnson (a strong president by anyone's standards) was in office, unusually large Democratic majorities in both houses of the eighty-ninth Congress supported his programs, and bold new policies were being forged that seemed certain to advance the nation's welfare. The American party system seemed to be in good shape. For more than a hundred years we had enjoyed a system of presidential nomination by conventions dominated by state and local party leaders and a general election campaign in which these institutional actors played a very strong role. The party system still enjoyed substantial public support. There was every reason to suppose that this "party game" was a more or less fixed feature of the American political system.[3] All the best professional political science literature of the time saw it as central to the process of selecting presidents and generating support for the business of national governance.[4]

What Young could not see in the mid-1960s as he concluded his study of the Jeffersonian era (he had plenty of company) is that things would soon look very different. The war in Vietnam and the very civil rights policies that were the crowning achievement of the Johnson administration would soon fracture the Democratic presidential coalition and create the setting for the disastrous confrontations in the streets of Chicago during the Democratic convention in 1968. The venerable convention system of presidential nomination so much admired by the best students of American political parties a generation ago would be swept away in the aftermath of the passions generated by the events of that incredible year.[5] The party system would be weakened at all levels during the 1970s by a combination of social, technological, and legal changes, the exact causal contribution of which still puzzles political scientists.[6] In general, the presidential selection process would become much more candidate-centered and less party-centered. If Young was correct that effective national governance in America has depended on the strong presidency supported by a vigorous partisan selection system, it should follow that problems of national governance would result from this transformation. The evidence, I believe, strongly supports this point of view.

I will argue here that the current presidential selection system is part of a larger process of party decomposition that has greatly weakened the governance capacity of the Washington community over the last twenty years. Because we have no better answer, we continue to rely on our historic formula for national leadership, presidential government, but "the party game" on which it depended for support has come unglued. A weakened presidency heavily dependent on public relations techniques, an individualistic Congress, divided partisan control of the two branches, and a House of Representatives all but divorced from the issue-related dynamic of presidential politics are all parts of the big picture of national governance pathologies that we now need to understand.

Very few whose experience in Washington goes back to the period before Vietnam think we are better governed now than then. A host of evidence suggests otherwise. There is certainly less institutional capacity in the Washington community to make coherent domestic and foreign policy, and citizens are much less effectively linked to the machinery of national government. Electoral participation has fallen off sharply, and an alarmingly large part of the public now regards the activities of the national governing community as baffling and uninteresting—an alien sphere, better kept out of sight and out of mind. The underlying dynamic in all of this, I believe, is party decomposition. The welcome evidence of the Reagan years that it is not an inevitable process should not lull us into complacency, but motivate us to find ways to strengthen the party system. I believe we can have stronger parties if we want them. In order to want them, we need to understand the negative governance consequences of not having them.

POLITICAL PARTIES: THE BLIND SPOT OF AMERICAN DEMOCRACY

The United States is the only democratic nation in the world in which it would be necessary to write this chapter—a polemic in favor of a strong role for political parties in the leadership selection process.[7] Everywhere else it is taken for granted that political parties as institutional organizations ought to nominate candidates for office and control the election campaigns conducted in their name. On this matter our understanding has always been unusual. Even while the American presidential selection process was party-dominated (roughly speaking, the hundred or so years from the administration of James K. Polk through that of Harry Truman), strong currents of opinion held that it should not be.

Our exceptional attitude toward the role of parties is deeply rooted in American political thought. Three distinct strains of ideas seem to be at work here. First, it is important to recognize that the founders of the American republic idealized a "partyless" politics of republican virtue. Although their actions quickly gave birth to the world's first modern political parties, they were never able adequately to conceptualize what they had done or develop an intellectual rationale for their unintended offspring. While party historians have amply demonstrated the failure of the partyless, gentry-based politics of the years before the invention of the popularly elected presidency and the national nominating convention, the framers' intellectual legacy has remained influential. Then, of course, there is the much more commonly recognized contribution of the Progressives and their distrust of party organizations and the "corrupt" motivations of traditional state and metropolitan party leaders (patronage, preferment, social mobility, etc.). Their most influential invention, the direct primary, was meant to be a party-weakening device, and after World War II, it belatedly began to exert its intended effect, even before the current nominating system was in place. Finally, the 1960s ushered in a new model of direct "participatory democracy" that had great influence on the antiwar and radical activists who visited their discontent on the traditional Democratic party elites in Chicago in 1968, setting in motion the forces that would "reform" the party's delegate selection processes and a movement to create new delegate selection primaries before the 1972 election.

All these ideas dispose many Americans to deny what is taken for granted elsewhere: that political parties are vitally important instruments of democratic government with specific functions to perform—among them, nomination, program formulations, and structuring the agenda of government. Each of these intellectual strains in its own way obscures a bedrock reality of government in all modern nation states—that it is simply impossible for citizens to govern directly. We alone among the world's democracies have yet to be convinced that parties are necessary precisely because they assist citizens who cannot or will not participate constantly at high levels in public affairs. As E. E. Schattschneider put the matter many years ago, Americans have a blind spot in the theory of democracy precisely in "the zone between the sovereign people and the government which is the habitat of the parties."[8]

Parties in the Nominating Process

The essential feature of the nomination system we fumbled our way into after 1968 is that it all but eliminates the critically important traditional functions of institutional party elites (party officials and officeholders) at the national conventions. The system has worked somewhat differently in every presidential election cycle since 1972, but it has retained the same essential structure whatever tinkering we have done with it. It is above all a system in which the nomination must be *won* by individual effort. All candidates *must* put together *personal* campaign organizations, raise their own money, contest a long "invisible primary" for media attention, and finally win enough delegates to clinch the nomination in the actual primary and caucus events of the election year. The nominating process is over when the primary season ends. The convention in this system is simply an afterthought—no more than a ratifying device for decisions reached elsewhere. The central feature of the nominating convention in the era of "the party game"—the ability of institutional party "professionals" (state and local party leaders and officeholders) to choose presidential candidates and package the issues on which the parties contest the election—has simply vanished.

In the last edition of his classic text on American parties and elections, published in 1964, V. O. Key, Jr., had observed that the use of primaries had not "produced conventions of automata." Party professionals, he thought, could still dominate the selection process. Less than ten years later, his discussion of the "discretion" that party leaders exercised at the convention to achieve party unity would read like ancient history.[9]

The trouble with the new nominating system is not, as I see it, that it produces presidential candidates who are poorly qualified for the presidency *as individuals*. Although it is often indicted on this ground, the evidence needed for conviction is simply not there. I agree in general terms with the conclusion of John Aldrich, whose careful analysis of the nominating process from the 1880s to the present has found that "presidential candidates look remarkably similar" in terms of their backgrounds and personal attributes over this long period.[10] The new nominating system is often accused of producing candidates with inadequate experience, poor "apprenticeships," unappealing personalities, and the like, but if this is so, it is certainly no worse than the old convention system.

Unlike the British parliamentary system with which comparisons (generally unfavorable to us) are often made, the American system has never required that presidents hold any certain combination of prior offices or serve any particular kind of apprenticeship.[11] In fact, there is no impressive correlation between prior experience of any particular sort and presidential success or failure. Good and bad presidents have come from the same kinds of "apprenticeships," whether they have been governors, senators, vice-presidents or military officers. Jimmy Carter and Ronald Reagan are only the most recent examples of remarkably different presidents who sprang from quite similar political backgrounds— mid-career entrance into electoral politics and service as governor.

It must also be said, after some fifteen years of trying, that our best efforts to predictively associate the observed personality attributes of presidential aspirants with later presidential behavior have yielded very unsatisfactory results.[12] It is certainly not my argument that the old convention system of nomination produced candidates whose personalities were superior to those nominated since 1972.

My own reading of the modern presidential "job description" is that it calls for such a remarkable personal combination of experience, skill, and winning ways that it will always be difficult if not impossible to locate the *individual* with "the right stuff." If we are really to believe the presidential literature, no one but Franklin Delano Roosevelt comes close to filling the bill since the modern expectations of presidential performance came into being some fifty years ago.[13] Here, in fact, is where the conundrum of modern presidential selection originates. Where, anywhere in the world, could there be found an *individual* so wise, energetic, elegant, inspiring? No other democratic system, of course, tries to resolve the leadership question in such starkly individualistic (and unrealistic) terms. No nominating system whatever could reliably bring forth the idealized, larger than life, *personal* leaders that much of the presidential literature tells us we must have.

Having understood this, we are in much better shape to see where the new nominating system really *is* deficient. From a perspective concerned with governance, it is severely flawed. It does not promote coalition-building inside the parties; rather, it creates intraparty divisions. If it does not nominate inferior candidates as individuals, it fails to generate support for them as party nominees. The system also places unrealistic demands on the electorate, producing an unenviable admixture of confusion, boredom, and distrust. On each of these counts the candidate-centered "primary game" is inferior to the convention-centered "party game" it replaced.

Coalition-Building and Cooperation

A concern with governance directs our attention to how the politics of the nominating process, other things being equal, contributes to the parties' ability to achieve internal unity and a sense of common purpose. It requires that we see the nomination contest not as a thing in itself (a "horserace," for example, as the dominant part of the media story has it), but a process that ought to generate support for presidents and their programs. It is exactly this concern that disposed students of the American party system like V. O. Key, Jr., and Clinton Rossiter to praise the national nominating convention as it had functioned for more than a hundred years after its routinization in the 1840s and to warn against the extension of presidential primaries in their writing a generation ago. Rossiter's warning is especially noteworthy. The practice of nominating presidential candidates by national convention, he thought, struck a "nice balance between the hard responsibilities of the professionals at the convention and the vague wishes of the voters at home." Unless it could be demonstrated that the presidency, the central institution on which we rely for national leadership, would not be damaged by altering the nominating system, "we ought to stand fast on tradition and prescription" and leave the historically validated convention system alone.[14]

What Rossiter felt would-be reformers did not see at the time, and what the actual reformers surely did not sufficiently understand in the late 1960s and early 70s is that primaries are inherently divisive and individualistic. Parties everywhere in the world experience internal quarrels arising out of rival personal ambitions and ideological differences. Generally, elsewhere, every effort is made to deal with these as quickly as possible in meetings held behind closed doors. Nowhere else has there been extensive use of the direct primary—an American invention that routinely invites co-partisans to compete with one another in a lengthy public campaign to determine whose personal qualifications and ideas are best in the general election.

Foreign observers of American presidential politics have always seen the national nominating convention as comparatively open and participatory. By the 1950s primary campaigns had become an important part of the normal nominating process. But despite the warnings of Rossiter and others, the new system of primaries and open caucuses put in place before the election of 1972 institutionalized openness to a new and extreme degree. In essence, we created then a nominating system that requires the parties to fight out their internal policy disputes and personal rivalries under the spotlight of modern media coverage for a period of more than two years. This unfortunate system not only fails to promote intraparty cooperation, it literally manufactures personal rivalries and individualistic policy positions. It inevitably creates a candidate-based rather than a party-based politics.

Ironically, the Democrats have suffered most under the new system—one that would not have been created, had it not been for the party's bitter internal divisions in the late 1960s and early 70s. To be sure, the nominating system is not the root of their problems in presidential politics over the last five elections, but it has made the party's age-old problem of finding common ground among its diverse coalitional elements much more difficult. There can be little doubt that the party would have fared better in presidential politics during these years if party "professionals" (state and local party leaders and office holders) were able to play a stronger role in selecting candidates and shaping campaign issues. While the Republicans have been less adversely affected by the new system, their time to suffer may yet come. The GOP has been unusually unified in the Reagan years, but it is hard to believe it will always fare so well. If and when internal divisions bedevil the party again, the long, public battles of the new nomination system will render them much more difficult to compromise.

Why do we want these long, public intraparty campaigns? Why would we want to invite co-partisans to undertake personal contests against one another for years on end? Why would we want to have a system that is virtually guaranteed to create intraparty divisions—even to invite intraparty assaults on presidents (Ford in 1976 and Carter in 1980)? Why would we want to deprive both parties of the mediating functions of "professionals" with an institutional interest in winning elections? From a governance perspective the answer is quite clear. The new system is sadly lacking in capacity to promote coalition-building and cooperation. It is a system with little ability to generate support for nominees, and after the election, for presidents who have to govern.

The Functionally Hollow Convention: No Glory to Bestow

The most unfortunate aspect of the current nominating system is its effects on the convention. Whatever is the exact causal contribution of each, a potent combination of new technologies, social change, and reformed delegate selection rules has utterly transformed this venerable institution, leaving it a functionally hollow shell, ill-equipped to perform any of the functions once thought so important by political scientists and other careful observers of American party politics. Not only is the nomination function gone, but the convention has also lost its ability to shape the issues and generate spirit and enthusiasm for the national fall campaign. Despite any attempts made so far to restore the "deliberative" functions of the delegates, it is all too clear that modern conventions are dominated not by institutional party actors, but by activists enlisted in individual candidates' campaigns. Delegates who have been selected to nominate particular candidates write platforms and make rules to suit particular candidates as well. This has been all too apparent at the Democratic conventions in 1984 and 1988. In both years defeated candidates for the nomination (Gary Hart in 1984 and Jesse Jackson in both years) extracted rules concessions for the next nominating round and for all practical purposes launched their next primary campaigns from the podium, while the nominees, Walter Mondale and Michael Dukakis, looked on nervously.

Whatever decisions conventions now make, they are in reality made by individual candidates and their managers. With so little for the convention to do, the networks now regard them as little more than entertainments with bad ratings. In 1988 only C-SPAN served up the full coverage for the few who still wished to watch.

The new nominating system, as we have seen, does not produce nominees inferior in experience or individual personal appeal to those produced by the old convention system. Nor does it, despite early fears to this effect, systematically produce candidates who are ideological extremists, who are hopelessly out of touch with their party's identifiers and the electorate as a whole. Yet the individuals it brings forth do not seem to satisfy. Each round of nomination brings the lament "Surely, we can do better than this! Why can't we find better candidates?" Something about this system makes the people in it *seem* inadequate. What is it? The answer, I think, lies in the greatly weakened role of political parties in the nomination process. Oddly enough, the system produces nominees with little party support.

In the nominating system of the old "party game," candidates came to wide public attention only when they emerged from the convention, having received the transforming gift of partisan symbolism. The nominee was seen not as a victorious individual, but as the party's spokesman. Whoever the nominee was, he looked more impressive for having been so anointed. Candidates in the new system, by contrast, undergo scrutiny for a seemingly endless period by media commentators who regard the "horserace" of the long "invisible primary" and the actual delegate selection events of the election year with considerable cynicism. The long, intra-party squabble of "the primary game" is inherently demeaning to those who choose to participate. By definition it requires candidates to engage endlessly in self-serving antics and to attempt to undermine their own partisan colleagues by hook or by crook at every opportunity.

The rules of this game make all its players look bad. Those who choose not to play, look better, but they would undoubtedly be demystified immediately if they entered the race. It is unfortunate, to be sure, that the contemporary system allows no late starters and permits no reluctant candidate to be drafted, but it is not likely that supposed "candidates of larger stature" like Mario Cuomo, Bill Bradley, or Sam Nunn would outshine the so-called dwarfs already in the race, were they to enter it. More likely, they too would be "dwarfed" by having to play the game.

No candidate can emerge from this nomination system unscathed. Someone has to win it by definition, but there is nothing at the moment of victory to equal the celebration of the tribal rites at the old convention. The victor and his personal campaign organization have triumphed, but the functionally hollow party convention has little glory to bestow.

Confusing and Boring the Electorate

A few years ago voters needed to pay relatively little attention to presidential politics until after the national conventions. Even so, the American presidential campaign was lengthy by comparative standards. The new nomination system has made the citizen's electoral function much more complex. First, the presidential campaign has been greatly lengthened. The nomination phase alone runs for well more than a year. To this must be added the large cast of characters in "the primary game"—as many as twenty or so, when as in 1988 the nomination in each party is up for grabs. In this strange new electoral world, the flow of information is mind-boggling. Years before the election the new "elections industry" grinds out coverage on the many candidates in the race, their staffs, their strategies, their funding, who is winning, their personalities, the issues, and the like. Ordinary voters should never have been expected to cope with this unwanted flood of information and commentary. The evidence is now substantial that they do not.

Although it was meant to empower the electorate, the new system has not done so. The information costs for citizens in this system are extraordinarily high. It is now quite clear after six rounds of the new system that most voters have neither the opportunity nor the inclination to act the part of the quidnuncs they would have to be in order to understand it. Most citizens pass through the long nominating season without knowing or caring much about what is going on. Strong interest in the nomination campaigns is limited to a small part of the electorate. Why, after all, *should* any reasonable democratic theory expect citizens to be interested in the doings and declamations of this small crowd of presidential aspirants? Why should voters be expected to sort through the endless statistics, and immodest claims, assertions that are the staples of nomination politics? In the general election, strong partisans, at least, thrive on such fare, but in the long nomination process, it is clearly beyond most voters' tolerance. They simply tune it out.

It is the strength of political parties in electoral politics that they help citizens to understand options and link their preferences to the public order. There is none of this healthy capacity in the partyless politics of the new nominating system. The hope that citizens would become more powerful in such a system was never realistic. They did not ask to do the work of partisan elites, and they have neither been willing nor able to do so. Our failure to think through the problems inherent in our fuzzy attraction to notions of direct democracy has been a costly one. The new nominating system puts voters into the business of selecting candidates and issues for the parties—tasks for which they are ill suited. We have yet to learn the lesson that E. E. Schattschneider tried so earnestly to teach over so many years—that the zone between the electorate and government is the natural realm of party organizations. The current nomination system, by depriving the parties of their most critical functions, has brought no gain to the electorate. It has simply promoted confusion, apathy, and distrust of politics.

Parties in the General Election

If the parties as organizations have lost the nomination function, they fare little better in the general election phase of the current presidential selection system. Again, American practice is at sharp odds with the vigorous role that party institutions continue to play in election campaigns elsewhere in the democratic world. In recent years the personal candidate organizations of the nominees have carried over from "the primary game" to play the central role in the management of the general election campaigns as well. So dominant now are the candidates' personal operatives and the fee-for-service media specialists, advertising and public relations types, pollsters, campaign management specialists, and the like, in the conduct of the general election campaign that it is sometimes hard, especially on the Democratic side, to see state or national party organizations at all. Movement in this direction has been underway for many years, at least since the 1950s, but it has seemed to most students of the party system to reach an entirely new level after 1972. The last four general election campaigns would not have had to be run very differently if we had no state and local party organizations whatever. Mainly, they have been waged on television.

It is also important to note the declining importance of party to individual voters in recent elections. In what political scientists have come to call a process of "dealignment," more and more voters have either lost the long-standing loyalty to the Democrats or Republicans that we have called "party identification," or they have been much more willing than in the past to depart from the ties they still profess in response to candidates' personal appeals and the issues of the particular election. Despite evidence since 1980 that the youngest age cohort in the electorate has shown a new and somewhat surprising proclivity to link up with the GOP, the surveys show that party ties now bind voters much more casually than they did in the heyday of "the party game."

"So what?," many will say. Why do we need strong parties and voters attached to them if we can conduct elections without them? My answer, grounded in what I have called here a governance perspective, is that individualistic elections produce incoherence or deadlock in Washington. Party decomposition has contributed mightily in recent years to the undermining of our one convincing answer to the leadership question—presidential government. No matter which party controls the White House, presidents are now systemically deprived of partisan support in Congress.

Most often, since 1968, national elections have produced "divided government," a situation in which there has been a Republican president and a Democratic majority in one or both houses of Congress. Against such a handicap, even an unusually gifted electoral politician like Ronald Reagan can only rarely muster support for his programs.[15] But that is not the whole story. The Carter years show how bad national governance can now be, even when a president is elected along with a majority of nominal co-partisans in both the House and the Senate. He and they, having hoisted themselves to Washington by their own boot straps, had little sense of common purpose and less disposition to see governance as a cooperative, collegial enterprise. The result is still painful to recall.

A Tale of Two Districts

In both 1984 and 1988 American voters chose Republican presidents, Ronald Reagan and George Bush, by strong popular and electoral majorities, and at the same time returned substantial majorities of Democrats to the House of Representatives. In 1986 Reagan, who tried more than any president in memory to play the role of "party leader," campaigned vigorously for congressional Republicans in the mid-term election. His effort failed. The Democrats to no one's surprise continued to enjoy a majority in the House of Representatives (as they had since 1954), and the Senate, having gone Republican to almost everyone's surprise in 1980, reverted to Democratic control. Students of American elections have come to expect such results in an era when nearly half the congressional districts in the nation are "split districts"—that is to say, carried by a president of one party and a House candidate of the other. What causes this is "split ticket" voting. In 1984 University of Michigan Survey data show that among voters casting ballots for president, senator, and representative, no less than 35 percent split the ticket—more than those who voted straight Republican (33 percent) or straight Democratic (32 percent).

Do voters really want this outcome? Many say they do. A considerable body of recent survey evidence suggests to some that American voters have become "cognitive Madisonians," intentionally disposed to set the president and Congress against one another. By 1988 it was not unusual to find a majority of respondents in national polls saying that they preferred "divided government." In Connecticut a strong majority of those who had voted for Bush (58 percent) said they thought it was "good for the country" that he would face a Congress controlled by the Democrats.[16] Yet it is doubtful that voters really intend this result. More likely, they are trying to implement another kind of logic.

To make my point, let me cite a personal conversation with two intelligent and well-informed voters in southwestern Ohio a couple of years ago. My wife's Uncle Sparky and his wife, Ginny, live in a "split district." Both were strong Reagan supporters, like the majority in their congressional district. Why, they asked me, disgustedly, was Congress so disposed to vex and oppose him? Why would they not cooperate? Are presidents not supposed to lead? When I asked about their own choice for the House, I was interested to learn that both knew the name of their representative and had voted for him with some enthusiasm as "a good man who had done things for the district." The only catch was that he was a fairly liberal Democrat. When I looked up his *Congressional Quarterly* "presidential support score" for the 100th Congress, it turned out to be 14 on a scale of 100—61 points lower than the score of a representative from a neighboring district who happened to be a Republican! The "good man/district service" logic had created the very problem that so perplexed them later.[17]

Many individuals in the substantial majority (61 percent) who voted for Reagan in my own Connecticut district in 1984 also split their tickets for the incumbent Democratic representative on much the same grounds, despite the availability at the time of a "party lever," which made it easy to vote the straight ticket.[18] Like his colleague from Ohio, this representative (a former student of mine) is a hard worker, and he tirelessly promotes the image of the "good man, serving the district." Again, it just so happens that his "presidential support score" was 13 in the 100th Congress, a stubborn fact of considerable importance to those who really wanted to see Reagan's policies implemented. Did all of those who split their tickets intend to hobble the president? If so, they chose the right man; if not, they made a serious mistake.

This tale of two districts is not a trivial one. It is now writ large across the nation. It goes far to explain how we got a 98.5 percent rate of reelection for House incumbents in 1988. It also shows how House elections have become all but divorced from the issue-driven dynamic of presidential politics and how we now routinely elect presidents (even unusually strong ones) who lack support for their programs. It is all part of the same big picture of

party decomposition—a picture sufficiently difficult to comprehend that most voters, whatever they tell pollsters, have not likely
thought it through. The trouble with electoral individualism is
that it does not generate the support that our only formula for national leadership, presidential government, requires. Why in the
world, if one found Reagan's clearly articulated policy goals attractive, would one want to elect a Congress guaranteed to implement
as few of his ideas as possible?

I happen to be a strong Democrat, but I happen also to be
persuaded that our system works best when presidents have the
support of co-partisans committed to their programs. As I told
Sparky and Ginny, I think they would have done better to have
voted a straight ticket. But I am not sure that I persuaded them to
my point of view. The problem, I could see, was the usual one, a
feeling that good politics ought to be "above" parties.

CONCLUSION

Unless we want a Washington that is unable to govern effectively, we should want political parties to play a strong role in
presidential *and congressional* selection. We have now become so
accustomed to the new, "partyless" world of the last twenty or so
years, that a kind of "crackpot realism" prevails (even among political scientists who ought to know better), to the effect that
strong parties are impossible in contemporary postindustrial
America.[19] Television, the fee-for-service professional of the "elections industry," and others have supposedly rendered them obso-
lete. Such a viewpoint is simple nonsense. Everywhere else in the
democracies parties remain centrally important despite a common
postindustrial socio-economic setting. It is we who are the exception. The problem of party decomposition is specifically an American one, and it is at root ideological.

E. E. Schattschneider got it exactly right half a century ago
when he wrote that the realm of political parties was then, and is
even more now, a blind spot in the theory of American
democracy.[20] We need now more than ever to return to the task to
which he devoted his long and productive academic career—convincing Americans that parties are indispensable instruments of
effective democratic governance in a large-scale polity.

Part 2

NO—
Political Parties Should Not Govern the
Presidential Selection Process

Allan J. Cigler

Virtually all political scientists hold the institution of political parties in high esteem, sharing the view that the party is the best organizational vehicle yet invented to aggregate and articulate the interests of the masses in a democratic polity.[1] Many would agree with E. E. Schattschneider, who proclaimed that "political parties created democracy and that modern democracy is unthinkable save in terms of party."[2] Parties are valued for being the glue that unites diverse elements within American politics; the only device capable of reconciling individual diversity and majority rule in both the electoral and policy processes, through coalition building—"the process of constructing majorities from the broad sentiments and interests that can be found to bridge the narrower needs and hopes of separate individuals and communities."[3]

In theory, the crucial party activity for accomplishing such grand tasks is the selection of public officials, from recruiting and training candidates and organizing the nomination process to running campaigns and mobilizing voters. The presidential selection process has generated the most interest. Ideally, a party-dominated presidential selection process creates a bond between the president and the organized representatives of the mass public, enhancing accountability, and creating an incentive for democratic responsiveness. A further bond between the president and the president's party in the legislature is also created, aiding in the ability to govern by overcoming many of the inherent antagonisms of the separation of powers. Party domination of presidential selection is a basic component of the thoughts of those who believe politics is best when it approaches responsible party government.[4]

There can be little doubt, however, that today's presidential selection system does not operate along the lines of this ideal model, and that parties, in practice, do not really "govern" the process. It is more accurate to say that political party organizations and their leaders have moved from being the major force determining presidential selection to being simply one interest in the process, and probably not the most important one.

Such a situation is disturbing to a number of political observers, who are upset with the plebiscitary characteristics of the contemporary presidential selection processes, and believe some effort should be made to again give party the primary role. But the answer to the question of whether or not parties, as they are or how they realistically could become, should govern the presidential selection process, is complex and multifaceted. Though the idealist in me wishes otherwise, the realist in me dictates that I answer *no* to such a question.

My argument has a number of interrelated components that reflect my view that the political party, as a mediating institution, can no longer play a paramount role in the postindustrial political environment. The dominant influence of the mass communications industry in contemporary political life, and the existence of highly educated and individualistic voters with intense democratic expectations, have created an environment hostile to partisanship in politics, a situation unlikely to be reversed.

American parties in the contemporary era not only have lost their impact in presidential selection to other mediating agencies, especially the media and professional campaign operatives and consultants, but today's party activists, leaders, and elected officials themselves are not the policy- and coalition-building cadres that the ideal party model envisions. Contemporary parties are made up of a heterogeneous mix of relatively narrow issue activists (many unwilling to compromise on central political issues), organizational managers, campaign professionals, and elected public officials. Even if achievable, strengthening their role in the process would accomplish little but perhaps the further alienation of the nation's electorate, already suspicious of parties and partisanship.

Nor would there necessarily be public policy benefits and more stability in the policy-making process accruing from a heightened role for parties in presidential selection, as some party supporters would have us believe. The institution of the modern presidency itself, and its meaning to the nations's public, has taken on a highly symbolic and nonpartisan character in recent decades. This trend is unlikely to be reversed even if parties were to increase their role in governing presidential selection. Political parties may hamper as much as help contemporary presidents as they attempt to secure and implement their programmatic concerns. indeed, if the contemporary presidency were to become more partisan, political conflict in the nation might be elevated to unhealthy levels.

With the exception of a number of academics and political analysts, there is limited support for a strong role for political parties in the presidential selection process. A strong party role is desired neither by the public at large, party activists, or elected public officials. In an environment where openness and internal democracy are norms that must not be violated, efforts designed to meaningfully strengthen the role of parties in the presidential selection process are doomed to failure. Efforts to improve the presidential selection process, which certainly has its flaws, should focus elsewhere. The clock for political parties cannot be turned back.

THE ROLE OF PARTIES IN PRESIDENTIAL
SELECTION—WHAT PARTIES?

Officially, political parties govern and are likely to continue to govern the presidential selection process, by nominating candidates for president under party rules, who will then run under the party banner in the general election. Unofficially, however, the party, in any meaningful sense of the term, has lost control of presidential selection and is unlikely to regain it in the future.

In practice, presidential campaigns, in both the nomination and general selection phases, are candidate-centered rather than party-centered. An individual politician's campaign organization raises funds, mobilizes activists, advertises on television, conducts sophisticated direct mail operations, and polls voters, all largely independent of party organizations—local, state, or national. Political consultants, pollsters, and outside strategists have replaced the party leadership as central figures in campaigns.

At the nomination stage, while the political parties do create the ground rules, nominations are far different than a generation ago, when candidates were nominated by party professionals who were typically chosen through state conventions or caucuses tightly controlled by the party organization. Eventual nominees usually had worked their way up the party hierarchy over a long period, had served in a number of elected positions in government, and were able to put together a coalition of state party delegations in order to win the nomination. Now nominations are often won or lost on the basis of the candidates' ability to put together an effective personal campaign organization and their appeal on television. Candidates now seek to construct coalitions of issue publics rather than state party delegations. "Peer review" by the party leadership plays a minor role, for candidates with a commanding media presence can gain recognition and stature almost overnight. Having held elected political office or worked for the party is now no longer a prerequisite to becoming serious candidates, as demonstrated by the nomination campaigns of television evangelist Pat Robertson and preacher/activist Jesse Jackson in 1988.

After the nomination, the presidential campaign is run by the candidate's organization rather than by the national party (since 1972, no general election campaign has been run by either the Republican or the Democrat national committee staffs). Clearly, presidential elections are more personal plebiscites than contests between rival candidates reflecting differences between the parties and beholden to party leaders and elected officials.

But would a presidential selection process dominated by political parties, as advocated by a number of political observers, improve the presidential selection process? I suspect not. Disenchantment with the current process, which is widespread, does not necessarily mean that a stronger role for parties in the process would improve the process. The process would certainly be different, diminishing the plebiscitary characteristics that now exist, but replacing them with a system characterized by bargained politics and control in the hands of an unrepresentive and unresponsive few does not seem to be an answer to the problem in an era of hyperpluralism and high democratic expectations.

The reasons for the decline of political parties have been well documented, and need not be commented upon in depth here.[5] Suffice it to say that the decline of American parties represents a long-term, secular trend that began around the turn of the century, well before the nomination rule changes and the spread of primary elections that have occurred over the past two decades, though such factors undoubtedly accelerated the decline of party in presidential selection. At base, parties, reflecting the imperatives of federalism, and strongest at the local and state levels, proved to be incapable of meeting national needs and aspirations, and declined in importance as a result.

Political observers who decry the role of the media, single-issue activists, and political amateurs in today's very open presidential selection process appear to convey a longing for the days of party domination of the process, characterized by local and state party leaders and bosses bargaining and compromising, selecting candidates with the support of the party coalition, and providing balanced tickets. There is a tendency to romanticize about how "functional" earlier party organizations were, to the point of not distinguishing their activities at the state and local levels from national politics.

There is no question that parties were invaluable in providing a number of welfare services and aiding in the assimilation of foreign immigrants and rural migrants into an increasingly urbanized and industrial nation,[6] but we should not forget that old-style parties were often genuine obstacles in national politics and opponents of progressive policy-making. The golden age of party in the late nineteenth century "was not a golden day for Presidents or for public policy or for politics as a profession."[7] As the eminent historian Arthur M. Schlesinger has noted, "not a single notable President led the nation in the forty years between Lincoln and the first Roosevelt; and Lincoln was a minority President and Roosevelt an accident."[8] A number of political movements arose during the period precisely because parties were inattentive and nonresponsive to a variety of important social forces.

Because of federalism, American parties have largely been dominated by local forces, yet such forces have typically denied, evaded, or been slow to respond to pressing national concerns. Their major aim in national politics was patronage, not national policies, yet "new ideas gain access to politics through hard-to-control reformers like Theodore Roosevelt, Woodrow Wilson, Franklin Roosevelt, John Kennedy and, in his peculiar way, Ronald Reagan,"[9] Such presidents have had to take control of the party from party leaders and remold it in their own image. They tried to make the party accountable to them!

The party reform movement in the late 1960s and early 70s, which essentially removed the nomination process from effective control by state and local party elites, rather than designed to weaken political parties, was designed "to tame the new social energies and incorporate them into the party process."[10] The changes were designed to accommodate the aspirations of newly "entitled" social groups—women, youth, and nonwhite minorities—a list of claimants that has since expanded. While most political observers probably believe the reforms went too far in decreasing party and elected official input, many fail to recognize that the reforms probably saved parties from becoming totally meaningless institutional entities in an era of rising expectations and democratic fervor.

A number of political observers feel that the new, media-dominated nomination process leads to the selection of presidential candidates who lack the capacity and talent to later govern effectively, because of the lack of peer review by party officials and officeholders, individuals seemingly most able to judge leadership potential. There is no question that such peer review means very little today. For example, ex-Senator Gary Hart in 1987 was the clear front-runner for the 1988 Democratic presidential nomination before alleged sexual escapades derailed his efforts, yet he had reached this position with the endorsement of only one of the Senators who had served with him. Contrast this to 1952, when the Democratic leadership at the convention rejected Senator Estes Kefauver (who had won nearly two-thirds of all votes cast in the primaries), because party leaders did not feel Kefauver could seriously challenge Eisenhower or become an effective president.

But, as political scientist Everett C. Ladd has convincingly argued, the contemporary peer review process simply recognizes the expansion of the players in American politics, ranging from more traditional party leaders, such as county and state chairpersons, to members of the press, to campaign operatives, financial contributors, and issue activists.[11] While such a heterogeneous and open community of peer reviewers may cause confusion in the process, and certainly has diminished the role of the political party, it is not empirically clear that the old party-dominated peer review process was superior in judging potential presidents than the current one. Indeed, the old process was probably more likely to produce a Harding than a Roosevelt. The current peer review process many be too open and perhaps examines the candidates in too much personal detail, but it is politically unrealistic to believe the process could or should be returned to a narrow group of party officials. This is even true of the nomination process, where "increasing the number of party 'leaders' at the convention is like bringing back knights in armor in the age of gunpowder."[12]

Attempts to institutionalize peer review by party and elected officials in nomination politics have not matched reformer expectations, as the Democrats found out in the 1980s. For example, the Hunt Commission (1980–1984) attempted to increase the role of party regulars in the nomination process by designating that a certain percentage of the national convention delegates would be "superdelegates" drawn from a pool of party and public officials (state chairpersons, governors, U.S. Representatives, etc.). The rationale for the effort was not simply self-interest by party professionals, but an expectation that their experience would be a moderating force, and that their convention participation would enhance ties between the party and its officeholders. The original hope was that the superdelegates would largely remain uncommitted throughout much of the nomination process, and perhaps play a compromising role at the national convention.[13]

But, given the realities of the contemporary presidential selection process, dominated by the media and candidate organizations, a great deal of pressure was put on the superdelegates to commit early to give various candidates momentum and an early advantage in the media's coverage of the nomination "horse race." In 1984 most superdelegates committed to Walter Mondale early, well before the Iowa and New Hampshire contests, and his selection looked "bossed" to some. In 1988 the clear preferences of the superdelegates for established political figures so angered insurgent candidate Jesse Jackson on fairness grounds that the procedure may be modified in the future. Like so many reforms to strengthen the party in the nomination process, such efforts seem undemocratic in the contemporary era, and are overwhelmed by other campaign factors.

Those who argue that parties ought to control the presidential selection process often fail to confront what U.S. political parties have become and the characteristics of today's party peers. Contemporary parties are hardly vehicles that would enable us to approach anything like a responsible party system, nor are they likely to become such vehicles. At the local and state level, organizational party leaders and activists interested in presidential nomination are typically not interested in either patronage or the long-term fortunes of the political party. Often their involvement is rather ephemeral, either candidate-specific or narrow-issue oriented, and their commitment to support a nominee not of their choosing is weak. Without a patronage base, it is simply impossible to develop local party leadership along the lines desired by those who advocate something approaching responsible parties.

The national party organizations do not hold much promise either. At the national level, each of the two major national parties is really three parties: a national committee, and a Senate and House party campaign committee. While it has become fashionable in recent years to comment upon the "resurgence" of the national parties, and how they have "adapted" to the new features in American politics,[14] it is important to understand exactly the role played by contemporary national parties and how far removed it is from anything approaching a responsible party model.

Today's national parties are less voter-mobilizing agencies and coalition-building vehicles, and more simply candidate safety organizations, dedicated primarily to the reelection of legislators who have a party label (largely unrelated to how they vote as legislators). Both national parties perform a variety of services for their members, ranging from coordination of fund-raising efforts to providing polling services. Recruitment of legislative candidates, especially for the Republican National Committee, is important as well. Involvement in presidential selection by the national parties is largely involved in setting the general rules, which broadly circumscribe how the nomination contests will be conducted.

Why should such organizations, largely dedicated to incumbent protection instead of policy considerations, be given more voice in presidential election? Such organizations in no way resemble the coherent, programmatic parties, which advocate responsible party desires, and it is hard to envision them becoming such vehicles.

There are, of course, significant differences between the two national parties. The Republicans appear to be much more "professional" than the Democrats, with more financial resources, more permanent staff, and a larger number of paid campaign operatives. Their Washington operation has more central control of the party. The Democrats, on the other hand, are more the activist party (a very loose coalition of intense special interests, in large part unrepresentative of the party rank and file), with neither the money nor staff to compete with the Republicans without other forms of assistance. Democrats rely more on volunteer and interest-group support.

But in neither party are significant decisions being made largely by people with a coalition-building orientation who are very sympathetic to the party as an institution. The major players differ between the two parties, but a high proportion tend to be special-interest advocates of some sort, including electoral consultants, and individuals interested in the fortunes of only one candidate. For example, since the early 1970s Democrats have used a number of rules commissions to develop the ground rules for presidential nominations. While reformers and "friends" of political parties as institutions did play a role, a large number of the party professionals involved were either rights activists seeking to expand their group's influence, or "delegate selection experts," professionals who have created a career by staffing rules commissions, attending delegate selection conferences, and serving as advisors in candidate campaign organizations.[15] For most, the concerns were group or candidate advantage, not party as a vehicle for responsible party government.

It is not likely that today's political parties could be converted into such a vehicle. Ironically, the major barrier is the activists in the party themselves, particularly party and elected officials. If, as James Sundquist suggests, "a stronger party is by definition one with a stronger center, possessing some institutional means of fostering unity and cohesion,"[16] state officials, be they governors or party chairpersons, would likely see the development of a strong, centralized party as a threat. National party intrusion into the selection of party nominees within the state, or attempts by a national party to impose its policy on the entire party, simply is not compatible with a party system that is and will remain federal in its structure, and where political self-interest is a powerful centrifugal force.[17]

Overall, there is simply no compelling advantage to be gained from making party forces more influential in presidential selection. The past track record of parties in presidential selection, when parties dominated the process, is not a particularly good one. And contemporary parties are a far cry from anything approaching responsible parties, and the barriers to meaningfully changing them seem overwhelming.

PARTIES, GOVERNING, AND THE MODERN PRESIDENCY

Those who advocate a stronger role for political parties in presidential selection see better national policy-making as the eventual result of change designed to strengthen political parties. The current presidential selection process, with parties playing a relatively minor role, is considered by some to be the culprit underlying many policy failures in Washington over the past two decades. The Carter years draw particular attention, seemingly illustrating the frustrations of a president elected largely due to appeals outside the party apparatus, who, once elected, experienced difficulty with his own party in Congress, even though Democrats controlled both houses. According to this perspective, a president selected in a process approximating a plebiscite comes to office lacking the basis for stable, programmatic leadership, especially the necessary connection between the president and his legislative party, essential to establishing a solid political base in Congress. "A presidency whose main constituency is public opinion may well be able to ride high when popularity is on the president's side, but party support is what helps to sustain a president in leaner seasons."[18]

As compelling as this argument is, it should be pointed out that it is one thing to assert that a strong connection between the president and his party in the legislature can be an aid in governing (which seems obvious), and quite another to link an increased role for party in presidential selection with an improved capacity for a president to govern effectively in the contemporary Washington environment. This is especially true in our separation of powers system, characterized by potential antagonism between the executive and legislative branches, particularly in situations when the party that controls the presidency may not be the same one that controls one or both houses of the legislature.

Unlike a parliamentary government system, a U.S. president is nominated by the party, but is not elected by it. Government does not fall if divided, and presidential legitimacy and authority often depend more on the executive's capacity to rise about partisanship and appeal to the masses, than the ability to muster partisan forces for programmatic purposes. While clearly good relations with the party in Congress are an asset, the modern president must not be too partisan.

As in the case with presidential selection, some political observers have a tendency in hindsight to glorify the role of political
parties in policy-making in previous periods of U.S. history. In reality, presidents and their parties were often competitors. In a variety of ways, "the modern presidency was crafted with the
intention of reducing the influence of the party system on American politics."[19] Franklin Roosevelt, for example, the first of the
modern presidents, quickly found that political parties, based on
state and local interests, were incapable of providing a base for programmatic politics, and moved to build a popular base among the
voters, through the skillful use of the medium of radio and manipulation of national newspapers and news services.[20] Party patronage was deemphasized, and Roosevelt attempted to construct an
administration of individuals loyal to him personally, and committed to an expanded regulatory and redistributive role for the federal
government. From Roosevelt through Bush, modern presidents
have often found that the political party can be a major obstacle to
an executive desirous of addressing pressing problems truly national in scope, and have developed strategies for "going public."[21]

It is hard to believe that a president elected in a process dominated by political parties would necessarily enjoy improved success in Congress. While there is no question that the political
party provides a basis for political capital, and that the president's
"party cohorts typically want to support his policies and despite
obstacles usually do"[22] the major problem of presidential party
programmatic leadership lies more with the Congress than with
the process by which we elect presidents.

Senators and Representatives may be elected on the party
banner, but in most cases they do not perceive themselves as beholden to party or to the presidential candidate. Most were elected
by their own individual efforts, largely separate from party, from
fund-raising to management of the campaign. They remain in office less because of any alliance to party in the legislature, and
more because of their constituent service efforts. They are individual political entrepreneurs who can be elected in spite of presidential candidates of their party who are not popular, and hence do
not necessarily see their fortunes linked to those of the chief executive. It is in no way assured that they would behave differently in
the face of a president selected by a party-dominated procedure.

In the contemporary era, characterized by the electorate's increasing lack of party loyalty and a tendency to split their tickets,

the electoral connection between congressmen and presidential candidates is virtually nonexistent. Even electoral landslides, such as the 1984 and 1988 presidential elections, see no evidence of a coattail effect.[23]

Not only are legislators elected and reelected without much help from party or its presidential candidate, once in Congress party has less control over them than in previous eras. The political party is now only one of the organizational referents that legislators must confront. Legislators now must deal with large numbers of congressional caucuses or working groups (like the Black Caucus and the Women's Caucus), which often compete with congressional party leaders for influence and votes,[24] as well as hordes of special interests in numbers far greater than even two decades ago.[25]

After the congressional reforms of the mid-1970s, the congressional parties emerged as coordinators of the legislative process, rather than as mobilizers of blocs of votes on major policy issues. Legislators are now far less dependent upon the legislative party for career advancement than previously. The number of important congressional actors has greatly increased with the rise in importance of subcommittee chairs. No longer can a president deal with a few congressional party leaders able to genuinely control the rank and file. As Paul Licht has noted, parties "now provide only a shallow base of support in the legislative process" for presidents.[26] It is hard to see how a change in presidential election would alter this situation.

Indeed, if the presidential selection process were to become more partisan, national policy-making might become even less predictable and manageable than it is today. Anything approaching the responsible party model necessitates that one party control the legislative and executive branches. Yet we have had divided government for twenty-three of the thirty-five years from the election of 1954. Voters apparently have come to rely upon the Democratic Party in Congress to defend government benefits and services, as well as to provide a "political umbrella under which a wide range of programmatic groups can gather" (particularly minority groups, senior citizens, and environmental and consumer groups).[27] They show a preference for Republicans at the presidential level and that party's foreign affairs and government management orientation. As Sundquist suggests, "stronger parties confronting each other from their respective redoubts in the White House and Capitol

Hill would reduce rather than enhance the prospects for governmental unity."[28] As long as divided government remains the norm in Washington, presidential leadership will involve negotiation and compromise with partisan opponents as well as supporters. An even more partisan presidential selection process would not help matters—it might actually make them worse.

CONCLUSION

In discussing the potential role of political parties in presidential selection, it is important to separate idealism from reality. While American politics seems lacking in effective mediating institutions, resurrecting political parties does not seem to be a viable answer to the nations's needs. Any attempt to strengthen the political party role runs counter to powerful trends in American politics, such as the growth of the personalized presidency and the increasing influence of the mass media on presidential selection. Any meaningful reforms directed toward strengthening the role of parties in presidential selection would have to contend with deep-seated, negative public attitudes toward partisanship and the self-interest of entrenched politicians who would be ultimately responsible for change. As long as the nation has a policy-making process that must operate within the framework of the separation of powers, and an electoral system based on federalism, it is hard to imagine how parties could ever play the role envisioned by those who advocate responsible parties.

My disagreement with those who advocate an expanded role for parties in presidential selection is over the viability of parties as mediating institutions, not over ultimate reform goals (more politically accountable public decision-makers and more coherence in the policy process, for example). While we should be careful not to diminish the party role further, expansion of their role is not warranted either.

Rather than attempting to resurrect political parties, inevitably by tinkering with a nomination process that has been changed in every election since 1968, and even now lacks legitimacy in some quarters as a consequence, efforts might be more focused upon other mediating institutions, particularly the media. As Everett Ladd has noted, "since political parties will never again dominate communication on candidates and elections as they once did, and an independent press certainly will dominate this vital process, the only question worth pondering is how the press can be helped to do its job better."[29]

The role of the mediating impact of interest groups in both the electoral and the governing process deserves increased scrutiny as well. The role of special-interest money and its contribution to incumbent safety is perhaps the biggest barrier to meaningful political accountability in American politics, and deserves particular attention. In an era of weak political parties, "the best solution may be for interest groups to become more democratic, less dominated by staff, more sensitive to their own internal conflicts, and more willing to accept compromises."[30]

No presidential selection process will ever satisfy all observers, and the search for a better system will surely continue. But the future debate over the role of parties in presidential selection is less likely to involve efforts to expand the party role, and more likely to be over defending what small role the party presently possesses. Dissatisfaction with presidential selection may eventually lead to Congress assuming jurisdiction over the nomination process. The party future is not bright.

Conclusion

Gary L. Rose

A TIME FOR GRAND REFORM

We now return to the central premise of this book: the modern presidential selection process, which has evolved from 1968 to the present, is failing with alarming regularity and appears to be in a serious state of crisis. The crisis state of presidential selection manifests itself in two important respects: a crisis in political linkage and a crisis in governance. The crisis in linkage is evident in low rates of voter turnout in presidential elections, abysmally low levels of participation in caucus contests and primary elections, deep disenchantment among the electorate with the presidential nominees of the two major parties, and declining confidence in the capacity of parties and elections to meet the needs and interests of the American people.

The current crisis in governance can be observed through a fairly steady decline in public approval ratings of recent American presidents; poor, and in some instances quite dismal, performance rankings of modern presidents; a high incidence of negative voting behavior in presidential elections; and perceptions among the electorate suggesting that the qualities associated with presidential greatness are absent among those individuals who seek the Oval Office. The evidence that directly points to a crisis in linkage and effective governance is empirical, scientifically obtained, and representative of nationwide political behavior and orientations. Such evidence therefore cannot be ignored or dismissed; a crisis does in fact exist.

To resolve the crisis state of presidential selection requires a very thorough examination of the entire process by which we select the American president. Indeed, the time has come to reevaluate the selection system in its entirety, rather than a partial reevaluation of component processes and mechanisms, the approach characteristic of modern reform commissions. Such commissions, it should be added, have done nothing more than apply band-aids to deep and very grave wounds. American politics would be better served by a holistic reevaluation of all dimensions of the presidential selection process, ranging from the nominating campaign to the national nominating convention, and through the general election. In this author's view, a major revamping of the process appears to be in order.

Dimensions of the selection process that require attention involve the various issues discussed in the preceding chapters: voter registration procedures, the representativeness of the nominating process, the role of the mass media, the power of delegates at national nominating conventions, the process for selecting vice-presidential candidates, public funding of presidential elections, the regulation of campaign commercials, the institutionalization of presidential debates, the continuation of the electoral college, and the proper level of political party influence throughout the course of the presidential selection process. These are the current and burning issues that require intense and thorough review. Such issues are very controversial and, as demonstrated from the content of this book, provoke debate among close observers of presidential politics.

How the critical issues facing the presidential selection process are addressed and ultimately resolved in the years ahead will have a direct bearing on the quality of our national leadership and the overall vitality of American democracy. Reformers should never lose sight of the deep interface between the process of presidential selection and the quality of the larger political system. As noted, the presidential selection process is the "foundation" of the American democracy; effective national leadership and a healthy democratic state depend heavily on the process we follow for selecting a president.

In this book a parallel was drawn between the presidential selection process of 1824 and the current process by which American presidents are chosen. Both processes, it was argued, led to a crisis in political linkage and effective governance. As it was noted, the "cobwebs" in which voters were caught in 1824 and the perceived illegitimacy of the selection process bear a very disturbing resemblance to the "modern" process of presidential selection, a process that began in the years following the tumultuous Democratic convention of 1968 and extending to the present.

While the notion that history tends to repeat itself is somewhat specious, American politics does appear once again to be facing a political condition experienced in the early decades of the nineteenth century. By 1824 the process was deemed broken and the outcome unrepresentative of the expectations, aspirations, and ideals of the American people. The process was doomed to failure and ultimately collapsed. Evidence presented in this text, most of which has been gathered over the past two decades, points to a similar development. It appears that we have once again reached a state where the ideals of American democracy are not being served through the process of choosing the president.

The presidential selection process in 1824, perceived as grossly dysfunctional for the welfare of the republic, was forced to undergo a radical transformation with respect to nominating procedures. It is possible therefore that the modern process could also experience a bold revision in selection processes and procedures in the not too distant future.

The 1990s might very well be characterized by reforms that go far beyond the normal activity of party reform commissions, such reforms conducted on a scale similar to that which followed the election of 1824. Granted, the events of 1824 were far more illegitimate and distressing compared with events in the modern era of presidential selection. One is hard pressed to claim that the two processes have yielded perfectly identical results; there is no such attempt made in this text. Nevertheless, it is difficult to avoid the parallel between the two processes in terms of representation, or lack thereof, and the fact that both processes have failed to mobilize the support of the American people. It is doubtful, therefore, that the process of presidential selection, as it is currently constructed, can endure for much longer.

The Bush Presidency: Some Explanations

At this point, it seems reasonable and fair to pose the following question: if the presidential selection process is in fact in a "crisis" state, how then does one explain the impressive public approval ratings currently enjoyed by President Bush? At the time of this writing, close to 80 percent of the American public approves of Bush's performance as president, evidence hardly indicative of a "crisis in governance." While the president's current approval ratings tend to challenge the thesis that a crisis in presidential selection is upon us, a closer inspection of the Bush phenomenon suggests that a substantial portion of Bush's popularity is attributable to variables unrelated to the process by which he was chosen president. Current approval ratings instead appear to be related to two significant factors. First, it is difficult to separate Bush's approval ratings from the recent and positive developments taking place in eastern Europe. The removal of the Berlin Wall, the emergence of democratic reform in Poland, Czechoslavakia, Romania, East Germany, and even the Soviet Union clearly reinforce the virtues of American democracy, and the American president appears to be the beneficiary of such developments. Enthusiasm among Americans with the spread of democracy in eastern Europe appears to manifest itself in enthusiastic and positive feelings towards the president, regardless of the fact that the president has had little direct involvement in such remarkable events.

A second factor that appears to account for President Bush's extraordinary appeal is a common perception that the president is a man of basic decency. Americans perceive President Bush as one who cares deeply about the welfare of the American family and his fundamental personality suggests sincerity, warmth, and integrity. The American people like President Bush very much and it appears that current approval ratings are closely tied to personality attributes. This is not to suggest that the president is performing poorly. In this author's view the invasion of Panama, the subsequent apprehension of General Noriega, the recent Colombian drug summit, and the president's effective working relationship with Mr. Gorbachev suggest a decisive American president with considerable expertise in foreign policy-making. Nevertheless, the consensus that surrounds the Bush presidency seems to be primarily attributable to factors that are not residual by-products of the process through which President Bush was selected. As such, the popularity of President Bush does little to soften criticism of the mechanism we employ for selecting the American president.

What Do We Really Want?

Perhaps what truly needs to be determined as we enter the final decade of the twentieth century is a firm understanding of what kind of presidential selection process best serves the interests of American democracy and what kind of process is most likely to produce American presidents who can effectively govern the nation. Put differently, what kind of democracy and what kind of presidency do we really want? Few would disagree that a selection process that contributes to enthusiastic political participation, rational voting behavior, and a high level of confidence in presidential nominees is somehow inconsistent with the goals and ideals of a democratic state. Few would also object to presidential nominees who are representative of the political party's rank and file, reflect the will of broad segments of the American population, and who are capable of forging stable governing coalitions. In an industrialized nation of 250 million persons, with a multitude of diverse interests, effective presidential leadership requires no less.

The concept of a representative American president therefore remains one of the chief concerns of those who seek to reform the process of presidential selection. Indeed, a president who represents the American people is fully consistent with the principal objective of the framers of the American Constitution. As Charles C. Thach notes in his classic work on the creation of the presidency: "With the abandonment of the idea of the supreme legislature went the concept of executive responsibility to the legislature, and in its place came that of the executive as representative of and responsible to the people."[1] The challenging task that awaits reformers therefore is how to redesign the presidential selection process in a manner consistent with the intentions of the founding fathers.

The Restoration of Parties

In my view, and in the view of several contributors to this volume, the restoration of political party influence within the context of the presidential selection process should constitute the very first order of business for political reformers in the 1990s. At this point in time, the evidence seems overwhelming regarding the interrelationship between party decline and the crisis state of the presidential selection process. If we truly desire a representative American president, then serious attention must be directed toward a revitalized role for political parties in the course of the selection process; the restoration of party influence is a prerequisite for obtaining this goal.

Unfortunately, however, to restore political parties to a more dominant role in presidential selection will not be an easy task: the road to restoration is long and filled with many obstacles. Clearly, the preceding two decades have been characterized by a wave of developments that are inconsistent with a more active and influential role for party leadership: the proliferation of presidential primaries, the rise of television as a principal campaign mechanism, the emergence of media consultants, the development of candidate-centered organizations, and the power afforded to party reform commissions that appear predisposed toward open and less party-oriented nominating procedures are all developments that have worked against the interests of party leadership in the modern era. Such developments are often depicted as part of a "new politics" that has penetrated all facets of presidential politics.

One can therefore expect substantial resistance to reform proposals that significantly strengthen party control over the selection of American presidents. Indeed, to many Americans, party leadership and party influence connotes bossism, smoke-filled rooms, and rule by a small elite, a decision-making process hardly consistent with democratic principles. Such perceptions are understandable given the blemished history of party organization leadership. Nevertheless, to focus on the misgivings and negative aspects of party leadership is to overlook and obfuscate the larger contributions of the parties.

One is better served by considering the role of parties in light of the writings of several leading scholars of American party politics. Consider the perspective of William N. Chambers, for example. In Chambers's view, political parties were the institutions that effectively met the political and economic challenges that surfaced during the early days of the republic, what Chambers refers to as the "loads of the new nation." According to Chambers, it was through the institutions of political parties that pragmatism was maintained in public policy-making, factionalism in American politics was kept at bay, and the American Constitution, a novel experiment in limited government, was set in motion.[2]

V.O. Key, discussing the central functions of political parties, identifies the parties as institutions "basic" to our democracy. In Key's perspective, political parties are needed to effectively manage the transfer of political power from one election to the next, and through parties broad popular support for public policy is acquired. According to Key, effective governance is greatly enhanced by a strong and meaningful system of political parties.[3]

One also needs to consider the perspective of Fred I. Greenstein. In Greenstein's view, American presidents are more likely to work effectively with Congress, as well as their cabinet, when political parties structure the course of national politics. Through parties a sense of partisan teamwork is facilitated, which, in turn, unites the presidency with the component parts of the federal government. Such teamwork is a necessary requirement for presidential coalition-building.[4]

It is important for future reformers to remain cognizant of the preceding perspectives as they contemplate new and innovative methods for choosing the American president. Political reforms in the 1990s must be implemented with an eye toward meaningful and influential political party participation as an effective system of linkage and governance fully depend upon it.

A SPECIFIC PROPOSAL: A PREPRIMARY NATIONAL CONVENTION

One proposal that has emerged from the field of political science would have the direct effect of strengthening the function of parties in the process of presidential selection. Such a proposal, which would radically revise the presidential nominating process, is worthy of serious consideration. This is the controversial proposal to have a national primary election preceded by a national party convention.[5] According to this plan, political parties would conduct a national nominating convention that would serve the purpose of "winnowing" viable presidential candidates. The delegates to the national party convention, most of whom would be party professionals, would formally endorse a presidential candidate, thereby creating the notion of an official party choice and front-runner. The convention, as a result, would serve a very critical screening and endorsing function within the context of the nominating process, rather than serve as an institution that simply ratifies those candidates who emerge as front-runners through the lengthy and faction-ridden process of state primaries and caucuses.

Following the national party convention, a national primary would be conducted. The convention-endorsed candidate would compete against other candidates who were able to demonstrate a respectable level of viability at the national convention, viability determined by acquiring a certain percentage of delegate support.

The national primary therefore would be contested by the party-endorsed candidate and only presidential candidates who are deemed competitive. The list of presidential candidates contesting the national primary would probably be much shorter compared with the lists that appear under the current nominating system. Presidential contenders would be those with a respectable base of support rather than support from narrow interests within the party. It is doubtful that the presidential nominating process under this system would be contested by relatively unknown presidential candidates collectively referred to as "the seven dwarfs." A viable candidate would most likely be an individual of substantial national stature.

The preprimary endorsement convention followed by a national primary is a bold recommendation, yet one with substantial merit. First, conducting a national primary following the nominating convention would eliminate the long and fractious nature of state primaries and caucuses, events and mechanisms that accomplish little in the way of mobilizing political consensus and governing coalitions. Second, the national primary would eliminate the enormous and grossly unfair momentum created by the results of one state's primary, most notably the state of New Hampshire. The nominating process therefore would truly be a national event, a process fully consistent with the concept of a national chief executive. Third, the national primary, due to a high concentration of media coverage, would also have the effect of stimulating interest in viable presidential candidates, thereby generating a higher and more respectable level of voter turnout. Fourth, the preprimary national convention would allow the political parties the opportunity to determine who the viable presidential candidates are and subsequently what the issues during the campaign will involve. In this respect, according to Martin Wattenberg, the parties, rather than the media, would have more influence in determining the key personalities and the content of the campaign. Put differently, the presidential campaign would unfold from the political party structure rather than the structure of the mass media. Of further merit is the fact that the national primary would be conducted fairly soon after the nominating convention, which would deny the media the opportunity to define the politics and character of the campaign.

To revitalize the role of political party leadership in the nominating process would yield positive consequences for the process of presidential selection as well as the general health of American democracy: factionalism would be significantly reduced, presidential nominees would be representative of their political party, a broad consensus would be achieved among the party's rank and file for those who emerge as nominees, and party as opposed to candidate-centered campaigns would resurface in presidential politics. These are several of the benefits that would flow from a resurrection of party organization influence in the presidential selection process.

In my view, the preprimary convention, followed by a national primary, is a proposal that should be enthusiastically pursued. Interestingly, the proposal would restructure the presidential nominating process on a scale very similar to that which followed the disastrous events of 1824. Given the gravity of the crisis facing presidential selection, the proposal, albeit a radical response, seems to be appropriate.

Notes

INTRODUCTION

1. ABC News, *The 88 Vote* (New York: Capital Cities/ABC Inc., 1988), p. xix.

2. Austin Ranney, "Participation in Precinct Caucuses" in James I. Lengle and Byron E. Shafer, *Presidential Politics*, 2nd edition (New York: St. Martin's Press, 1983), p. 174. Study applies to Democratic caucuses.

3. ABC News, *The 88 Vote*, p. 15.

4. Anthony King, "How Not to Select Presidential Candidates" in Austin Ranney, ed., *The American Elections of 1980* (Washington, D.C.: American Enterprise Institute for Public Policy Research, 1981), p. 306; see Table 9–1 for data.

5. Gallup Poll, September 21–24, 1984.

6. Gallup Poll, October 23–26, 1988 (registered voters only).

7. Gallup Poll, October 20–21, 1988.

8. Herbert Asher, *Presidential Elections and American Politics*, 3rd edition (Homewood, Ill.: Dorsey Press, 1984), p. 15. See Figure 1.1

9. Gerald Pomper with Susan Lederman, *Elections in America*, 2nd edition (New York: Longman, 1980), p. 75.

10. Everett Carll Ladd, Jr., *Where Have All the Voters Gone?*, 2nd edition (New York: Norton, 1982), p. 127.

11. Richard Rose, *The Postmodern President* (Chatham, N.J.: Chatham House, 1988), p. 270. See Table 13.1.

12. Larry Berman, *The New American Presidency* (Boston: Little, Brown, 1987), p. 125. See Table 4.2.

13. Robert Shogan, *None of the Above* (New York: Nal Books, 1982), p. 251.

14. Quoted in Shogan, *None of the Above,* p. 259.

15. Theodore C. Sorensen, *A Different Kind of Presidency* (New York: Harper and Row, 1984), p. 45.

16. Ibid., pp. 46–47.

17. ABC News, *The 88 Vote,* p. 27.

18. Ibid., p. 26.

19. Gerald Pomper, *Nominating the President* (New York: Norton, 1966), p. 20.

20. George Dangerfield, *The Era of Good Feelings* (New York: Harcourt, Brace and World, 1952), p. 314.

21. Ibid., p. 335.

22. Robert V. Remini, *The Election of Andrew Jackson* (Philadelphia: Lippincott, 1963), p. 19.

23. Excellent sources for examining questions pertaining to the representativeness of the presidential nominating process include: Dennis G. Sullivan et al., *The Politics of Representation* (New York: St. Martin's Press, 1974); Jeanne Jordon Kirkpatrick, *The New Presidential Elite* (New York: Russell Sage, 1976); William J. Crotty, *Political Reform and the American Experiment* (New York: Harper and Row, 1977); James Ceaser, *Presidential Selection* (Princeton: Princeton University Press, 1979); James I. Lengle and Byron E. Shafer, eds., *Presidential Politics,* 2nd edition (New York: St. Martin's Press, 1983), part 3; Nelson Polsby and Aaron Wildavsky, *Presidential Elections,* 7th edition (New York; Free Press, 1988).

24. For an examination of the distinction between a political "professional" and political "amateur," see James Q. Wilson, *The Amateur Democrat* (Chicago: University of Chicago Press, 1966).

25. A review of criticisms directed toward primaries can be found in William J. Crotty, *Political Reform and the American Experiment,* pp. 208–28).

26. For a discussion of media, momentum, and the impact of the New Hampshire primary, see Gary Orren and Nelson Polsby, eds., *Media and Momentum* (Chatham, N. J.: Chatham House, 1987).

27. Issues pertaining to national nominating conventions receive very clear examination in Judith H. Parris, *The Convention Problem* (Washington, D.C.: Brookings Institution, 1972).

28. The evidence reveals that ten vice-presidents have become president through succession: Tyler, Fillmore, Andrew Johnson, Hayes, Arthur, Theodore Roosevelt, Coolidge, Truman, Lyndon Johnson, and Ford. Five were elected in their own right: Adams, Jefferson, Van Buren, Nixon, and Bush. See Barbara Hinckley, *Problems of the Presidency* (Glenview, Ill.: Scott, Foresman, 1985), Chap. 6.

29. The reliance on media, especially television, for forming opinions regarding politics and politicians is discussed and documented in Austin Ranney, *Channels of Power* (New York: Basic Books, 1983), Chap. 1 and 4.

30. L. Sandy Maisel, *Parties and Elections in America* (New York: Random House, 1987), p. 227. According to Maisel, of the $29.4 million allocated to the two major candidates for the 1980 presidential campaign, President Carter spent $20.5 million and Governor Reagan $16.8 million on media advertising.

31. The role and influence of media consultants receives extensive treatment in Larry J. Sabato, *The Rise of Media Consultants* (New York: Basic Books, 1981). A concise review of image building and expenditures is found in Stephen J. Wayne, *The Road to the White House*, 3rd edition (New York: St. Martin's Press, 1988), Chap. 7. According to Wayne, the Reagan campaign of 1984 spent $27 million on media advertising, while Mondale's media efforts consumed $23 million.

32. Herbert Alexander, *Financing Politics*, Chap. 1.

33. A variety of issues pertaining to presidential debates can be found in Austin Ranney, ed., *The Past and Future of Presidential Debates* (Washington, D.C: American Enterprise Institute for Public Policy Research, 1979).

34. An excellent examination of the Electoral College can be found in Wallace S. Sayre and Judith H. Parris, *Voting for President: The Electoral College and the American Political System* (Washington, D.C.: Brookings Institution. 1970).

35. For very recent comparative figures, see Milton C. Cummings, Jr., and David Wise, *Democracy under Pressure*, 6th edition (San Diego: Harcourt, Brace, Jovanovich, 1989), p. 349.

36. The literature on political party decline within the context of the presidential selection process is vast. See, for example: Jeanne Jordon Kirkpatrick, *Dismantling the Parties* (Washington, D.C.: American Enterprise Institute for Public Policy Research, 1978); Ruth K. Scott and Ronald J. Hrebenar, *Parties in Crisis*, 2nd edition (New York: John Wiley, 1984); and William J. Crotty, *American Parties in Decline*, 2nd edition (Boston: Little, Brown, 1984).

CHAPTER ONE, PART 1

1. Hanna F. Pitkin, *The Concept of Representation* (Berkeley: University of California Press, 1967), Chap. 4–6.

2. William Crotty and John S. Jackson III, *Presidential Primaries and Nominations* (Washington, D.C.: Congressional Quarterly Press, 1985).

3. Commission on Party Structure and Delegate Selection, *Mandate for Reform* Washington, D.C.: Democratic National Committee, 1970).

4. U.S. Department of Commerce, *1989 Statistical Abstract of the U.S.*, 109th edition (Washington, D.C.: Bureau of the Census, 1989), p. 13.

5. Ibid., p. 23.

6. Ibid., p. 13.

7. John S. Jackson III, Barbara L. Brown, and David Bositis, "Herbert McClosky and Friends Revisited," *American Politics Quarterly*, 10 (April 1982): 158–80; Warren E. Miller, *Without Consent: Mass-Elite Linkages in Presidential Politics* (Lexington: University of Kentucky Press, 1988); Byron E. Shafer, *Bifurcated Politics: Evolution and Reform in the National Party Convention* (Cambridge: Harvard University Press, 1988).

8. Jackson, Brown, and Bositis, "McClosky and Friends"; Shafer, *Bifurcated Politics*.

9. Jackson, Brown, and Bositis, "McClosky and Friends."

10. Anthony Downs, *An Economic Theory of Democracy* (New York: Harper and Row, 1957); V.O. Key, Jr., *Politics, Parties and Pressure Groups*, 5th edition (New York: Crowell, 1964).

11. Jeanne J. Kirkpatrick, *The New Presidential Elite* (New York: Russel Sage Foundation, 1976); James W. Ceaser, *Reforming the Reforms* (Cambridge, Mass.: Ballinger, 1982).

12. Warren E. Miller and M. Kent Jennings, *Parties in Transition: A Longitudinal Study of Party Elites and Party Supporters* (New York: Russell Sage Foundation, 1986); Shafer, *Bifurcated Politics*; Miller, *Without Consent*, 1988.

13. Miller and Jennings, *Parties in Transition*, 1986.

14. Austin Ranney, *The Doctrine of Responsible Party Government* (Urbana: University of Illinois Press, 1962).

CHAPTER ONE, PART 2

1. Howard L. Reiter, *Selecting the President* (Philadelphia: University of Pennsylvania Press, 1985), Chap. 1.

2. Larry M. Bartels, *Presidential Primaries and the Dynamics of Public Choice* (Princeton: Princeton University Press, 1988), p. 23. Also Rhodes Cook, "The Nominating Process" in Michael Nelson, ed., *The Election of 1988* (Washington, D.C.: Congressional Quarterly Press, 1989), p. 28.

3. Herbert B. Asher, *Presidential Elections and American Politics* (Chicago: Dorsey Press, 1988), p. 249.

4. Walter Lippmann, *Public Opinion* (New York: Free Press, 1965), p. 19.

5. Thomas W. Patterson, "The Press and its Missed Assignment" in Michael Nelson, ed., *The Election of 1988* (Washington, D.C.: Congressional Quarterly Press, 1989), pp. 97–98.

6. Quoted in Bartels, *Presidential Primaries*, pp. 40–41.

7. Ibid., p. 36.

8. Ibid., pp. 37–38.

9. Cook, "The Nominating Process." p. 31.

10. Ibid., p. 35.

11. William G. Mayer, "The New Hampshire Primary" in Gary R. Orren and Nelson W. Polsby, eds., *Media and Momentum* (Chatham, N.J.: Chatham House), pp. 26–29.

12. Bartels, *Presidential Primaries*, p. 261.

13. V.O. Key, Jr., *American State Politics: An Introduction* (New York: Knopf, 1956), chap. 5.

14. Austin Ranney, "Turnout and Representation in Presidential Primary Elections," *American Political Science Review* 66 (1972): 21–37.

15. James I. Lengle, *Representation and Presidential Primaries: The Democratic Party in the Post Reform Era* (Westport, Conn.: Greenwood Press, 1981), p. 78.

16. Quoted in Bartels, *Presidential Primaries*, p. 141.

17. Ibid., pp. 140–48.

18. Ibid., pp. 166–71.

19. Ibid., p. 203.

20. Reiter, *Selecting the President*, pp. 61–63.

21. David E. Price, *Bringing Back the Parties* (Washington, D.C.: Congressional Quarterly Press, 1984), p. 195.

22. Warren E. Miller and M. Kent Jennings, *Parties in Transition* (New York: Russell Sage Foundation, 1986), pp. 221–23.

23. Nelson W. Polsby and Aaron Wildavsky, *Presidential Elections*, 7th edition (New York: Free Press, 1988), pp. 127–43.

24. Gerald M. Pomper, "The Presidential Nominations in Gerald M. Pomper, ed., *The Election of 1988* (Chatham, N.J.: Chatham House, 1989), pp. 68–69.

25. Reiter, *Selecting the President*, pp. 65–71.

26. Ibid., p. 50.

27. Ibid., p. 130.

28. Lester Seligman and Cary R. Covingtion, *The Coalitional Presidency* (Chicago: Dorsey Press, 1989), pp. 7–16.

29. Nelson W. Polsby, *Consequences of Party Reform* (New York: Oxford University Press, 1983), pp. 105–14.

CHAPTER TWO, PART 2

1. Democratic National Committee, *Delegate Selection Rules for the 1980 Democratic National Convention* (Washington, D.C.: Democratic National Committee, (1978).

2. Since the rules of the convention must be adopted before any other votes, including the votes on platform and presidential nomination, they are particularly useful in testing the strength of a candidate at the convention.

3. For example, in 1968, the last year prior to the McGovern-Fraser reforms, there were only nine presidential primaries with the names of the presidential candidates on the ballot. Of those only three bound the delegates to vote for the winner of the primary. By 1980 there were thirty-five primaries with the names of the presidential candidates on the ballot and thirty-three of these primaries were binding on the delegates.

4. The Gallup Opinion Index, Report #180 (Princeton, New Jersey, August 1980).

5. Nelson W. Polsby, "The Democratic Nomination" in *The American Elections of 1980*, Austin Ranney, ed. (Washington, D.C.: American Enterprise Institute for Public Policy Research, 1981).

6. Minnesota is a special case. Because it was the vice-president's home state, those who wished to oppose Carter ran as uncommitted—in order to avoid embarrassing Mondale. The thirty "yes" votes came from uncommitted delegates. On the face of it, it looks like Representative Nolan picked up thirty votes for the open convention position, while in fact the open convention advocates lost seven votes.

7. Nelson W. Polsby and Aaron B. Wildavsky, *Presidential Elections: Strategies of American Electoral Politics*, 7th edition (New York: Free Press, 1988); Byron E. Shafer, *Bifurcated Politics: Evolution and Reform in the National Party Convention* (Cambridge: Harvard University Press, 1988).

8. Shafer, *Bifurcated Politics*, pp. 152–54.

9. For example, at the end of the primary season in 1968 Hubert Humphrey had 662.5 delegates formally pledged to him out of 1,312 needed to nominate, or 50 percent of what he needed. Although he was the presumptive nominee, much activity remained before the convention. Whereas at the end of the 1984 primary season Walter Mondale had 1967 pledged delegates out of 1,974 needed to nominate or 99 percent of what he needed. See *Congressional Quarterly*, June 14, 1968, p. 1477, and June 9, 1984, p. 1345.

10. Shafer, *Bifurcated Politics*, pp. 276–80.

11. Elaine Ciulla Kamarck, "Who Will Control Coverage of the Convention," *Newsday*, July 11, 1988.

12. In the gubernatorial primary in Illinois in 1986, a very small turnout allowed a follower of Lyndon LaRouche, a right-wing extremist, to win the primary—forcing the Democratic Party of Illinois to disavow its elected candidate and endorse Adlai Stevenson III, who ran on the ticket of a new party. In Louisiana in 1988 the neo-Nazi David Duke embarrassed the Republican Party by winning the primary for a seat in the state legislature and then going on to win the seat under the Republican label.

13. Democratic National Committee, *Delegate Selection Rules for the 1984 Democratic National Convention* (Washington, D.C.: Democratic National Committee, 1982).

CHAPTER THREE, PART 1

1. This was at an off-the-record breakfast in Washington, D.C., sponsored by the Presidential Campaign Hotline.

2. Quoted in Jack Germond and Jules Witcover, *Whose Broad Stripes and Bright Stars? The Pursuit of the Presidency, 1988* (New York: Warner Books, 1989), p. 441.

3. Ibid., p. 437.

4. Gallup Poll, March 8–11, 1990. Survey among 1,228 adults nationwide.

5. Quoted in Ann Devroy, "Good News for Quayle: Lots of People Have No Opinion of Him," *Washington Post National Weekly Edition*, August 21–27, 1989, p. 37.

6. Gallup Poll, March 8–11, 1990. It is obvious that doing a good job as vice-president and being equipped to be president are not the same thing in the public mind.

7. Sam Donaldson and Diane Sawyer, interview with J. Danforth Quayle, "Prime Time Live," ABC News broadcast, August 17, 1989.

8. Poll data cited in Devroy, "Good News for Quayle."

9. Donaldson and Sawyer, interview with Quayle.

10. Quoted in Everett Carll Ladd, *The American Polity: The People and their Government* (New York: Norton, 1989), p. 228.

11. Thomas E. Cronin, "Rethinking the Vice-Presidency" in Thomas E. Cronin, ed., *Rethinking the Presidency* (Boston: Little, Brown, 1982), p. 326.

12. For further elaboration on this, see Arthur M. Schlesinger, Jr., "The Vice Presidency: A Modest Proposal" in Arthur M. Schlesinger, Jr., *The Imperial Presidency* (New York: Popular Library, 1974), esp. p. 474.

13. Quoted in Paul C. Light, *Vice-Presidential Power: Advice and Influence in the White House* (Baltimore: Johns Hopkins University Press, 1984), p. 13.

14. Quoted in Schlesinger, "The Vice Presidency," p. 474.

15. Adams served as George Washington's vice-president from 1789 to 1797. Calhoun served as Andrew Jackson's vice-president from 1829 to 1833.

16. Bush cast no tie-breaking votes in 1981 and 1982, two in 1983, one each in 1984 and 1985, two in 1986, one in 1987, and none in 1988. In 1983 Bush voted twice to continue U.S. production of nerve gas. A year later he voted for continued production and eventual deployment of the MX missile. In 1985 Bush voted to reduce the budget deficit by $56 billion for fiscal year 1986 and $295 billion over the following three years. In 1986 he voted in favor of Ronald Reagan's selection of Daniel Manion to be a U.S. circuit judge for the Seventh Court of Appeals. He also voted to continue U.S. production of nerve gas. In 1987 Bush voted against an amendment that would have reduced federal funding for the Strategic Defense Initiative (popularly known as Star Wars). Thus, three of Bush's seven tie-breakers involved U.S. production of nerve gas.

17. Remarks of Vice-President Dan Quayle, luncheon with the *Los Angeles Times* Washington bureau September 6, 1989.

18. Quoted in Schlesinger, "The Vice Presidency," p. 475.

19. Ibid., p. 474.

20. Quoted in Light, *Vice-Presidential Power*, p. 13.

21. These are frequently quoted remarks about the vice-presidency.

22. Previously, the runner-up served as vice-president. Thomas Jefferson did not welcome the prospect of a political antagonist becoming his vice-president, so he conspired with Aaron Burr to produce an electoral college tie—a plot to get Burr the vice-presidency. Having tasted political power Burr decided he wanted the top job after all, and forced a constitutional crisis that produced the Twelfth Amendment.

23. Thus, the House of Representatives in addition to the Senate would have a say in naming a vice-president.

24. Under section three of the Twenty-Fifth Amendment, a president may pronounce himself or herself unable to perform the duties of the office. This is done by writing the Speaker of the House of Representatives and the President pro tempore of the Senate. A president may resume office by transmitting a letter to the Speaker and President pro tempore stating that the temporary disability has ended. Ronald Reagan transmitted such letters prior to and just after his cancer surgery in 1985. Section four of the amendment allows a vice-president and a majority of the cabinet to declare a president disabled. If that happens, the vice-president becomes acting president. If the president disagrees with the cabinet decision, an appeal may be lodged with the Congress. Should two-thirds of both houses of Congress agree with the cabinet finding, the vice-president continues as acting president; otherwise the president regains the office.

25. Roosevelt removed Wallace from this latter position, after he tangled with the Secretaries of State and Commerce.

26. Quoted in *RN: The Memoirs of Richard Nixon* (New York: Grosset and Dunlap, 1978), pp. 87–88.

27. Quoted in Jimmy Carter, *Keeping Faith* (New York: Bantam Books, 1982), p. 35.

28. See James Fallows, "The Passionless Presidency," *Atlantic Monthly* (May 1979): 42. The example is often cited as a reminder of how not to run the White House.

29. Carter, *Keeping Faith*, 40.

30. Mondale kept his advice to Carter strictly confidential. He and Carter also integrated their staffs, something that had never happened before. Heretofore, vice-presidential staffers were jealous of slights by presidential assistants, reflecting their bosses' animosities.

31. In 1960 Vice-President Richard Nixon received the Republican presidential nomination. Four years later, former vice-president Lyndon Johnson, now president, was nominated by the Democrats. In 1968 Hubert Humphrey, the incumbent vice-president, and Nixon headed the Democratic and Republican tickets, respectively. Nixon led the GOP ticket again in 1972. In 1976 former vice-president Gerald R. Ford, now president, wrested the Republican presidential nomination from Ronald Reagan. In 1984 former vice-president Walter Mondale won the Democratic presidential nomination. Finally, George Bush captured the 1988 Republican presidential nomination.

32. Schuyler Colfax served as vice-president during the first administration of U.S. Grant (1860–1873). Grant resented Colfax's presidential

aspirations and replaced him with Henry Wilson who served 1873–1875. Wilson died in office. William Wheeler served one term as vice-president during the administration of Rutherford B. Hayes (1877–1881). Thomas Hendricks formed the other half of the Democratic ticket with Grover Cleveland in 1884. Both were elected, but Hendricks died during his first year in office. Levi P. Morton was elected vice-president in 1888, and served during the administration of Benjamin Harrison (1889–1893). Garret A. Hobart was elected vice-president in 1896, the year that William McKinley was chosen president in a landslide. But Hobart served only two years, dying in 1899. He was replaced by Theodore Roosevelt in 1901. Until passage of the Twenty-Fifth Amendment in 1967, if a vice-president died in office or succeeded to the presidency, the vice-presidential position remained vacant until the next election.

33. Quoted in Light, *Vice Presidential Power*, p. 1.

34. Ibid., p. 137.

35. The four conventions were 1900 when Republican leaders replaced the late Garret A. Hobart with Theodore Roosevelt; 1904, 1924, and 1948, when the vice-presidency was vacant.

36. Quoted in Gerald M. Pomper, "The Nomination of Hubert Humphrey for Vice President," in Norman L. Zucker, ed., *The American Party Process: Readings and Comments* (New York: Dodd, Mead, 1968), p. 132. This article was first published in *The Journal of Politics*, volume 28, number 3 (August 1966): 639–59.

37. See, for instance, Ted Morgan, *FDR: A Biography* (New York: Simon and Schuster, 1985), esp. pp. 725–30.

38. The others were Congressmen Charles Halleck and Walter Judd, Governors Dan Thornton and Arthur Langlie. See Dwight D. Eisenhower, *Mandate for Change: The White House Years, 1953–56* (Garden City, N.Y.: Doubleday, 1963).

39. Quoted in Pomper, "The Nomination of Hubert Humphrey," p. 122.

40. Ibid., p. 131.

41. Ibid. At the time of his nomination, Humphrey was a United States Senator.

42. John Ehrlichman, *Witness to Power: The Nixon Years* (New York: Pocket Books, 1982), p. 122.

43. The Hunt Commission created the position of "superdelegate" at the Democratic convention. Party leaders—including members of Con-

gress, Democratic state chairs, and governors—could attend the convention automatically, without having previously announced their presidential preference.

44. Quoted in Germond and Witcover, *Whose Broad Stripes and Bright Stars?*, p. 334.

45. Ibid, p. 379.

46. Quoted in David Hoffman, "For Bush, the Baton at Last," *Washington Post*, January 20, 1989. p. F-3.

47. Muskie was Hubert Humphrey's choice to receive the Democratic vice-presidential nomination in 1968; Eagleton was George McGovern's handpicked candidate in 1972; Ferroro was Walter Mondale's choice in 1984.

48. The Bush campaign never considered dropping Quayle from the ticket, even after it was alleged that he was the beneficiary of favoritism in gaining a post in the Indiana National Guard.

49. Cited in Cronin, "Rethinking the Vice-Presidency," p. 341.

50. The first simultaneous vote for president and vice-president came in 1984 when Republican delegates renominated Ronald Reagan and George Bush.

51. This was Jesse Jackson's argument in support of his being named a vice-presidential candidate in 1988. In recent years, however, only Lyndon Johnson, a runner-up in the 1960 convention balloting, was chosen as a vice-presidential candidate.

52. Arthur M. Schlesinger, Jr., is a noted advocate of this idea. See Schlesinger, "The Vice Presidency."

53. Carter, *Keeping Faith*, p. 36.

CHAPTER THREE, PART 2

1. "Official Report of the Vice Presidential Selection Commission of the Democratic Party," December 19, 1973, 5 pp.

2. Irving G. Williams, *The Rise of the Vice Presidency* (Washington, D.C.: Public Affairs Press; 1956).

3. Joel K. Goldstein, *The Modern American Vice Presidency: The Transformation of a Political Institution* (Princeton: Princeton University

Press; 1982), and Marie D. Natoli, *American Prince, American Pauper* (Westport, Conn.: Greenwood Press, 1985).

4. The Wallace-Roosevelt correspondence at Hyde Park includes serious substantive exchanges on foreign affairs as well as seed swapping between gentleman farmers.

5. The Barkley-Truman correspondence at Independence is largely nostalgic World War I patter.

6. Paul T. David, "The Vice Presidency: Its Institutional Evolution and Contemporary Status," *Journal of Politics*, vol. 29, no. 4 (November 6 1967).

7. The folders of hate mail are preserved at the Lyndon B. Johnson Library in Austin, Texas.

8. Conversations with John Stewart and other former aides to Hubert Humphrey when he was vice-president, during 1974.

9. Conversations in May of 1974 with C.D. Ward, Jean Spencer, and other Agnew staff members.

10. Contemporary articles catching this unusual spectacle are David Broder's "Ford's Three Pitches," *Washington Post*, June 23, 1974, and Rowland Evans and Robert Novak's "Ford: a Time for Independence," *Washington Post*, August 1, 1974.

11. Conversations with Susan Herter, Vice-President Rockfeller's administrative assistant, during 1977–80.

12. John Saxon, a Mondale aide in 1978–79, says that Mondale reasoned that a long-term assignment such as a commission chairmanship might preclude his being available for more important ad hoc assignments from the president.

13. Conversations with Joan Abrahamson, aid to Vice-President Bush in the first Reagan administration.

14. Frederick C. Thayer lauded the idea in "Was a Good Idea Lost in the Media Shuffle?" in *Pitt*, November 1980, supplement, p. 1. George Will commented favorably in "Reagan Can Win," in *Newsweek* March 31, 1980, p. 92.

CHAPTER FOUR, PART 1

1. Holli A. Semetko, "The Role of Mass Media in Elections: What Can We Learn From 1988?," *The Political Science Teacher*, 1 (Summer 1988): 18.

2. Henry E. Brady and Richard Johnston, "What's the Primary Message: Horse Race or Issue Journalism? in *Media and Momentum*, Gary Orren and Nelson Polsby, eds. (Chatham, N.J.: Chatham House, 1987), pp. 127–86, and see Dan Nimmo, "Handicapping in the Early Campaign: Frontrunners, Dark Horse, and Also Rans in the Polls," *Political Communication Review*, 11 (1986): 19–32.

3. David Broder, "Political Reporters in Presidential Politics," in *Presidential Politics*, James Lengle and Byron Shafer, eds. (New York: St. Martin's Press, 1980).

4. David Weaver, Doris Graber, Maxwell McCombs, and Chaim Eyal, *Media Agenda-Setting in a Presidential Election* (New York: Praeger, 1981).

5. Edward Epstein, *News from Nowhere* (New York: Random House, 1973); Herbert Gans, *Deciding What's News* (New York: Pantheon, 1979); and Michael Robinson and Margaret Sheehan, *Over the Wire and on TV* (New York: Russell Sage Foundation, 1983).

6. Keith Blume, *The Presidential Election Show* (S. Hadley, Mass.: Bergin and Garvey, 1985), and Neil Postman, *Amusing Ourselves to Death: Public Discourse in the Age of Show Business* (New York: Viking Penguin, 1985).

7. Robert Agranoff, *The New Style in Election Campaigns* (Boston: Holbrook Press, 1976); Kathleen Jamieson, *Packaging the President* (New York: Oxford University Press, 1984); and Robert Spero, *The Duping of the American Voter: Dishonesty and Deception in Presidential Television Advertising* (New York: Lippincott, Crowell, 1980).

8. Robert Cantor, *Voter Behavior and Presidential Elections* (Itasca, Ill.: Peacock Publishers, 1975) pp. 104–5.

9. Philip Converse, "The Concept of the Normal Vote," in Angus Campbell et al., *Elections and the Political Order* (New York: John Wiley, 1966), pp. 9–39.

10. Daniel Boorstin, *The Image* (New York: Harper and Row, 1964).

11. Doris Graber, *Verbal Behavior and Politics* (Champaign: University of Illinois Press, 1976), p. 249.

12. Becker, McCombs, and McLeod in *Political Communication*, Steven Chaffee, ed. (Beverly Hills: Sage Publications, 1975).

13. Paul Lazarsfeld, Bernard Berelson, and Hazel Gaudet, *The People's Choice* (New York: Columbia University Press: 1944, 1948, and 1968).

14. See Leon Festinger, *A Theory of Cognitive Dissonance* (Stanford: Stanford University Press, 1957); J.T. Klapper, *The Effects of Mass Communications* (New York: Free Press, 1960); and see Lewis Froman and John Skipper, "Factors Related to Misperceiving Party Stands on Issues," *Public Opinion Quarterly*, 26 (1962): 265–71.

15. See McCombs, in Chaffee, *Political Communication*, p. 174.

16. Sidney Kraus, *Televised Presidential Debates and Public Policy* Hillsdale: Lawrence Erlbaum Associates, 1988).

17. Doris Graber, *Processing the News* (New York: Longman, 1984); Carl Bybee, Jack McLeod, William Luetscher, and Gina Garramone, "Mass Communication and Voter Volatility,," *Public Opinion Quarterly*, 45 (Spring 1981): 69–90; and see Paul Hagner and John Orman, "A Panel Study of the Impact of the First 1976 Presidential Debate: Media-Events, 'Rootless Voters' and Campaign Learning," paper presented to the annual meeting of the American Political Science Association, Washington, D.C., September 1977.

18. Thomas Patterson and Robert McClure, *The Unseeing Eye* (New York: Putnam's, 1976).

19. Lazarsfeld et al., *The People's Choice*.

20. Murray Edelman, "The Politics of Persuasion," in *Choosing the President* James Barber, ed. (New York: Columbia University, Prentice-Hall, 1975), p. 154.

CHAPTER FOUR, PART 2

The author would like to thank Ms. Sandra Hensley for her assistance in this research project.

1. Mickey Kaus, Howard Fineman, and John McCormick, "Adventures in Campaignland" in *Behind the Scenes in American Government: Personalities and Politics*, 7th edition, Peter Woll, ed. (Boston: Scott, Foresman, 1989), p. 38.

2. *Newsweek*, October 31, 1988, p. 19.

3. David H. Weaver et al., *Media Agenda-Setting in a Presidential Election: Issues, Images, and Interest* (New York: Praeger, 1981), p. 5.

4. Albert R. Hunt, "The Media and Presidential Campaigns" in *Elections American Style*, A. James Reichley, ed. (Washington, D.C.: Brookings Institution, 1987), p. 53.

5. David Broder, *Behind the Front Page: A Candid Look at How the News is Made* (New York: Simon and Schuster, 1987), p. 216.

6. Roger Mudd, "Television Network News in Campaigns" in *Political Persuasion in Presidential Campaigns*, L. Patrick Devlin, ed. (New Brunswick, N.J.: Transaction Books, 1987), p. 91.

7. Andrew Radolf, "Television News Rates High," *Editor and Publisher*, vol. 118 (April 13, 1985): 10.

8. John Mashek, "News Magazines in Campaigns" in Devlin *Political Persuasion*, p. 123.

9. Christopher F. Arterton, *Media Politics: The New Strategies of Presidential Campaigns* (Lexington, Mass.: Lexington Books, 1984), p. 44.

10. Ibid., p. 45.

11. *Mass Media and American Politics* (Washington, D.C.: Congressional Quarterly Press, 1980), p. 179.

12. Michael Robinson and Margaret Sheehan, *Over the Wire and on TV: CBS and UPI in Campaign 80* (New York: Russell Sage Foundation, 1983), p. 6.

13. James G. Stovall, "Coverage of the 1984 Presidential Campaign," *Journalism Quarterly*, vol. 65 (Summer 1988): 444.

14. Thomas E. Patterson, "The Press and its Missed Assignment" in *The Elections of 1988*, Michael Nelson, ed. (Washington, D.C.: Congressional Quarterly Press, 1989], p. 97. The study is based on a content analysis of *Time* and *Newsweek* coverage of the 1988 elections.

15. Anthony Lewis, "NYT's Lewis Criticizes Media's Performance," *Broadcasting*, vol. 115 (December 26, 1988), p. 67.

16. Bruce Babbitt, "A Candidate's Farewell: An Inside Look at What It's Like to Run and Lose" in Woll, *Behind the Scenes in American Government*, p. 47.

17. Albert R. Hunt, "The Media and the Presidential Campaign" in Reichley, *Elections American Style*, p. 67.

18. Cited in Thomas E. Patterson, "The Press and its Missed Assignment" in Nelson, *The Elections of 1988*, p. 103.

19. Cited in Albert R. Hunt, "The Media and Presidential Campaigns" in Reichley, *Elections American Style*, p. 53.

20. Ibid., p. 63.

21. Ibid., p. 53.

22. Thomas E. Patterson, "The Press and its Missed Assignment" in Nelson, *The Elections of 1988*, p. 99.

23. Hunt, "The Media and Presidential Campaigns" in Reichley, *Elections American Style*, p. 73.

24. George Garneau, "Latest Public Perception of the Press," *Editor and Publisher*, vol. 120 (November 28, 1987), p. 32.

25. Quoted in Arterton, *Media Politics*, p. 52.

26. Nicholas Von Hoffman, "Public Opinion Polls: Newspapers Making Their Own News?" *Public Opinion Quarterly*, vol. 44 (Winter 1980): 573.

27. James G. Stovall, "Coverage of 1984 Presidential Campaign," *Journalism Quarterly*, vol. 65 (Summer 1988): 449.

28. Anthony C. Broah, "Horse-Race Journalism: Reporting the Polls in the 1976 Presidential Elections," *Public Opinion Quarterly*, vol. 55 (Winter 1980): 528.

29. Thomas E. Patterson, "The Press and its Missed Assignment," in Nelson, *The Elections of 1988*, p. 101.

30. Thomas E. Patterson, *The Mass Media Election: How Americans Choose their President* (New York: Praeger, 1980), pp. 41–42.

31. Michael Robinson and Margaret Sheehan, *Over the Wire and on TV: CBS and UPI in Campaign 80*, p. 303.

32. David Broder, "Columnists is Campaigns" in Devlin, *Political Persuasion*, pp. 100–101.

33. William E. Bricker, "Network TV News and the 1976 Presidential Primaries" in *Race for the Presidency: The Media and the Nomination Process*, James D. Barber, ed. (Englewood Cliffs, N.J.: Prentice-Hall, 1978), p. 105.

34. Lewis, "NYT's Lewis Criticizes Media's Performance," p. 67.

CHAPTER 5, PART 1

1. The arguments contained within this article have also been presented by the author in formal testimony before the United States Senate

Committee on Rules and Administration, September 29, 1983, and the Senate Committee on Commerce, Science, and Transportation, September 10, 1985.

2. Keith Melville, John Doble, and Mary Komarnicki, "Money and Politics," paper presented at the Aspen Institute Conference on Campaign Finance, Queenstown, Maryland, January 24–26, 1985.

3. Figures on campaign costs based on data supplied by the Federal Election Commission.

CHAPTER FIVE, PART 2

1. Patrick Devlin, "An analysis of Presidential Television Commercials: 1952–1984" in Linda Lee Kaid, Dan Nimmo, and Keith R. Sanders, eds., *New Perspectives on Political Advertising* (Carbondale: Southern Illinois University Press, 1986), p. 26.

2. Bruce L. Felknor, *Dirty Politics* (New York: Norton, 1966), Chap. 1.

3. In a snit, the Kennedy White House canceled its subscription to the *New York Herald Tribune*.

4. Edwin Diamond and Stephen Bates, *The Spot: The Rise of Political Advertising on Television*, rev. edition (Cambridge: MIT Press, 1988), p. 28. For a review of presidential campaign advertising, see Kathleen Hall Jamieson, *Packaging the President: A History and Criticism of Presidential Advertising* (New York: Oxford University Press, 1984).

5. Michael Mansfield and Katherine Hale, "Uses and Perceptions of Political Television: An Application of Q Technique" in Kaid et al., *New Perspectives*, p. 286.

6. See Leonard Shyles, "Political Spot Advertising," in Kaid et al., *New Perspectives*, p. 115.

7. Richard Joslyn, "The Content of Political Spot Ads," *Journalism Quarterly*, 57 (1980): 92–98; Thomas Patterson, *The Mass Media Election* (New York: Praeger, 1980), p. 28.

8. Leonard Shyles, "Political Spot Advertising," in Kaid et al., *New Perspectives*, p. 138.

9. Viewing advertisements correlated .34 with knowledge about the campaign: Atkin and Heald, as quoted in Donald T. Cundy, "Political

Commercials and Candidate Image: The Effect Can Be Substantial," Kaid et al., ibid., p. 213.

10. Joslyn in Kaid et al., ibid., pp. 196–97.

11. Gina Garramone, "Voter Response to Political Ads," *Journalism Quarterly*, 61 (1984): 25—59. See also Alice Isen, "Influences of Affect on Cognitive Processes," in Patricia Cafferata and Alice Tybout, eds., *Cognitive and Affective Responses to Advertising* (Lexington, Mass.: Lexington Books, 1989), and Tony Schwartz, *The Responsive Chord* (Garden City, N.Y.: Doubleday, 1973).

12. Bruce L. Felknor, *Dirty Politics* (New York: Norton, 1966), p. 247.

13. Montague Kerns, *30 Second Politics: Political Advertising in the Eighties* (New York: Praeger, 1989), p. 212.

14. T. Barton Carter, Marc A. Franklin, Jay B. Wright, *The First Amendment and the Fourth Estate: The Law of Mass Media*, 4th edition (Westbury, N.Y.: Foundation Press, 1988), p. 600.

CHAPTER SIX, PART 1

1. Herbert E. Alexander, *Strategies for Election Reform*. (Washington, D.C.: Project for Comprehensive Campaign Reform, April 1989), p. 29–43.

2. The historical overview is based on Herbert E. Alexander, *Financing Politics*, 3rd edition (Washington, D.C.: Congressional Quarterly, 1984), chap. 3 and 4, pp. 55–112.

3. Fred Wertheimer, "Let's get Serious about Ethics," *Washington Post*, February 21, 1988.

4. Herbert E. Alexander and Brian A. Haggerty, *Financing the 1984 Election* (Lexington, Mass.: Lexington Books, 1987), pp. 84–88.

5. Herbert E. Alexander, "The Price we Pay for our Presidents," *Public Opinion*, vol. 2, no. 6 (March/April 1989), pp. 46–48.

6. Alexander and Haggerty, *Financing the 1984 Elections*, pp. 291–92.

7. "General Motors' Generosity: 250 Cars Per Convention," *PACs & Lobbies*, vol. 9, no. 14 (July 20, 1988), pp. 1, 4; also Brooks Jackson, "Big Business is Back in Thick of Things at Conventions," *Wall Street Journal*, August 16, 1988.

8. Paul Houston, "Bush, Dukakis got Record big Gifts," *Los Angeles Times*, December 10, 1988.

9. Paul Houston, "Big Cash Gifts to Parties Skirt Election Laws," *Los Angeles Times*, October 3, 1988.

10. Gary C. Jacobson, "Public Funds for Congressional Campaigns: Who Would Benefit?" in Herbert E. Alexander, ed., *Political Finance* (Beverly Hills: Sage Publications, 1979), pp. 99–127.

CHAPTER SIX, PART 2

This chapter is based on a speech delivered before the U.S. Senate on February 17, 1988. That text can be found in the *Congressional Record* of February 17, 1988, pp. 804–13. Senator McConnell would like to acknowledge the assistance of Steven J. Law, legislative assistant, in the preparation of this article.

CHAPTER SEVEN, PART 1

1. Theodore White, *The Making of the President 1960* (New York: Signet Press, 1967), pp. 319–20.

2. Ibid., p. 33

3. Theodore White, *The Making of the President, 1968* (New York: Signet Press, 1970), p. 460.

4. Hunter S. Thompson, *Fear and Loathing on the Campaign Trail* (New York: Fawcett Popular Library, 1973), p. 416.

5. Gerald M. Pomper, ed., *The Election of 1976* (New York: Longman, 1977), pp. 68–69.

6. Stephen Wayne, *The Road to the White House*, 2nd edition (New York: St. Martin's Press, 1984), p. 22.

7. Ibid.

8. John H. Kessel, *Presidential Campaign Politics*, 3rd edition (Chicago: Dorsey Press, 1988), pp. 214–17.

9. Herbert B. Asher, *Presidential Elections and American Politics*, 4th edition (Chicago: Dorsey Press, 1988), p. 192.

10. Thomas R. Dye and Harmon Zeigler, *American Politics in the Media Age*, 3rd edition (Pacific Grove, Calif.: Brooks/Cole, 1989), pp. 19–21.

11. Marjorie Randon Hershey, "The Campaign and the Media" in *The Election of 1988*, Gerald M. Pomper, ed. (Chatham, N.J.: Chatham House, 1989), pp. 88–94.

12. Asher, *Presidential Elections*, pp. 178–79.

13. Wayne, *The Road to the White House*, pp. 224–28.

14. Steven H. Chaffee and Jack Dennis, "Presidential Debates: An Empirical Assessment" in *The Past and Future of Presidential Debates*, Austin Ranney, ed. (Washington, D.C.: American Enterprise Institute, 1979), pp. 87–88.

15. Ibid., p. 82.

16. Robert G. Meadow and Marilyn Jackson-Beeck, "A Comparative Perspective on Presidential Debates: Issue Evolution in 1960 and 1976" in *The Presidential Debates: Media, Electoral and Policy Perspectives*, George F. Bishop, Robert G. Meadow, and Marilyn Jackson-Beeck, eds. (New York: Praeger, 1978), pp. 33–58; Hershey, "The Campaign and the Media," pp. 88–96.

17. Hershey, "The Campaign and the Media," pp. 88–94.

18. Meadow and Jackson-Beeck, "A Comparative Perspective," pp. 33–58.

19. Gladys Engel Lang and Kurt Lang, "The Formation of Public Opinion: Direct and Mediated Effects of the First Debate" in Bishop, Meadow, and Jackson-Beeck, *The Presidential Debates: Media, Electoral, and Policy Perspectives*, pp. 61–80.

CHAPTER SEVEN, PART 2

1. Plato, *The Republic*, Allan Bloom ed. (New York: Basic Books, 1968).

2. John Locke, *Two Treatises of Government*, Peter Laslett, ed. (Cambridge: Cambridge University Press, 1970); Alexis de Tocqueville, *Democracy in America*, Phillips Bradley, ed. (New York: Vintage Books, 1945).

3. Thomas Jefferson, *The Portable Jefferson*, Merrill D. Peterson, ed. (New York: Viking Press, 1975), p. 253.

4. Alexander Hamilton, James Madison, and John Jay, *The Federalist*, Benjamin Fletcher Wright, ed. (Cambridge: Harvard University Press, 1961.

5. James Madison, *The Debate in the Federal Constitution of 1787 which Framed the Constitution of the United States of America*, Gaillard Hunt and James Brown Scott, eds. (New York: Oxford University Press, 1920).

6. For an excellent analysis of the changing nature of presidential campaigning, see M. J. Heale, *The Presidential Quest* (New York: Longman, 1982).

7. Joel L. Swerdlow, "The Strange—and Sometimes Surprising—History of Presidential Debates in America" in *Presidential Debates 1988 and Beyond*, Joel L. Swerdlow, ed. (Washington, D.C.: Congressional Quarterly, 1987); Kathleen Hall Jamieson and David Birdsell, *Presidential Debates* (New York: Oxford University Press, 1988); and Heale, *Presidential Quest*.

8. For an excellent account of the campaign, see Theodore H. White, *The Making of the President 1960* (New York: Atheneum, 1961).

9. Lee Becker et al., "Debates' Effects on Voters' Understanding of Candidates and Issues" in *Presidential Debates*, George F. Bishop, ed. (New York: Praeger, 1978), pp. 126–39; Jamieson and Birdsell, *Presidential Debates*; Steven H. Chaffee and Jack Dennis, "Presidential Debates: An Empirical Assessment" in *The Past and Future of Presidential Debates*, Austin Ranney, ed. (Washington, D.C.: American Enterprise Institute, 1979), pp. 75–101; Commission on National Elections, "Choosing the President," (Washington, D.C.: Center for Strategic and International Studies, 1985).

10. Angus Campbell, Philip Converse, Warren Miller, and Donald Stokes, *The American Voter* (New York: John Wiley, 1964); Philip Converse, "The Nature of Belief Systems in Mass Publics" in David Apter, ed., *Ideology and Discontent* (New York: Free Press, 1964); Philip Converse and Gregory Markus, "Plus ca change . . . : The New CPS Election Study Panel," *American Political Science Review* (March 1979): 32–49.

11. Evron M. Kirkpatrick, "Presidential Candidate Debates: What Can We Learn from 1960?" in *The Past and Future of Presidential Debates*, Austin Ranney, ed. (Washington, D.C.: American Enterprise Institute, 1977), pp. 1–50; Paul R. Hagner and Leroy N. Rieselback, "The

Impact of the 1976 Presidential Debates: Conversion or Reinforcement?" in Bishop, *Presidential Debates*, pp. 157–78.

12. Frederick T. Steeper, "Public Response to Gerald Ford's Statements on Eastern Europe in the Second Debate" in Bishop, *Presidential Debates*, pp. 81–101; Gladys Engel Lang and Kurt Lang, "The Formation of Public Opinion: Direct and Mediated Effects of the First Debate" in Bishop, *Presidential Debates*, pp. 61–80.

13. Jack W. Germond and Jules Witcover, *Blue Smoke and Mirrors* (New York: Viking Press, 1981), pp. 116–140; Jack W. Germond and Jules Witcover, *Wake Us When It's Over* (New York: MacMillan, 1981), pp. 533–34.

14. Germond and Witcover, *Blue Smoke and Mirrors*, pp. 267–85.

15. Germond and Witcover, *Wake Us When It's Over*, pp. 523–38; Gerald Pomper, "The Presidential Election" in *The Election of 1984*, Gerald Pomper, ed. (Chatham, N.J.: Chatham House, 1985), p. 77; Elizabeth Drew, *Campaign Journal* (New York: MacMillan, 1985), pp. 706–8; Albert R. Hunt, "The Campaigns and the Issues" in *The American Elections of 1984*, Austin Ranney, ed. (Washington, D.C.: American Enterprise Institute, 1985), pp. 157–58; Paul C. Light and Celinda Lake, "The Election" in *The Elections of 1984*, Michael Nelson, ed. (Washington, D.C.: Congressional Quarterly, 1985), pp. 102–3.

16. Germond and Witcover, *Wake Us When It's Over*, pp. 187–88 and 309; Drew, *Campaign Journal*, pp. 380–89; Gerald M. Pomper, "The Nominations" in *The Election of 1984*, pp. 11–23.

17. Paul J. Quirk, "The Election" in *The Elections of 1988*, Michael Nelson, ed. (Washington, D.C.: Congressional Quarterly, 1989), pp. 77–78; Marjorie Randon Hershey, "The Campaign and the Media" in *The Election of 1988*, Gerald M. Pomper, ed. (Chatham, N.J.: Chatham House, 1989), pp. 91–93.

18. Martin Schram, *Running for President* (New York: Pocket Books, 1977), pp. 348–64.

19. James David Barber., *The Presidential Character* (Englewood Cliffs, N.J.: Prentice-Hall, 1977).

20. C. David Heymann, *A Woman Named Jackie* (New York: Lyle Stuart, 1989); Kitty Kelly, *Jackie O* (New York: Ballantine, 1979).

21. Marjorie Randon Hershey, "The Campaign and the Media," pp. 93–94.

22. Daniel J. Boorstin, *The Image: A Guide to Pseudo-Events in America* (New York: Harper and Row, 1964), p. 42.

23. For self-described levels of interest in 1940 and from 1952 to 1984, see Bernard Hennessy, *Public Opinion*, 5th edition (Monterey, Calif.: Brooks/Cole, 1985), p. 36. The 1988 data taken from the 1988 National Election Studies, University of Michigan Center for Political Studies.

24. Hennessy, *Public Opinion*, p. 36.

CHAPTER EIGHT, PART 2

1. *Federalist # 68*. This number of the *Federalist Papers* includes Hamilton's comments on the Electoral College. See also Martin Diamond, *The Electoral College and the American Idea of Democracy* (Washington, D.C.: AEI, 1977), p. 5.

2. Wallace S. Sayre and Judith H. Parris, *Voting for President* (Washington, D.C.: Brookings Institution, 1970), p. 29.

3. Judith Best, *The Case against Direct Election of the President: A Defense of the Electoral College* (Ithaca: Cornell University Press, 1975), p. 54.

4. Paul L. Haworth, *The Hayes-Tilden Disputed Presidential Election of 1876* (Cleveland: Burrows Brothers, 1906.; repr., New York: AMS Press, 1979), Passim.

5. Best. *Case against Direct Election*, pp. 65–66.

6. Ibid., chap. 2 passim.

7. Neal R. Pierce and Lawrence D. Longley, *The People's President: The Electoral College in American History and the Direct Vote Alternative*, rev. edition (New Haven and London: Yale University Press, 1981), pp. 120–30.

8. Nelson W. Polsby and Aaron Wildavsky, *Presidential Elections*, 7th edition (New York: Free Press, 1988), pp. 276–77.

9. Sayre and Parris, *Voting*, pp. 48ff.

10. An excellent analysis of this issue written several years ago is Allen P. Sindler's "Presidential Election Methods and Urban-Ethnic Interests," *Law and Contemporary Problems*, vol. 27 (Spring 1962): 213–33.

11. Alexander Bickle, *Reform and Continuity: The Electoral College, the Convention and the Party System* (New York: Harper and Row. 1971), pp. 4–36. See also Martin Diamond, *The Electoral College and the American Idea of Democracy* (Washington, D.C.: A.E.I., 1977), pp. 7–8

12. See the section on electoral college votes in *Congressional Quarterly's Guide to U.S. Elections*, 2nd edition (Washingtion, D.C.: Congressional Quarterly, 1985), pp. 253–315, esp. p. 259.

13. Polsby and Wildavsky, *Presidential Elections*, p. 277.

14. Best, *Case against Direct Election*, p. 84.

15. Diamond, *Electoral College*, pp. 19–20.

16. Ibid., pp. 13–15.

CHAPTER NINE, PART 1

1. Curtis Gans, "Voter Participation Revisited," *The FEC Journal of Election Administration*, 16 (Summer 1989): 8–11.

2. Arthur H. Miller, "Is Confidence Rebounding?" *Public Opinion*, 6, 3 (1983): 16–20; Miller, "Political Issues and Trust in Government: 1964–1970," *American Political Science Review*, 68 (1974): 951–72; Jack Citrin, "Comment: The Political Relevance of Trust in Government," *American Political Science Review*, 68 (1974): 973–88.

3. Citrin, "The Alientated Voter," *Taxing and Spending* (October 1978): 1–7; Raymond E. Wolfinger, David P. Glass, and Peverill Squire, "Predictors of Electoral Turnout: An International Comparison," paper presented at the International Political Science Association XIII World Congress, Paris, 1985.

4. Wolfinger, Glass, and Squire, "Predictors of Electoral Turnout," 1985.

5. Ibid.

6. Ibid., p. 15.

7. Wolfinger, Glass, and Squire, "Predictors of Electoral Tournout," 1985; G. Bingham Powell, Jr., "American Voter Turnout in Comparative Perspective," *American Political Science Review*, 80 (1986): 17–43; Robert W. Jackman, "Political Institutions and Voter Turnout in Industrial Democracies," *American Political Science Review*, 81 (1987): 405–23.

8. Walter Dean Burnham, *The Current Crises in American Politics* (New York: Oxford University Press, 1982).

9. Powell, "American Voter Turnout in Comparative Perspective," 1986.

10. Raymond E. Wolfinger and Steven J. Rosenstone, *Who Votes?* (New Haven: Yale University Press, 1980), p. 66.

11. Joseph Albright and Marcia Kunstel, "Most Non-Voters Don't Fit Stereotype of Ignorance, Apathy, Survey Reveals," *The Atlanta Journal and the Atlanta Constitution*, 2 (October 1988).

12. David Glass, Peverill Squire, and Raymond Wolfinger, "Voter Turnout: An International Comparison," *Public Opinion*, 6, 6 (1984): 49–55 Powell "American Voter Turnout in Comparative Perspective," 1986.

13. Peverill Squire, Raymond E. Wolfinger, and David P. Glass, "Residential Mobility and Voter Turnout," *American Political Science Review*, 81 (1987): 45–65.

14. Glass, Squire, and Wolfinger, "Voter Turnout," 1984.

15. Wolfinger and Rosenstone, *Who Votes?*, 1980; Squire, Wolfinger, and Glass, "Residential Mobility and Voter Turnout," 1987.

16. Wyoming has election-day registration only for primaries.

17. Wolfinger and Rosenstone, *Who Votes?*, 1980.

18. "House Passes Bill to Lure Voters to Register," *Iowa City Press Citizen*, February 21, 1989.

19. Wolfinger and Rosenstone, *Who Votes?*, 1980; Squire, Wolfinger, and Glass, "Residential Mobility and Voter Turnout," 1987.

20. Squire, Wolfinger, and Glass, "Residential Mobility and Voter Turnout," 1987.

21. Wolfinger and Rosenstone, *Who Votes?*, 1980. See also survey results in *New York Times*, November 2, 1988.

CHAPTER NINE, PART 2

1. See, for example, Robert Kuttner, "Why Americans Don't Vote," *The New Republic*, September 7, 1989: 19–21.

2. See, for example, Ruy Teixeira, "Will the Real Nonvoter Please Stand Up?, *Public Opinion*, July/August 1988: 41–44.

3. For a full listing of currently applicable state registration requirements, see p. 211, Table 5.9, in *The Book of the States*, 1988–89 edition (Lexington, Kentucky, the Council of State Governments).

4. For a good overview of proposed reforms, see Ruy A. Teixeira, "Registration and Turnout," *Public Opinion*, January/February 1989: 12–13, 56–58.

5. See various books and articles by Raymond E. Wolfinger and his associates: Raymond E. Wolfinger and Steven J. Rosenstone, *Who Votes?* (New Haven: Yale University Press, 1980); David Glass Peverill Squire, and Raymond Wolfinger, "Voter Turnout: An International Comparison," *Public Opinion* (Dec./Jan. 1984: 49–55); Peverill Squire, Raymond E. Wolfinger, and David P. Glass, "Residential Mobility and Voter Turnout," *American Political Science Review*, 81 (1987): 45–65. Also see Frances Fox Piven and Richard Cloward, *Why Americans Don't Vote* (New York: Pantheon, 1988).

6. Estimates of the increase in turnout that might be induced by same-day registration are actually moderate, about 9 or 10 percent.

7. See James J. Kilpatrick, "Instant Voter Registration is an Invitation to Fraud," *The Atlanta Journal and Constitution*, June 13, 1989, p. A-21.

8. Kuttner, "Why American Don't Vote," *The New Republic*, September 7, 1987, quoting a 1929 book authored by historian Joseph P. Harris.

9. For a good overview of this literature, see chap. 6 of Lester W. Milbrath and M. L. Goel, *Political Participation: How and Why Do People Get Involved in Politics?*, 2nd edition (Chicago: Rand McNally, 1977).

10. "Registration and Turnout," *Public Opinion*, January/February 1989: 12.

11. Teixeira, "Will the Real Nonvoter Please Stand Up?," *Public Opinion*, July/August 1988.

12. The poll was taken by ABC News in cooperation with Harvard University. See Adam Clymer, "Voter Turnout to Remain Low, Poll Says," *The Dallas Morning News*, September 25, 1983; and "Survey Shows Moving Election Day to Sunday Could Trim Voter Turnout," *The Houston Post*, September 25, 1983.

13. Clymer, "Voter Turnout to Remain Low, Poll Says," 1983.

14. Barry Sussman, *What Americans Really Think and Why our Politicians Pay No Attention* (New York: Pantheon, 1988), p. 74.

CHAPTER TEN, PART 1

1. See especially Bert A. Rockman, *The Leadership Question: The Presidency and the American System* (New York: Praeger, 1984). The leadership question is the central concern of the literature of the presidency. Rockman's book is a good place to start for those coming newly on the literature.

2. James Sterling Young, *The Washington Community: 1800-1828 (New York: Columbia University Press, 1966), pp. 250–54.*

3. This nice conceptualization of the American party system and presidential selection is from Richard P. McCormick, *The Presidential Game: The Origins of American Presidential Politics* (New York: Oxford University Press, 1982), pp. 164–206.

4. See especially V.O. Key, Jr., *Politics, Parties, and Pressure Groups* (New York: Crowell, 1964), pp. 398–412.

5. See especially Byron E. Shafer, *The Quiet Revolution: The Struggle for the Democratic Party and the Shaping of Post-Reform Politics* (New York: Russell Sage, 1983).

6. The main argument here seems to be between those who think the party system has mainly been transformed by social and technological changes and those who blame the work of "party reformers." For the former view, see Howard Reiter, *Selecting the President: The Nomination Process in Transition* (Philadelphia: University of Pennsylvania Press, 1985), and for the latter view, Nelson W. Polsby, The Consequences of Party Reform (New York: Oxford University Press, 1983). It is highly likely that both factors are at work, but I would argue that the way we think about parties is not the result of any rigid social or technological determinism. Our negative attitudes toward parties has permitted them to be more affected by the social and technological changes of postindustrialism than in other democratic polities.

7. Virtually anyone writing from the experience of living abroad sees the exceptionalism of our thinking about political parties immediately. See, for example, Richard Rose, *The Postmodern President: The White House Meets the World* (Chatham, N.J.: Chatham House, 1988).

8. E.E. Schattschneider, *Party Government* (New York: Rinehart, 1942), pp. 13–15.

9. Ibid., pp. 411–12.

10. John H. Aldrich, "Methods and Actors: The Relationship of Processes to Candidates" in Alexander Heard and Michael Nelson, eds. *Presidential Selection* (Durham: Duke University Press, 1987), pp. 155–187.

11. See, for example, Anthony King, "How Not to Select Presidential Candidates" in Robert E. DiClerico, ed., *Analyzing the Presidency* (Guilford, Conn.: Dushkin, 1985), pp. 6–24.

12. See, for example, James David Barber, *The Presidential Character: Predicting Presidential Performance in the White House* (Englewood Cliffs, N.J.: Prentice-Hall, 1985). In general terms Barber's analysis would predict success for Carter and failure for Reagan. Although Professor Barber continues to argue that he got this more or less right, a fairly large crowd of presidential scholars might be assembled from those who remain unpersuaded.

13. See my tongue-in-cheek version of the "job description" in Everett Carll Ladd, *The American Polity: The People and Their Government* (New York: Norton, 1989), p. 219.

14. Clinton Rossiter, *The American Presidency* (New York: Mentor, 1964), pp. 183–92.

15. Reagan enjoyed his greatest success in 1981, largely because the 1980 elections "shook up" the Washington community. The 1981 legislative victories on the ERTA tax bill and the spending adjustments of the reconciliation bill were enormous ones, the effects of which are still apparent after many years. But he would never again command such influence in Congress. His success in 1981, easily the most impressive since Lyndon Johnson's in 1965–66, is all the more impressive because he has nothing like the party support Johnson had enjoyed. On Reagan as a legislative leader, see Charles O. Jones, "Ronald Reagan and the U.S. Congress: Visible Hand Politics" in Charles O. Jones, ed., *The Reagan Legacy: Promise and Performance* (Chatham, N.J.: Chatham House, 1988), pp. 30–59.

16. On these points, see Everett Carll Ladd, "The 1988 Elections: Continuation of the Post-New Deal System," *Political Science Quarterly* (Spring 1989): 4–5.

17. I have received permission to tell this personal story, My relatives know that I respect them greatly. The point is that they, like most Americans, get less service and more grief by voting for congressional imcumbents than they realize.

18. It has since been abolished.

19. This nice phrase was used often by the sociologist C. Wright Mills in the 1950s to refer to pretentious sounding "scientific" arguments that had no real claim to scientific status.

20. Schattschneider, *Party Government*, pp. 1–16.

CHAPTER TEN, PART 2

1. An excellent discussion of how political scientists view the institution of political parties is found in Leon D. Epstein, "The Scholarly Commitment to Parties" in Ada W. Finifter, ed., *Political Science: State of the Discipline* (Washington, D.C.: American Political Science Association, 1983), pp. 127–53.

2. E. E. Schattschneider, *Party Government* (New York: Holt, Rinehart and Winston, 1942), p. 1.

3. David S. Broder, "Introduction" in Seymour Martin Lipset, ed., *Emerging Coalitions in American Politics* (San Francisco: Institute for Contemporary Studies, 1978), p. 3.

4. For a classic statement of the responsible party view, see Committee on Political Parties of the American Political Science Association, *Toward a More Responsible Two Party System* (New York: Holt, Rinehard and Winston, 1950).

5. See, for example, Everett Carll Ladd, *Where Have All the Voters Gone?* 2nd edition (New York: Norton, 1982); David Broder, *The Party's Over* (New York: Harper and Row, 1971); Martin Wattenberg, *The Decline of American Political Parties* (Cambridge: Harvard University Press, 1984.

6. Robert Merton, *Social Theory and Social Structure* (New York: Free Press, 1957), pp. 72–82.

7. Arthur M. Schlesinger, Jr., *The Cycles of American History* (Boston: Houghton Mifflin, 1986), p. 264.

8. Ibid.

9. Ibid., p. 269.

10. Ibid, p. 267.

11. Everett C. Ladd, "Misstating the Problems," *Public Opinion*, vol. 11 (May/June 1988): 4.

12. Howard L. Reiter, *Parties and Elections in Corporate America* (New York: St. Martin's Press, 1987), p. 230.

13. Stephen E. Frantzich, *Political Parties in the Technological Age* (New York: Longmans, 1989), p. 128.

14. See, for example, Xandra Hayden, "Alive and Well and Living in Washington: The American Political Parties" in Michael Margolis and Gary Mauser, eds., *Manipulating Public Opinion* (Pacific Grove, Calif.: Brooks/Cole, 1989), pp. 70–94.

15. James Ceaser, "Improving the Nomination Process" in A. James Reichley, ed., *Elections American Style* (Washington, D.C.: Brookings Institution, 1987), p. 31.

16. James L. Sundquist, "Strengthening the National Parties," ibid., p. 213.

17. Ibid., pp. 206, 213–14.

18. Ceaser, "Improving the Nomination Process," p. 43.

19. Sidney M. Milkis, "The Presidency and Political Parties," in Michael Nelson, ed., *The Presidency and the Political System* 2nd edition (Washington: CQ Press, 1988), p. 331.

20. Theodore J. Lowi, "Constitution, Government, and Politics" in George Grassmuch, ed., *Before Nomination: Our Primary Problem* (Washington: American Enterprise Institute, 1985), p. 17.

21. For a discussion of presidential leadership in the contemporary political environment, see Samuel Kernell, *Going Public* (Washington, D.C.: CQ Press, 1986).

22. George Edwards, *At the Margins* (New Haven: Yale University Press, 1989), p. 70.

23. While the lack of association between presidential and congressional elections appears to represent a secular trend, the weak connection was particularly pronounced in 1988. See Gary Jacobson, "Congress: A Singular Continuity" in Michael Nelson, ed., *The Election of 1988* (Washington, D.C.: CQ Press, 1988), pp. 127–47.

24. Susan Webb Hammond, Author G. Stevens, Jr., and Daniel P. Mulhollan, "Congressional Caucuses: Legislators as Lobbyists" in Allan J. Cigler and Burdett A. Loomis, *Interest Group Politics* (Washington, D.C.: CQ Press), pp. 275–97.

25. Burdett A. Loomis and Allan J. Cigler, "The Changing Nature of Interest Group Politics," ibid., pp. 1–30.

26. Paul Light, *The Presidential Agenda* (Baltimore: Johns Hopkins University Press, 1982), p. 210.

27. Francis E. Rourke and John T. Tierney, "The Setting: Changing Patterns of Presidential Politics, 1960 and 1988" in Nelson, *The Election of 1988*, p. 20.

28. James L. Sundquist, "Strengthening the National Parties," p. 220.

29. Everett C. Ladd, "Misstating the Problems," p. 4.

30. Norman J. Ornstein and Mark Schmitt, "The New World of Interest Politics," *The American Enterprise*, vol. 1 (Jan./Feb. 1990): 51.

CONCLUSION

1. Charles C. Thach, Jr., *The Creation of the Presidency 1775–1789* (Baltimore: Johns Hopkins University Press, 1922), p. 167.

2. William N. Chambers, "Parties and Nation Building in America," in *Political Parties and Political Development*, Joseph LaPalombara and Myron Weiner, eds. (Princeton: Princeton University Press, 1966), p. 93.

3. V.O. Key, *Politics, Parties and Pressure Groups* (New York: Crowell, 1964), p. 9.

4. Fred I. Greenstein, "Change and Continuity in the Modern Presidency" in Harry A. Bailey, Jr., ed. *Classics of the American Presidency* (Illinois: Moore Publishing, 1980), pp. 388–416.

5. For a full review of the preprimary convention/national primary proposal, see Martin P. Wattenberg., "When You Can't Beat Them, Join Them: Shaping the Presidential Nominating Process to the Television Age," *Polity*, 21 (Spring 1989): 587–97. Also Jerome M. Mileur and John Kenneth White, "Where Angels Fear to Tread: Toward a Larger National Role in a Federal System of Presidential Nomination," paper presented at the annual meeting of the Midwest Political Science Association, April 13–15, 1989; and Thomas Cronin and Robert Loevy, "The Case for a National Pre-Primary Convention," *Public Opinion* (Dec.-Jan. 1983): 5–53.

Suggested Bibliography

THE PRESIDENTIAL NOMINATING PROCESS

Ceaser, James W. *Reforming the Reforms*. Cambridge: Ballinger, 1982.

Crotty, William. *Political Reform and the American Experiment*. New York: Harper and Row, 1977.

Crotty, William, and Jackson, John S. III. *Presidential Primaries and Nominations*. Washington, D.C.: Congressional Quarterly Press, 1985.

Lengle, James I. *Representation and Presidential Primaries: The Democratic Party in the Post-Reform Era*. Westport, Conn.: Greenwood Press, 1981.

Polsby, Nelson W. *The Consequences of Party Reform*. New York: Oxford University Press, 1983.

Pomper, Gerald. *Nominating The President*. New York: Norton, 1966.

Ranney, Austin. *Curing the Mischiefs of Faction*. Berkeley: University of California Press, 1975.

Reiter, Howard. *Selecting the President: The Nomination Process in Transition*. Philadelphia: University of Pennsylvania Press, 1985.

Shafer, Byron E. *The Quiet Revolution: The Struggle for the Democratic Party and the Shaping of Post-Reform Politics*. New York: Russell Sage, 1983.

Sullivan, Dennis G. et al. *The Politics of Representation.* New York: St. Martin's Press, 1974.

CONVENTION POLITICS

Jackson, John S. III, Brown, Barbara L., and Bositis, David. "Herbert McClosky and Friends Revisited." *American Politics Quarterly,* 10 (April 1982): 158–80.

Kirkpatrick, Jeanne Jordon. *The New Presidential Elite.* New York: Russell Sage 1976.

Miller, Warren E., and Jennings, M. Kent. *Parties in Transition: A Longitudinal Study of Party Elites and Party Supporters.* New York: Russell Sage Foundation, 1986.

Miller, Warren E. *Without Consent: Mass Elite Linkages in Presidential Politics.* Lexington: University of Kentucky Press, 1988.

Parris, Judith H. *The Convention Problem.* Washington, D.C.: Brookings Institution, 1972.

Plissner, Martin, and Mitofsky, Warren J. "The Making of the Delegates: 1968–1988." *Public Opinion* (Sept./Oct. 1988).

Shafer, Byron E. *Bifurcated Politics: Evolution and Reform in the National Party Convention.* Cambridge: Harvard University Press, 1988.

VICE-PRESIDENTIAL SELECTION

Cronin, Thomas E. "Rethinking the Vice-Presidency" in Thomas E. Cronin, ed. *Rethinking the Presidency.* Boston: Little Brown, 1982.

David, Paul T. "The Vice Presidency: Its Institutional Evolution and Contemporary Status," *Journal of Politics,* vol. 29, no. 4 (November 1967).

Goldstein, Joel K. *The Modern American Vice Presidency: Transformation of a Political Institution.* Princeton: Princeton University Press, 1982.

Hinkley, Barbara. *Problems of the Presidency.* Glenview, Ill.: Scott, Foresman, 1985. Chap. 6.

Light, Paul C. *Vice-Presidential Power: Advice and Influence in the White House.* Baltimore: Johns Hopkins University Press, 1984.

Pomper, Gerald M. "The Nomination of Hubert Humphrey for Vice President." *Journal of Politics,* vol. 28, no. 3 (August 1966): 639–59.

Schlesinger, Arthur M. "The Vice Presidency: A Modest Proposal" in Arthur M. Schlesinger, Jr., *The Imperial Presidency.* New York: Popular Library, 1974.

Williams, Irving G. *The Rise of the Vice Presidency.* Washington, D.C.: Public Affairs Press, 1956.

MASS MEDIA

Arterton, Christopher F. *Media Politics: The New Strategies of Presidential Campaigns.* Lexington, Mass.: Lexington Books, 1984.

Barber, James D., ed. *Race for the Presidency: The Media and the Nomination Process.* Englewood Cliffs, N.J.: Prentice-Hall, 1978.

Devlin, Patrick L., ed. *Political Persuasion in Presidential Campaigns.* New Brunswick, N.J.: Transaction Books, 1987.

Graber, Doris. *Mass Media and American Politics.* Washington, D.C.: Congressional Quarterly Press, 1980.

———. *Processing the News.* New York: Longman, 1984.

Orren, Gary, and Polsby, Nelson, eds. *Media and Momentum.* Chatham, N.J.: Chatham House, 1987.

Patterson, Thomas, and McClure, Robert. *The Unseeing Eye.* New York: Putnam's, 1976.

Patterson, Thomas. *The Mass Media Election.* New York: Praeger, 1980.

———. "The Press and its Missed Assignment" in *The Elections of 1988* Michael Nelson, ed. Washington, D.C.: Congressional Quarterly Press 1989.

Robinson, Michael, and Sheehan, Margaret. *Over the Wire and On T.V.: CBS and UPI in Campaign '80.* New York: Russell Sage Foundation, 1983.

Weaver, David, Graber, Doris, McCombs, Maxwell, and Eyal, Chaim. *Media Agenda-Setting in a Presidential Election.* New York: Praeger, 1981.

CAMPAIGN COMMERCIALS

Agranoff, Robert. *The New Style in Election Campaigns*. Boston: Holbrook Press, 1976.

Carter, T. Barton, Franklin, Marc A., Wright, Jay B. *The First Amendment and the Fourth Estate: The Law of Mass Media*, 4th edition Westbury, N.Y.: Foundation Press, 1988.

Diamond, Edwin, and Bates, Stephen. *The Spot: The Rise of Political Advertising on Television*, Rev. edition Cambridge: MIT Press 1988.

Felknor, Bruce L. *Dirty Politics*. New York: Norton, 1966.

Garramone, Gina. "Voter Response to Political Ads." *Journalism Quarterly*, 61 (1984): 250–59.

Jamieson, Kathleen Hall. *Packaging the President: A History and Criticism of Presidential Advertising*. New York: Oxford University Press, 1984.

Joslyn, Richard. "The Content of Political Spot Ads." *Journalism Quarterly*. 57 (1980): 92–98.

Kaid, Linda Lee, Nimmo, Dan, Sanders, Keith R., eds. *New Perspectives on Political Advertising*. Carbondale: Southern Illinois University Press, 1986.

Kerns, Montague. *30-Second Politics: Political Advertising in the Eighties*. New York: Praeger, 1989.

Sabato, Larry. *The Rise of Media Consultants*. New York: Basic Books, 1981.

Spero, Robert. *The Duping of the American Voter: Dishonesty and Deception in Presidential Television Advertising*. New York: Lippincott, Corwell, 1980.

PUBLIC FUNDING AND CAMPAIGN FINANCE

Adamany, David, and Agree, George E. *Political Money*. London: Johns Hopkins University Press, 1975.

Alexander, Herbert E. *Money in Politics*. Washington, D.C.: Public Affairs Press, 1972.

———. *Financing Politics*, 3rd edition. Washington, D.C.: Congressional Quarterly, 1984.

———."The Price We Pay For Our President." *Public Opinion*, vol. 2, no. 6 (March/April 1989).

———. *Strategies for Election Reform*. Washington, D.C.: Project for Comprehensive Campaign Reform, April 1989.

———,ed. *Campaign Money*. New York: Free Press 1975.

———,ed. *Political Finance*. Beverly Hills: Sage Publications, 1979.

———,and Haggerty, Brian A. *Financing the 1984 Election*. Lexington, Mass.: Lexington Books, 1987.

Malbin, Michael J., ed. *Parties, Interest Groups and Campaign Finance Laws*. Washington, D.C.: American Enterprise Institute for Public Policy Research, 1979.

Sorauf, Frank J. *Money in American Elections*. Glenview, Ill.: Scott, Foresman, 1988.

PRESIDENTIAL DEBATES

Bishop, George F., Meadow, Robert G., and Jackson-Beeck, Marilyn, eds. *The Presidential Debates: Media, Electoral and Policy Perspectives*. New York: Praeger, 1978.

Jamieson, Kathleen Hall, and Birdsell, David. *Presidential Debates*. New York: Oxford University Press 1988.

Ranney, Austin, ed. *The Past and Future of Presidential Debates*. Washington, D.C.: American Enterprise Institute, 1979.

Swerdlow, Joel L., ed. *Presidential Debates 1988 and Beyond*. Washington, D.C.: Congressional Quarterly, 1987.

THE ELECTORAL COLLEGE

Best, Judith. *The Case Against Direct Election of the President: A Defense of the Electoral College*. Ithaca: Cornell University Press, 1975.

Bickel, Alexander M. *Reform and Continuity: The Electoral College, the Convention, and the Party System.* New York: Harper and Row, 1971.

Diamond, Martin. *The Electoral College and the American Idea of Democracy.* Washington, D.C.: American Enterprise Institute for Public Policy Research, 1977.

Pierce, Neal R., and Longley, Lawrence D. *The People's President: The Electoral College in American History and the Direct Vote Alternative,* rev. edition. New Haven: Yale University Press, 1981.

Sayre, Wallace S., and Parris, Judith H. *Voting for President: The Electoral College and the American Political System.* Washington, D.C.: Brookings Institution, 1970.

VOTER REGISTRATION AND VOTER TURNOUT

Gans, Curtis. "Voter Participation Revisited." *The FEC Journal of Election Administration,* 16 (Summer 1989): 8–11.

Glass, David, Squire, Peverill, and Wolfinger, Raymond. "Voter Turnout: An International Comparison." *Public Opinion* (Dec.-Jan. 1984): 49–55.

Hill, David B., and Luttbeg, Norman. *Trends in American Electoral Behavior.* Itasca: F. E. Peacock, 1980.

Kilpatrick, James J. "Instant Voter Registration is an Invitation to Fraud." *The Atlanta Journal and Constitution*(June 13, 1989): 21, section A.

Kuttner, Robert. "Why Americans Don't Vote." *The New Republic* (September 7, 1987): 19–21.

Milbrath, Lester W., and Goel, M. L. *Political Participation: How and Why Do People Get Involved in Politics?* 2nd edition. Chicago: Rand McNally, 1977.

Piven, Frances Fox, and Cloward, Richard. *Why Americans Don't Vote.* New York: Pantheon, 1988.

Powell, Bingham G., Jr. "American Voter Turnout in Comparative Perspective." *American Political Science Review,* 80 (1986): 17–43.

Squire, Peverill, Wolfinger, Raymond E., and Glass, David P. "Residential Mobility and Voter Turnout." *American Political Science Review,* 81 (1987): 45–65.

Teixeira, Ruy A. "Will the Real Nonvoter Please Stand Up?" *Public Opinion* (July/Aug. 1988): 41–44.

———."Registration and Turnout." *Public Opinion* (Jan./Feb. 1989): 12–13, 56–58.

Verba, Sidney, and Nie, Norman H. *Participation in America.* New York: Harper and Row, 1972.

Wolfinger, Raymond E., and Rosenstone, Steven J. *Who Votes?* New Haven: Yale University Press, 1980.

POLITICAL PARTIES

Abbott, David W., and Rogowski, Edward T. *Political Parties: Leadership, Organization, Linkage,* 2nd edition. Chicago: Rand McNally, 1978.

Broder, David S. *The Party's Over.* New York: Harper and Row, 1971.

Committee on Political Parties of the American Political Science Association. *Toward a More Responsible Two-Party System.* New York: Rinehart, 1950.

Cotter, Cornelius P., and Hennessy, Bernard C. *Politics Without Power.* New York: Atherton Press, 1964.

Crotty, William J. *American Parties in Decline,* 2nd edition. Boston: Little, Brown, 1984.

James, Judson. *American Political Parties in Transition.* New York: Harper and Row, 1974.

Key, V. O., Jr. *Politics, Parties and Pressure Groups,* 5th edition. New York: Basic Books, 1964.

Kirkpatrick, Jeanne Jordon. *Dismantling the Parties.* Washington, D.C.: American Enterprise for Public Policy Research, 1978.

Ladd, Everett Carl, Jr. *Where Have All The Voters Gone?* New York: Norton, 1978.

Ladd, Everett Carl, Jr. and Hadley, Charles D. *Transformations of the American Party System.* New York: Norton, 1975.

LaPalombara, Joseph, and Weiner, Myron, eds. *Political Parties and Political Development.* Princeton: Princeton University Press, 1966.

Lawson, Kay. *Political Parties and Democracy in the United States.* New York: Charles Scribner's Sons, 1968.

Ranney, Austin. *The Doctrine of Responsible Party Government.* Urbana: University of Illinois Press, 1954.

Ranney, Austin, and Kendall, Willmore. *Democracy and the American Party System.* New York: Harcourt, Brace, 1956.

Schattschneider, E. E. *Party Government.* New York: Rinehart, 1942.

Scott, Ruth K., and Hrebanar, Ronald J. *Parties in Crisis.* New York: John Wiley, 1979.

Sorauf, Frank J., and Beck, Paul A. *Party Politics in America*, 6th edition. Glenview, Ill.: Scott, Foresman, 1988.

PREPRIMARY NATIONAL CONVENTION

Cronin, Thomas, and Loevy, Robert. "The Case for a National Pre-Primary Convention." *Public Opinion* (Dec./Jan. 1983): 50–53.

Mileur, Jerome M., and White, John Kenneth. "Where Angels Fear to Tread: Toward a Larger National Role in a Federal System of Presidential Nomination." Paper presented at the annual meeting of the Midwest Political Science Association, April 13–15, 1989.

Wattenberg, Martin P. "When You Can't Beat Them, Join Them: Shaping the Presidential Nominating Process to the Television Age." *Polity* (Spring 1989): 587–97.

GENERAL WORKS

Ceaser, James W. *Presidential Selection: Theory and Development.* Princeton: Princeton University Press, 1979.

DiClerico, Robert E. and Uslaner, Eric M. *Few are Chosen: Problems in Presidential Selection.* New York: McGraw-Hill, 1984.

Polsby, Nelson, and Wildavsky, Aaron. *Presidential Elections.* 7th edition. New York: Free Press, 1988.

Wayne, Stephen J. *The Road to the White House.* 3rd edition. New York: St. Martin's Press, 1988.

Contributors

Herbert E. Alexander is director of Citizens' Research Foundation and professor of political science at the University of Southern California. Regarded as the nation's foremost authority on campaign finance, Professor Alexander served as the executive director of the Commission on Campaign Costs under President John F. Kennedy. Professor Alexander's work includes quadrennial volumes regarding campaign finance in presidential elections from 1960 to 1988, as well as broad treatments of the role of money in elections. His publications include *Money in Politics* (1972); *Campaign Money: Reform and Reality in the States* (1976); *Political Finance* (1979); *Financing Politics* (1976, 1980, 1984) and many others. Professor Alexander's work serves as a principal database for students of campaign finance.

William Carroll is assistant professor in political science at Sam Houston State University in Texas. His research interests include the policy leadership role of the American presidency and the performance of political parties in the governing process. Professor Carroll's most recent publication is the introductory chapter to *Perspectives on American and Texas Politics: A Collection of Essays* (1987), edited by Donald S. Lutz and Kent L. Tedin. Professor Carroll is also a student of British and European politics.

Allen J. Cigler is a professor of political science at the University of Kansas. His research interests include American political behavior, interest-group politics, and political parties. He is currently involved in a long-term project concerning the evolution of the American agricultural movement from a protest group to a Washington-based interest group. Professor Cigler's work includes two co-edited books, *Interest Group Politics* (1983, 1986) and *Agriculture Groups* (1990). His articles appear in *American Politics Quarterly, Western Political Quarterly, Policy Studies Journal,* and *Journal of Urban Affairs* among others.

Curtis B. Gans is director of the Committee for the Study of the American Electorate in Washington, D.C. On matters of voting, Mr. Gans has become the primary source of information for most newspapers, wire services, news magazines, and columnists. His writings have appeared in a number of publications including *The Atlantic, Public Opinion, The Washington Monthly,* and *The New York Times.* He has appeared on "Today," "Good Morning America," "All Things Considered," "The NcNeil-Lehrer Report," and other talk shows. In a career that straddles both politics and journalism, Gans is also well known for leading the effort against the reelection of President Lyndon Johnson in 1967 and directing the presidential campaign of Senator Eugene J. McCarthy the following year.

David B. Hill, director of Hill Research Consultants, has conducted public opinion polls since 1974 for clients in politics, government, public affairs, and business. Dr. Hill has been a faculty member at Texas A & M University and Kansas State University. The author of numerous articles in scholarly journals such as *The Journal of Politics, Public Opinion Quarterly,* and *Social Science Quarterly,* Dr. Hill is also co-author of *Trends in American Electoral Behavior* (1983) and *Election Demographics* (1988).

John S. Jackson III is professor of political science and Dean of the College of Liberal Arts at Southern Illinois University. His research interests include political parties, voting behavior, public opinion, and political elites. Professor Jackson is the co-author of *Presidential Nominations and Primaries* (1985) and has published articles regarding presidential politics in *American Politics Quarterly, Journal of Politics, Polity,* and other scholarly journals.

Landis Jones is professor of political science and Interim Director of the School of Urban Policy at the University of Louisville. He was director of the President's Commission on White House

Fellowships during the Carter administration. From 1969 to 1970 he was a White House Fellow and served as the Special Assistant for Urban Affairs to the Vice-President, Spiro T. Agnew. Professor Jones testified before the commission on Vice-Presidential Selection of the Democratic National Committee in 1973 and was the author of the working papers on the vice-presidency for the National Academy of Public Administration's 1979–80 study "Managing the Federal Government: The Role of the President."

Marion R. Just is professor of political science at Wellesley College in Massachusetts. She has been a visiting fellow at the Press and Politics Center of the Kennedy School of Government at Harvard University and the Research Program in Communications Policy at M.I.T. Her publications are in the field of political behavior, focusing on the mass media. She is the author of *Coping in a Troubled Society* (1974) and many articles in political science and communication journals. She is vice-chair of the Political Communication Section of the American Political Science Association and current president of the New England Political Science Association.

Elaine Ciulla Kamarck is a Senior Fellow at the Progressive Policy Institute in Washington, D.C. In 1977 Professor Kamarck served as research director of the Winograd Commission, which wrote the 1980 delegate selection rules for the Democratic Party. In 1978–1980, she served as executive director of the Compliance Review Commission, the body that enforces the rules of the Democratic Party, and then as executive director of the Platform Committee to the 1980 Convention. At the 1980 Convention, she was a member of the team that ran the rules fight on behalf of President Carter. She served as director of Delegate Selection for the Mondale for President Campaign and as a member of the technical Advisory Committee for the Hunt and Fairness Commissions. Professor Kamarck is co-author of *Practical Politics in the United States* (1972) and has written numerous articles in the popular and academic press.

James I. Lengle is an associate professor in the department of government at Georgetown University in Washington, D.C. He is the author of *Representation and Presidential Primaries* (1981), co-editor of *Presidential Politics* (1980, 1983), and author of numerous articles on presidential selection. *Dianne C. Lambert* is a legislative affairs specialist at NASA in Washington, D.C., and a doctoral candidate in American politics in the department of government at Georgetown University.

Lawrence D. Longley is associate professor of government at Lawrence University in Wisconsin. He is the author of *The Politics of Electoral College Reform* (1975), *The People's President* (1981), as well as articles regarding the politics of the Electoral College. Professor Longley was a Presidential Elector in the presidential election of 1988 and has served as a consultant to U.S. Senate hearings on electoral college reform. Current research of Professor Longley includes a forthcoming book comparing electoral reform movements in America and Britain: *Changing the System: Electoral Reform Politics in Great Britain and the United States*.

Mitch McConnell is a United States Senator from Kentucky. Elected to the Senate in 1984, Senator McConnell serves on the Senate Agriculture Committee, Energy and Natural Resources Committee, Foreign Relations Committee, and Rules Committee. He is currently the leading critic on Capitol Hill of public funding for presidential elections, and has introduced and sponsored legislation to repeal federal financing provisions.

Sarah McCally Morehouse is a professor of political science at the University of Connecticut. She is author of *State Politics, Parties and Policy* (1981) as well as articles and chapters on state governors, legislatures, and political parties. Her recent research has concentrated on gubernatorial nominations, much of it under the auspices of the Russell Sage Foundation. She has served on the council of the American Political Science Association and was a consultant to the National Governors' Association. She is currently on the National Executive Committee of the Committee for Party Renewal.

Robert T. Nakamura is associate professor and chair of political science at the State University of New York at Albany. His research interests include policy implementation, legislative policy making, and presidential nominating conventions. Professor Nakamura is the co-author of four books and several professional articles. His professional publications appear in *American Journal of Political Science, Political Science Quarterly, Legislative Studies Quarterly*, among others.

John Orman is professor of politics at Fairfield University in Connecticut. He is the author of several books including *Presidential Secrecy and Deception: Beyond the Power to Persuade* (1980); *Comparing Presidential Behavior: Carter, Reagan and the Macho Presidential Style* (1987); and *Presidential Accountability: New and Recurring Problems* (1990). Professor Orman's articles and reviews regarding American politics have appeared in *Presidential Studies Quarterly, PS*, and the *American Political Science Review*, among others. In 1984 Professor Orman was the Democratic candidate for Congress in the Fourth Congressional District in Connecticut.

Kant Patel is a professor of political science at Southwest Missouri State University. His research interests involve various aspects of American politics and public administration. Professor Patel's articles appear in *Political Methodology, Youth and Society, American Politics Quarterly*, and the *Journal of Political Science*. Professor Patel has conducted extensive research involving politics in the Bible Belt and the American evangelical movement. He is currently at work on a text concerning public policy.

Denny Pilant is professor and head of political science at Southwest Missouri State University. Professor Pilant has published articles on topics concerning American politics in the *Journal of Black Studies, American Politics Quarterly*, and *Journal of Political Science*. In addition, he has contributed chapters on issues in state and national politics in several university presses. He has done extensive research on both the relationship between religion and politics, and the unintended political consequences of institutional reform.

W. Wayne Shannon is a professor of political science and coordinator of the M.A. Concentration in Survey Research at the University of Connecticut. He has written widely about various aspects of American national politics. Most recently, he has edited with Ann Serow and Everett Ladd *The American Polity Reader* (1990).

Peverill Squire is associate professor of political science at the University of Iowa. He is the editor of *The Iowa Caucuses and the Presidential Nominating Process* (1989). His articles on various aspects of American politics have appeared in the *American Politi-*

cal Science Review, Journal of Politics, Public Opinion Quarterly, and other scholarly journals.

John Kenneth White is an associate professor of politics at the Catholic University of America. He is the author of *The Fractured Electorate: Political Parties and Social Change in Southern New England* (1983); *The New Politics of Old Values* (1990), and co-editor of *New York State Today: Politics, Government, and Public Policy* (1988). Professor White is the executive director of the Committee for Party Renewal, an organization consisting of political scientists and political practitioners dedicated to the revitalization of political parties in American politics. He is also the general editor of the SUNY series, The Presidency: Contemporary Issues.

Gary L. Rose is an associate professor of political science at Sacred Heart University in Connecticut. His research interests include political parties, political movements, and issues facing presidential selection. His publications appear in *Youth and Society, American Politics Quarterly, Journal of Political Science,* and *Connecticut Review.* Professor Rose is an active member of the Committee for Party Renewal and serves as the coach of the Sacred Heart University Debating Society. He has appeared on television to discuss the presidential selection process and is currently at work on a project concerning the Connecticut party system in transition.

Index

Adams, John, 82–84, 95, 143, 219
Adams, John Quincy, 9
Agnew Spiro, 82, 88, 94, 99–100, 105
Ailes, Roger, 115–116
Allen, Richard, 99
Anderson, John, 213, 231
Angotti, Joe, 74
Arledge, Roone, 74
Atwater, Lee, 30

Babbitt, Bruce, 91, 122
Bailey, Lloyd W., 208
Baker, Jim, 101
Barber, James David, 197
Barkley, Alben, 97, 104
Bartels, Larry, 45
Beauty Contests, 61
Beckel, Robert, 170
Bentsen, Lloyd, 88–89; and debate against Quayle, 186, 196
Berlin Wall, 284
Biden, Joseph, 16, 112, 126
Billygate, 70
Black Caucus, 277
Boorstin, Daniel, 199

Boston Harbor, 116, 150
Bradley, Bill, 53, 194, 260
British Parliament, 16
Broder, David, 45, 119, 176
Brokaw, Tom, 73
Brountas, Paul, 88
Buckley, Jill, 137
Buckley v. Valeo, 139, 167
Bush, George, 14–15, 30, 79, 81, 246, 276; and choice of Defense Secretary, 91; and choice of vice president, 88–90, 92–93; and debates against Dukakis, 186–188, 195; and electoral college, 210; and Iowa caucus, 125; and media coverage, 113, 116; nomination of, 36–37, 46; public attitudes towards, 3, 8, 283–284

California General Assembly, xi
California primary, 69
Calhoun, John C., 83, 192
Campaign commercials, 16–17, 131–132, 136, 140; and cost of campaigns, 135–136; and demagoguery, 137–139; and First

Amendment, 132, 150, 153; and
party decline, 136; regulation of,
141–143, 147–148; and studies
concerning content, 146–147
Canzeri, Joseph, 81
Carter, Jimmy, 6, 160; and conven-
tion controversy, 13, 67, 69–71;
and debate against Ford, 184–
185, 188, 193, 196; and debate
against Reagan, 185; and elec-
toral college, 209, 212; and
media coverage, 124, 126; nomi-
nation of, 21, 35, 51, 54–55, 64–
65, 256; and relationship to vice
president, 85–86, 91–92, 101
Casey, Bill, 113
Castro, Fidel, 141
Chambers, William N., 286
Chappaquidick, 70
Cheney, Richard, 90
Chicago Tribune Poll, 6
Church, Frank, 92
Clay, Henry, 9, 192, 219
Clean Campaign Act, 143
Cleveland, 214, 220
Colombian Drug Summit, 284
Convention Without Walls, 74
Connally, John, 18, 159
Convention Delegates, 13–14, 23–
25, 57–59; behavior of, 34–37;
demographic characteristics of,
26–30, 50–51; ideology of, 30–
32, 51–52, 55; issue positions of,
32–34; pledged to candidates,
60–66, 76–77; and Rule IIH con-
troversy, 68–73; and superdele-
gates, 52, 58, 62, 76–77, 272
Colfax, Schuyler, 86
Crawford, William, 9, 219
Crisis, x, 1, 22, 282; in election of
1824, 9–11, 282–283; in election
of 1988, 8; in governance, 5–8,
281, 284; in linkage, 2–5, 281;
in vice presidency, 89–90

Cronin, Thomas E., 82
Cuomo, Mario, 53, 260

Dangerfield, George, 10
Daley, Mayor, 42, 211
David, Paul T., 87
Declaration of Independence, 237
Democratic Party, xi, 5, 12, 21, 31,
38, 40, 45–46, 54–55, 58, 63–65,
101, 143, 258, 277; and 1968
convention, x, 5, 27, 42, 252,
254; and 1980 convention, 13,
51, 68, 72; and 1984 convention,
259; and 1988 convention, 15,
74, 259; National Committee of,
xi, 67–68, 90, 209; reforms of,
24, 27–29, 35, 41–43, 50–52, 88,
271–274
Democratic–Republican Party, 9
Dewey, Thomas E., 87
Dixiecrats, 231
Dole, Elizabeth, 112
Dole, Robert, 14, 89, 91, 101–102,
112, 125, 161, 185, 194
Douglas, William O., 87
Downs, Anthony, 34; model of,
35–36, 38–39
Dukakis, Kitty, 198
Dukakis, Michael: and campaign
commericals, 138, 150; and campaign spending, 161, 163–164;
and 1988 campaign, 31, 36, 37;
and debates against Bush, 186–
188, 195, 197–198; and electoral
college, 210; and media coverage, 112–113, 116, 122, 128;
nomination of, 12, 46–48, 64,
77, 259; public attitudes toward,
3, 8; and selection of running
mate, 88–89
DuPont, Pierre, 91, 112

Eagleton, Thomas, 89, 94, 105
Edelman, Murray, 115

Ehrlichman, John, 88
Eisenhower, Dwight, 6, 87, 94, 104, 271
Electoral College, 19, 58, 60, 73–74, 95, 117, 203, 219, 223, 231; and apportionment of electoral votes, 211–212; and constitutional theory, 225–226; and contingency procedure, 212–213, 224; and disfranchisement, 221–222; and faithless elector, 208–209, 223; history of, 204–207, 216–218; and interest groups, 222; and shift in votes critique, 220–221; and Twelfth Amendment, 207, 218, 224; and undemocratic results, 213–214, 218–220; and voter turnout, 223–224; and winner-take-all, 210–211

Fair Campaign Practices Committee, 148
Favorite sons, 61
Federal Comunications Commission, 151
Federal Election Campaign Act, 43, 158, 169
Federal Election Commission, 162–163, 165, 170, 178
Ferraro, Geraldine, 14, 89, 116
Ford, Gerald R., 6–7, 35, 54, 64, 100–101, 103; and debate against Carter, 184–185, 188, 193, 196; and electoral college, 210, 212
Freud, Sigmund, 198
Frontloading, 46
Fulani, Lenora, 172

Gallup Poll: and Dan Quayle, 81–82; and presidential approval, 6, 70; and presidential nominees, 2–4
Garner, John Nance, 84, 96

Gephardt, Richard, 91, 112
Germond, Jack, 81
Glenn, John, 124
Goldwater, Barry, 35, 38, 133, 137, 183
Gorbachev, Mikhail, 284
Gore, Albert, 91, 112
Graber, Doris, 114, 121
Grant, Ulysses, S., 158
Great Debates, 182–183, 193
Greenstein, Fred I., 287

Haig, Alexander, 91, 112
Harding, Warren, 250, 271
Hart, Gary, 16, 45, 50, 91, 110, 112, 116, 124, 160, 259, 271
Hart, Peter, 119
Hayes, Rutherford B., 219
Hayne, Robert, 192
Hendricks, Thomas, 86
Hinckley, Barbara, 87–88
Hobart, Garret A., 86
Hollings-Danforth Bill, xi, 143, 147–148, 151–152
Horton, Willie, 116, 128, 138
Hospers, John, 208
Huddleston, Walter, 137
Humphrey, Hubert, 42, 73, 82, 86–87, 90, 98–99, 183, 210
Hunt, Albert, 123

Invisible Primary, 255, 260
Iowa Caucus, 13, 15, 45–47, 49, 53, 111, 124, 125–126, 272
Iran-Contra Scandal, 113

Jackman, Robert W., 231
Jackson, Andrew, 9, 219
Jackson, Henry, 92, 160
Jackson, Jesse, 14, 29, 45, 74, 91, 113, 116, 160–161, 259, 272
Jacksonian Revolution, 251
Jacobson, Gary, 166–167

Jefferson, Thomas, 143
Jennings, Peter, 73
Johnson, Lyndon B., 6, 42, 83–85,
  88, 98–99, 133, 251, 283

Kefauver, Estes, 271
Kemp, Jack, 89, 91, 102, 112
Kennedy, Edward, 13, 51, 67, 69–
  71, 102, 110
Kennedy, John F., 6, 88, 98–99,
  125; and debate against Nixon,
  182–183, 188, 193, 197, 199; and
  electoral college, 212
Kennedy, Robert, 42, 158
Key, V. O., 34, 48, 257, 286
Kimmitt, Robert, 88
King, Anthony, 3
King Caucus, 9–10
King, Martin Luther, Jr., 42
Kissinger, Henry, 99
Krushev, Premier, 98
Kuttner, Robert, 243

Ladd, Everett, Carll Jr., 5, 271
LaRouche, Lyndon, 172
Lewis, Anthony, 122, 129
Libertarian Party, 208
Licht, Paul, 277
Lincoln-Douglas Debates, 193
Lippman, Walter, 44

MacBride, Roger, 208
MacNeil, Lehrer Newshour, 130
Madison, James, 192, 251
Malbin, Michael, 174
Marshall, Thomas, 82
Mason, George, 206
Mass Media, 15–16, 109, 118, 259;
  and character issues, 125–126;
  credibility of, 120; and general
  election coverage, 114–117; and
  horserace, 110, 121–123, 146,
  257, 260, 272; and issue coverage, 127–129; and media con-

sultants, 17, 20–21, 112; and
  nominating process, 44–46,
  109–113, 123–125; and party de-
  cline, 119
McCarthy, Eugene, 211
McCombs, Maxwell, 115
McGovern, 21, 35, 53, 65, 94, 102,
  124, 133, 183
Mitchell, John N., 88
Modern presidential selection:
  characteristics of, ix–x, 5–7
Mondale, Walter, 3, 14, 35, 45–46,
  48, 50–52, 54, 64–65, 71, 77,
  91–92, 116, 119, 124, 160, 170,
  259; and debates, 185–186, 196;
  and modern vice presidency, 85–
  86, 101
Monroe, James, 9
Morton, Levi P., 86
Mott, Stewart, 175
Mudd, Roger, 120
Murray Poll, 6
Muskie, Edmund, S., 47, 71, 89

National Conservative Political
  Action Committee, 137
National Security Council, 97, 101
National Voter Registration Act, xi
Naval Observatory, 101
New Deal, 91, 96–97
New Hampshire Primary, xi, 12–
  13, 16, 45–49, 53, 75, 111, 113,
  124, 272
New Politics, 20, 250
Newsweek Poll, 118
New York Primary, 69
New York Times Survey, 33
New York Times v. Sullivan, 152
Nightline, 130
Nixon, Richard, 6, 99–100; and
  debates against Kennedy, 182–
  183, 188, 193, 199; and electoral
  college, 210, 212; presidential
  campaigns of, 133, 159, 183;

and vice presidency, 85, 87–88, 94, 97–98, 104
Nominating process, 11–13, 23–24, 26, 40–41, 43; and role of media, 44–46; and primary votes, 48–49, 60; and representation of nominees, 53–54. *See also* Convention Delegates; Democratic Party, reforms of
Noriega, General, 284
North, Oliver, 113
Nunn, Sam, 194, 260

Old Executive Office Building, 98–99
O'Neill, Thomas (Tip), 137
Open Convention Committee, 70

Padden, Mike, 209
Participatory democracy, 254
Patterson, Thomas, 44, 128
Peabody, Endicott, 105
Pennsylvania Primary, 75
Pitkin, Hanna, 23, 26
Political Amateurs, 5, 12
Political parties, 2, 4–5, 7, 11–12, 15–16, 20–21, 24–25, 36, 40, 75, 119, 249, 258, 264, 270, 273, 277; American attitudes toward, 253–254; and coalition building, 256–258, 266; decline of, 120, 136, 252–253, 262, 265, 267, 269–270, 271–272; and divided government, 262–263; and party game, 260, 262; and post 1968 nominating process, 254–256, 260–261, 268–269; and pre-primary convention proposal, 287–288; and primary game, 260, 262; and reasons for restoring, 285–287; and relationship to governing, 253, 266, 275–278
Political Professionals, 5, 12, 258
Polk, James, 253

Polls, 2–4, 6, 8, 33, 70, 81–82, 118, 120, 126–127
Polsby, Nelson, 54
Pomper, Gerald, 4, 87–88
Powell, G. Bingham, 230
Presidential Debates, 18–19, 181; audience for, 199; and clues to leadership, 189, 197–198; fairness of, 194; and voter education, 187–188, 194; of 1960, 182–183, 193; of 1976, 184–185, 193; of 1980, 185; of 1984, 185–186, 193; of 1988, 186–187
Presidential Election Campaign Fund, 161
Progressives, 231, 254
Public funding, 17–18, 20, 155–156; and cheating, 170–171; and cost in 1988, 160–164; history behind, 157–159; and impact on democracy, 175–176; and proposal for congressional elections, 159, 166–167; and report of Kennedy School, 172–173, 175–177; and soft money, 163–165, 173; and tax check-off, 165–166, 172

Quayle, Dan, 14–15, 74, 79, 81–83, 89, 92–93, 102, 113, 126, 186, 196

Rajneesh, Bhagwan, 235
Ranney, Austin, 236
Ray v Blair, 223
Reagan, Ronald, 100, 103; and debates against Carter, 185, 186; and debates against Mondale, 185–186, 196; media coverage of, 113, 116; nomination of, 35, 54, 65; and presidential campaign, 5; and primary debate, 196; and public attitudes toward, 3, 6

Red Lion case, 151
Reiter, Howard, 41, 54
Remini, Robert, 10
Republican Party, 88, 99; and convention delegates, 63, 65, 68; National Committee of, 91, 137, 269, 273–274; National Convention of, 81, 94; and representation in nominating process, 27–33, 35–40, 45, 51–52
Rice, Donna, 16, 26
Rizzo, Mayor, 211
Robertson, 45, 91, 112, 125, 161–162
Roche, John, 206
Rockefeller, Nelson, 86, 100–101, 104
Roemer, Roy, 139
Rollins, Ed, 89
Romney, George, 110
Roosevelt, Franklin D., 87, 95–97, 144, 158, 256, 271, 276
Rose, Richard, 6
Rossiter, Clinton, 257

Salgo, Nicholas, 164
Sandinistas, 246
Schattschneider, E. E., 254, 261, 265–266
Schroder, Pat, 112
Seligman, Lester, 54
Seven Dwarfs, 288
Shafer, Byron, 73
Shaw, Bernard, 198
Sherman, Roger, 83
Shogan, Robert, 7
Simon, Paul, 91, 112
Sorensen, Ted, 7
Stevenson, Adlai, 73
Stoner, J. B., 150–151
Stovall, James, 127
Stone, Clement, 158
Sundquist, James, 274
Super Tuesday, 45, 46, 112–113, 123, 161

Survey Research Center/Center for Political Studies, 4

Taft, Robert, 94
Teixeira, Ruy, 245
Thach, Charles C., 285
Thompson, Hunter S., 184
Throttlebottom, Alexander, 82, 95
Thurmond, Strom, 16, 231
Tilden, Samuel J., 219
Tower, John, 90
Truman, Harry, 6, 83–84, 87, 97, 153, 253
Tuesday Team, 145

Vice Presidency, 79–80, 82–85, 90, 95–102; constitutional amendments concerning, 84, 86, 100; constitutional duties of, 83; modernization of, 84–86, 95–103; reform proposals for, 90–92; and selection process, 87–89, 93–94; and vice presidential debates, 185–186; and vice presidents, 82–85, 95–102
Vietnam, 30, 42, 53, 113, 126, 188, 192, 230, 252–253
Vinich, John, 139
Voter registration, 19–20, 227, 231, 242, 244–245; and motivation of reformers, 238–239; reform proposals concerning, 233–235, 239–241; and relationship to voter turnout, 231–233
Voter turnout, in caucus contests, 2, 10, 12; in comparison to other nations, 20, 229; explanations for decline of, 230, 232; in general election, 2, 10, 19–20, 175, 229; in primary elections, 2, 10, 12, 40, 75; and relationship to election day registration, 233–235
Voting behaivor, 8, 119, 263–264

Wallace, George, 208, 210, 213, 231
Wallace, Henry, 80, 85, 87, 96–97, 231
Washington, George, 205–206
Webster, Daniel, 192
Wheeler, William, 86

Wilson, Henry, 86
Wilson, Woodrow, 82
Women's Caucus, 277

Yankelovich, Daniel, 135
Young, James, Sterling, 251